Economic Disparity:

*PROBLEMS AND
STRATEGIES FOR
BLACK AMERICA*

William L. Henderson and

Economic Disparity:

Larry C. Ledebur

PROBLEMS AND STRATEGIES FOR BLACK AMERICA

 THE FREE PRESS, *New York*

Collier-Macmillan Limited, London

The Free Press
A Division of The Macmillan Company
866 Third Avenue, New York,
New York 10022

Collier-Macmillan Canada Ltd., Toronto,
Ontario
Library of Congress Catalog Card Number:
79-96833

printing number

1 2 3 4 5 6 7 8 9 10

to

James Boggs,

Dunbar McLaurin,

and Daniel Watts

Contents

Foreword

In the Spring of 1968, Daniel Watts, the editor of the Negro militant monthly *The Liberator*, visited the campus of Denison University, Granville, Ohio. At that time the authors began the first of a series of discussions with Mr. Watts regarding the economic goals of black militants. Mr. Watts made the significant point that most of the black organizations had only recently turned to consideration of economic-related activity. A survey of the available literature reinforced his point. Little information was available to provide an understanding as to what type of economic improvement or what changes in economic institutions were advocated by black militants. The quest for an orientation and answers to these questions were the basis on which the authors undertook to gather information about the economic programs of Negro organizations.

The search for current or older economic ideas or views espoused by black organizations was frustrating. Most of the literature available on black activity in the United States is in the historical, cultural, and sociological context. There are few works devoted to economic concerns of the black American. Harold Cruse's book, *Crisis of the Negro Intellectual,* and several articles written by Herbert Hill were the only significant sources available on this topic in the early stages of writing this book.

The frustration in determining the nature of economic goals of the Negro was amplified by the fact that the programs structured by Negroes for attacking economic ills are so new. There are no comparative compilations of the programs, nor has sufficient time elapsed to produce complete economic analysis of such programs. The available literature and reviews of the black economic development programs provide only a taxonomic listing of the ideas and tactics, as opposed to evaluative analysis of the feasibility or acceptability of the economic elements of those programs.

The authors also encountered significant difficulty in classifying the ideological propensities of Negro leaders with reference to whether they advocated economic development within the system or outside the system. The difficulties of classification relate to such terms as *militants, moderates, separatists, black nationalists,* and *nationalism.* For purposes of the review of the materials in this book, the authors have elected two ideological bases of Negro economic programs. In one, the term *moderate* is used, and in the other category the word *militant* is applied. The term *moderate* refers to an orientation toward implementation of programs on an evolutionary basis. The evolution implies slow and accumulative movement, and a biological-like, or anthropomorphic, alteration in institutional structures as a result of implementing various programs. The term *militant* characterizes a different manner of approach to the implementation of black economic programs. Militancy is identified with aggressive activity and implies that blacks are willing to undertake vigorous action to bring abrupt changes in any institutional framework that constricts efforts to achieve economic improvements. Within both the moderate and militant category, the term *separatist* may be applicable. A Negro may advocate programs to separate the black and the white community in regard to economic institutions and not be a black nationalist. A militant, nationalist, or separatist seeks aggressively to implement programs that would provide for black control over economic processes in an economic entity uniquely isolated from the institutional structure of white America. A militant is not necessarily a black nationalist, although he typically espouses the need for black political power before economic development can be undertaken. A black nationalist need not be a separatist, nor need he be a militant, but one who works for black political control.

Throughout the remainder of the book, the term *moderate* is

identified with programs implemented on an evolutionary basis where
no cataclysmic episodes interdict with the normal institutional processes.
The militant reference typifies Negroes who are interested in precipi-
tating immediate change in the structure and processes of the
American economic system. The ends to which the moderates are
slowly working and the ends to which the militant aggressively reacts
may be the same. However, there is no reason to believe that all
moderates are seeking integration within the total white institutional
framework, nor that all militants are seeking to separate the Negro
economically, politically, and socially from white institutional arrangements.

The problems regarding definition and sources of information
illustrate the difficulties in preparing a survey on this topic at this
time. The information presented in this book is an introduction to a
series of economic-oriented problems and programs which typify the
embryonic stages of the push for full black participation in American
economic life. Most of the questions raised as issues in black economic
development cannot be assessed until later evaluation is undertaken,
using traditional economic frames of reference; for example, are the
programs feasible, operative, and efficient on an alternative-cost basis?
The work of evaluating and assessing the significance of early attempts
to achieve economic equality or economic improvement for the Negro
must await future events and future studies by economic analysts. A
significant and definitive implication of the introduction of programs
and alternative strategies which can be drawn at this time is that the
information reflects a beginning of a long-term reassessment of American economic institutions. Although the problems are a century old,
the current trend toward solutions has produced less than half a decade
of experience of direct attacks upon the economic ills and economic
deprivation of the black.

The Development of Topics. Although historically the Negro's concern with poverty and his economic condition has been characterized
as a contemporary phenomenon, the "current" reference overstates the
contemporary case. It is true that the Negro organizations have only
recently structured programs aimed at economic deprivation. However, historical precedences of black attacks on deprivation and other
economic ills are well established. Chapter 2 reviews the sources of
economic ideas and philosophical orientation of the predecessors of
the contemporary black leadership and provides a perspective on the

manner in which the Negro has historically viewed and attacked economic problems. Subsequent chapters present a survey of the alternative current attitudes of black militants and moderates in regard to whether or not the institutional structure of free enterprise capitalism is an acceptable framework or can provide the mechanisms through which the economic ills of the Negroes can be solved. Chapters 4 and 5 introduce specific programs advocated by black militant and moderate leadership and organizations. A series of evaluations, including the financial and resource impact of implementing such programs, begins with Chapter 8. Chapter 9 evaluates the progress made in improving the economic conditions of the Negro as a result of the new emphasis on economic development programs. The final chapter provides a perspective by which the economic problems of the Negro can be associated with the broader implications of the need for a national urban policy.

W. L. H.
L. C. L.

Acknowledgments

The authors are deeply indebted to James Boggs, Dunbar McLaurin, and Daniel Watts for their graciousness and cooperation in providing advice and information. These gentlemen generously provided substantive information, unique insights, and expertise. The opportunity to discuss various points and issues with them was a rewarding educational experience. Their help and our gratitude are hereby acknowledged.

The work on this book was made possible because of the organizational skill and typing competence of Mrs. Marian Krieger and Mrs. Burton Dunfield. The authors wish to acknowledge publicly their gratitude for this important assistance.

Economic Disparity:

*PROBLEMS AND
STRATEGIES FOR
BLACK AMERICA*

CHAPTER 1

The Problem and Strategy

The Prosperous 1960's

During the 1960 decade, the American economy functioned at unprecedentedly high levels. The economic system produced the largest volume of goods and services and provided for a higher level of employment than in any other decade in history. Average earnings from private industry jobs continued in a long-term advancement. Average hourly compensation, including social security and supplements, showed a ten-year rise. The leading objective economic indicators revealed substantial strength in the system. The economy was creating new jobs at the rate of 1,500,000 per year. (The assumption is that the investment boom continues unimpeded.) Credit availability and rising disposable personal income, combined with increasing population and family

For Notes to Chapter 1 see pages 333–334.

formation, produced demand for durable and nondurable goods at unprecedented levels.

Despite this pattern of continued prosperity, inflationary pressures continued to be a primary policy focus. Manpower programs also had to be strengthened to assure that the poor were not bearing unusual burdens of unemployment or other costs from being excluded from the mainstream of American economic activity. There is statistical evidence that the continued high level of economic activity has not produced substantial inroads into the fundamental economic problems that have adversely affected minority groups for many years. Aggregatively, the economy was functioning well, but a closer look at selected indicators such as employment and income distribution reflected fundamental distortion and an uneven pattern of growth. Early in 1969 the National Commision on Urban Problems produced a document that included assessments of the critical factors of this economic imbalance. The syndrome of problems in the cities, as summarized in the Commission's report, is in sharp contrast to the optimistic report of overall economic performance:

From a cotton field in the South, big cities look like the only chance left for the rural poor, but city slums become prisons for the disinherited when they arrive.

Our big cities are hard up, costs of local government are skyrocketing, and the representation for the poor in slums is almost nonexistent.

Those most likely to live in substandard housing are the poor, nonwhites who have big families and who are renters, but they are not alone. A third of our affluent nation cannot afford adequate, nonsubsidized housing today despite great gains in our housing stock.

Over the years accomplishments in subsidized housing are extremely inadequate. The nation, in thirty years of public housing, has built fewer units than Congress, back in 1949, said were needed in the immediate six years.

Escalation of land prices adds to every bigger increment in the price of housing, and further explains the squeeze on low-income families seeking decent housing.

Zoning was intended to control land development, but fiscal considerations often lead to economic and racial exclusion.

Orderly urban growth can be the result of a political commitment on land-use decisions, who makes them and how they are made, plus the will to spend money on cities . . . to do something about the urban crisis, as political commitment grows, . . . the solutions called for are a tall order, but they are in proportion to the enormity of the problems of our urban areas.[1]

The Rural Elements in Distorted Prosperity

An earlier report by another Presidential Advisory Commission on Rural Poverty ("The People Left Behind") noted a similar listing of economic and social conditions which raised questions about any positive assessment of the system. The focus of this report was on those who do not live in the city. For these 14 million people, their socioeconomic status is bleak and a basis for despair. *Their income is low; 70 per cent of these 14 million have family incomes below $2,000.* An accompanying low quality of schooling is self-perpetuating and leads to surpluses of unskilled labor in areas where jobs are scarce. Rural poverty is most extreme for Negroes, Indians, and Mexican Americans.

These 14 million are typically from large families, and family size militates against a rising standard of living. Large family size typically stretches income beyond limits. The birth rate is higher than the United States average. The youth tend to move to the cities. Thus, for the family, few workers, persistent low incomes, and more people to support create serious dependency problems in the rural area. The population in the rural area has a higher proportion of older people. Sparser population density makes a viable social system more difficult. The measurements of rural poverty are extended to include other elements. Lack of access to respected positions in society and the lack of power to do anything about it lead to insecurity and unstable homes, an existence that tends to perpetuate itself from one generation to the next.

The cure, if implemented, must not only bring about increases in income, but amelioration of the lack of self esteem. The culture of poverty in the rural areas tends to be fatalistic and pessimistic, compounded by the vicious cycle of poverty. There is also a lack of traditional values, or the natural reaction of people living without a future. The pattern of emigration has been from rural areas to towns and cities, and heaviest from the South— north to Maryland, Indiana, Missouri, and west to California.

Unemployment and the Urban Nonwhite Poor

When a Negro moves into an urban area, he automatically complicates his employment pattern. "In 1940 (when 41% of Negro males were employed in agriculture, where unemployment rates were low), the nonwhite unemployment rate was slightly less than the white rate. It should be noted, however, that while unemployment rates in agriculture were low, so were wages. Employment did not necessarily spell economic well-being. Furthermore, in agriculture, underemployment is almost as serious a problem as unemployment."

Negroes were leaving the farms, however (since 1930 the proportion of Negroes living in cities has nearly doubled), and by 1960 only 9.1% of the experienced nonwhite labor force remained in agriculture.

The lowest point Negro unemployment reached in the years since World War II was 4.5% in 1953, but with the end of the Korean War, the rate doubled and then remained high throughout the 1950's and the early 1960's. In 1958 and 1961, both recession years, nonwhite unemployment rose about 12%. Since 1954 the 2-to-1 unemployment ratio has become a stubborn economic fact of life.[2]

In 1967, in twenty of the largest metropolitan areas in the United States, the central cities' unemployment rate for nonwhite was about twice as high for the whites in the central cities. In the suburban fringes, in that same year and in those same areas the white unemployment rate was less than half of the nonwhite. The movement to the industrial North into the central cities, has compounded the Negroes' employment problem and concentrated Negroes in the central city.

Industry has emigrated from the central city. This has resulted in an emigration of jobs and fewer jobs accessible to the central city residents. Between 1954 and 1965, more than half of new industrial and merchandising construction in metropolitan areas was outside central cities. Commuting costs and inconvenience added to the job-access problem of the central city nonwhite resident.

The high unemployment rate in the central city for nonwhites is, however, not wholly attributed to central-city-to-suburb commuting problems. White collar jobs, which are generally increasing at a faster rate than blue collar jobs, are in the main located in the central cities. But it is this source of employment —which would not involve commuting difficulties just described —that the nonwhite finds largely inaccessible to him because of his lack of skills or outright discrimination.[3]

The concentration of unemployed workers in the city has far-reaching implications. The urban poor tend to find out about their jobs and determine their opportunities for employment through informal as opposed to formal contacts. Jobs for this group are typically recommended by a relative or friend. A small percentage of jobs are actually discovered through employment agencies and newspaper advertising. Thus, labor market information is inadequate in the cities for the non-white unemployed.

Another dimension of the nature of the non-white unemployed is described in *Tally's Corner*, by Elliott Liebow:

When we look at what men bring to the job rather than at what the job offers men, it is essential to keep in mind that we are not looking at men coming to the job fresh, just out of school perhaps, and newly prepared to undertake the task of making a living, or from another job where they earned a living and are prepared to do the same on this job. Each man comes to the job with a long history characterized by his not being able to support himself or his family. Each man carries this knowledge, born of his experience, with him. He comes to the job flat and stale, wearied by the sameness of it all, convinced of his own incompetence, terrified of responsibility—of being tested again and found wanting.[4]

A former director of the U.S. Employment Service assessed the job-holding problem in this manner

The job-holding ability of gang members, school dropouts, and the unprepared is usually poor in relation to the regular work force . . . many such people lack staying power in training programs, preferring a job now with money to spend now. Their expectations are often unrealistic in terms of their background. Merely creating jobs will not correct this; the creation processes in the absence of a job retention effort ends in more failure for both the individual and the employer . . . what may be understandable behavior to the psychologist, is to the employer laziness and lack of responsibility; he cannot condone this. . . .[5]

Subemployment, or part-time employment and lower participation rates, for non-white males and low earners are much greater for nonwhites than for whites. The magnitude of this problem is understated in U.S. Department of Labor Statistics by the undercount of non-white males. These essential points add up to a bleak picture of the capacity of our prosperous system to provide the mechanisms to permit nonwhites and other hard-core unemployed to gain access to employment opportunities.

The period 1960 to 1967 reflected a slight gain in white-collar occupations formerly closed to Negroes, plus an opening for more apprenticeship opportunities and the upgrading of Negro employment in the federal government. The 1968 Manpower Report conceded that job discrimination continued to play a role in unequal occupational opportunities for Negroes. The extent of the job discrimination was difficult to determine. Another characteristic of the Negro employment problem noted was that as higher-paying jobs increase in industry, the probability of Negro employment in it is lowered. This condition is more pronounced for Negro men than for women. But for men and women, employment compared to that of whites is many times greater in low-wage industries. Occupational discrimination increases in direct relation to the concentration of Negroes in an industry, the ratio of well-paid occupations in the industry, the level of education of the Negroes involved and the proportion of the industry's employment found in the South.[6]

The heavy overrepresentation of Negro males in the low wage industries indicates that, even if they were given equal opportunity to rise, promotion would promise only limited financial rewards. What is required to solve the problem is not only opportunity for occupational upgrading for Negro men in industries where they are, but also greatly increased opportunities for entrance into industries with more high paid skilled jobs.[7]

Housing Environment
Disparities

The housing situation in urban areas or in rural areas also indicates the great disparity between whites and nonwhites or those people excluded from participating in a full share of the nation's economic wealth. In central city poverty areas, the density of housing was 100 times (1960) as great as in suburban poverty areas. The central-city average is distorted because of the high density in large metropolitan areas in New York, but these figures illustrate sharply contrasting conditions in poverty areas. Within the center city there is an acute shortage of open space, or an absence of recreational areas. Only about a third of the housing units in the central city are found in the poverty areas, but they were found on less than one fourth of the total land areas in the cities. There is continual crowding of transportation and all other public facilities. There are incipient higher land prices. A sense of containment pervades the ghetto. Residents of central city poverty areas are typically renters and not home owners.

These poverty urban areas contain the following: Four out of five of all housing units are occupied by nonwhites in the cities; three out of four of the substandard units are in the central cities; nine out of ten of the substandard units are occupied by nonwhite in these central cities; five out of six of the overcrowded units occupied by nonwhites were built before 1940, and about a third were 100 years old or older. Race, therefore, seems to be a significant factor in bad housing.[8] In these statistics, as in the poverty figures, substantially higher incidents of bad housing among nonwhites is more than offset by the almost nine-to-one ratio of whites to nonwhites in metropolitan populations. The task of replacing substandard units with decent homes is not limited to any one racial or ethnic group.

The areas within the urban core reflect the weaknesses of the private enterprise system and democratic government, which have preserved a syndrome of alienating factors. The alienating factors seem to be most severe for the Negro, despite the fact that cities have attracted other ethnic groups. The problems for the poor urban white and nonwhite are the same in kind, but different in degree. Even though the pace of immigration to the cities is slackening, the handicaps of deprivation appear in the children of earlier migrants because of isolation in one locality.

Fiscal Pressures
in the City

In terms of the impact on the city government, this concentration of the disadvantaged poor means high welfare costs and expensive police and fire protection activity. In other services such as schools, snow removal, street repair, garbage and trash collection, replacement of utility services, the central cities perform less well than the suburbs; the central cities seem to be unable to keep the streets clean. But conditions in ghetto neighborhoods are almost always intolerable. The magnitude of the problems in the central cities makes it difficult for neighborhoods to develop any effective relationships with city government. The residents of slum neighborhoods may discover that city department personnel, including administrators of the school system and the public welfare department, do not appear to be accountable to the people in the poor areas.

The decline of services is a function of the growing difference in the fiscal abilities of the central cities and the suburban fringe areas. The per capita tax base in the central cities is in many cases below that of the suburbs. In earlier periods most economic activity in cities was concentrated in central cores and was reached by city taxes. Today, wealth and tax capacity are dispersed more widely throughout the metropolitan areas and outside the scope of central city tax sources. The demands for public services are still concentrated in central cities with a lessened tax base.[9]

Although the fiscal capacity or tax base of the central city has declined, the need for higher expenditures has risen. At least three fundamental factors contribute to the heavy fiscal requirements of the central city. The central city is where the poor and dis-advantaged are concentrated. Thus there is a greater need for the high-cost services relating to poverty, such as public assistance or public hospital care, housing, and other social services. High population density necessitates increases in services such as police and fire protection, and sanitation. For most central cities, furthermore, these services—as well as local highway and traffic control activities—must meet the needs of an expanded "daytime" population that includes a net inflow of nonresident suburban community commuters.[10] Because the central cities were settled before suburbia, most public facilities include a large proportion of deteriorated structures and equipment, in need of constant repair or replacement. Expanding suburbs must also build new "public plants," but these facilities are considered in the context of pros-pective growth rather than declining population and sluggish economic environment found in the central cities.

The publication of a study by the Advisory Commission on Intergovernmental Relations, "Fiscal Balance in the American Federal System," produced a similar description of urban fiscal ills. This ACIR report described fiscal disparities in thirty-seven metropolitan areas for the years 1962–1965. For example:

☐ **1**   A deepeningly fiscal crisis reflects the exodus of middle- and high-income families and businesses from the central city to suburbia.

☐ **2**   In central cities, the burden of local taxes averages 7.6 per cent of the personal income compared with only 5.6 per cent of income from residents outside central cities.

☐ **3**   Central cities increased their relative tax effort during the period when their property tax base experienced a deceleration in rate of growth or absolute decline.

☐ **4**   In the thirty-seven largest metropolitan areas, current public school expenditures in 1965 averaged $449 per pupil in the central cities, compared with $574 per pupil in suburbia. "Children who need education the most are receiving the least."

☐ **5**   Per capita noneducational (municipal) outlays of $232 per capita were made by the thirty-seven largest central cities in 1965—$100 greater than their suburban counterparts. The Commission on Urban Problems noted with some emphasis that there is a crisis in urban government finance and the crisis continues to mount and seems to feed upon itself.

The level of municipal services in the low-income areas is inadequate. The evidence of deterioration in municipal services is matched or perhaps exceeded by the poor upkeep and maintenance of other private structures, with the exception of some retail shops and an occasional church. "These conditions add to the unattractiveness of these districts, and contribute to an unhealthy living environment."[11]

The Central City— "Melting Pot"?

In the earlier "melting-pot" era, the urban slum was simply a stopping place before residents moved on to a better life within the system. "Now, however, instead of sending forth the residents that characterize it—the urban nonwhites—the city poverty area appears to be concentrating them still further. The nonwhite component of the central city poverty areas has increased decidedly; their high proportion of poor households appears to be nearly stationary. Apparently there is a hard core of nonwhite families whose situation improves slowly, if at all."[12]

The Ghetto—A Capsule Description   A summary description of the pattern of life in the ghetto is provided by Herbert Hill, Labor Secretary of the National Association for the Advancement of Colored People. In addition to the ordinary reference that the physical status reflects the lack of employment opportunities and the presence of low incomes, additional dimensions are significant.

The ghetto is a place of concentration, not only of people of a particular race but of particular problems of cultural deprivation, high infant mortality rates, high rates of unemployment, short lifespan, second-rate education, and economic underdevelopment.

The life of the ghetto permits only the most limited opportunities for migrating out of the ghetto environment. There is an absence of choice of jobs, education, and places to live, a lack of choice that is a controlling element in ghetto life. Although equal opportunity is promised, it is unfulfilled if opportunity means access only to second-class schools, second-class homes, menial jobs, or long-term unemployment. There is no measure of human degradation and deprivation of the victims. There are more than 10 million Americans in ghettos concentrated in the metropolitan areas. The metropolitan urban ghettos are mainly Negro, but also include Mexican-Americans, Americans of oriental extraction, and Puerto Ricans, and for the American Indian the reservation is often a ghetto.[13]

Ed Bullins in his black theatre play, "In the Wine Time," has provided a fruitful reference to the exhaustion and the hopelessness of the ghetto.

. . . . on a worn, wooden porch on a simmering August night, a family marinates in cheap port, while a strolling cop swats his club against a wire fence, neighborhood voices yell down the block and people mutter through screen doors. A husband bickers with his pregnant wife. She berates him for being jobless while she goes to work : again and again she says that he is not a man . . . . it is the recurrent theme of poverty; that women have the authority (which they also resent), because more jobs are open to them and because whites have crippled the black male.

. . . . .

Bullins has distilled the language and the experience of the ghetto . . . . where the fatigue that oozes out of the suppressions seems even stronger than despair.[14]

Ghetto Removal   To eliminate the ghetto requires the provision of the material basis as well as the legal processes to achieve equality of opportunity. Included in the options of opportunity must be the ability to make choices in regard to jobs, housing, education, health care. There are really few choices under present conditions. Even the quality of opportunity available within the no-choice environment is extremely limited. Elimination of economic inequities may be a first step and the logical primary focus of blacks who attempt to solve their own economic problems.

Recognition—An Evolution

By 1967 it was apparent to most private citizens and public officials that ghetto conditions and the plight of the Negro represented need for a commitment to problem-solving action. The recognition of the problems as a reflection of inadequate market function, either because of discrimination or other factors, was a first step. Segments of the white community seem to be responding to the obvious human problems of ghetto existence. The white communities were made more aware of the magnitude of the necessary commitment by the Kerner Commission Report, the Report on the Commission on Urban Problems, and other documents provided chiefly through the executive office of the President. But the precipitous nature of the problems appeared only after the riots in Newark, Detroit, Harlem, and Washington and the destruction of public and private property. There has been a short period of a few years since the majority white community were willing to recognize the factors that led, in part, to the eruption and the breakdown in civil order in 1967 and 1968.

Black-Originated Problem-Solving It would seem that for the Negro the syndrome of the problem was apparent and need not be identified. As a product of and a resident in this disadvantaged environment, he was obviously aware of the nature of the deprivation and discrimination that prevented him from fully enjoying American citizenship. The Negroes' apparent concern with the economic status of the Negro is recent. Since 1965 there has been evidence of significant new activity by Negro organizations in economic areas. Bayard Rustin of the A. Philip Randolph Institution offered a perceptive analysis of why the Negro has been only recently concerned with using leverage of economic programs to solve ghetto or minority group problems.

Periods of Civil Rights Activity Rustin indicates that there have been three distinctly different periods in the Negro civil rights movement. The first, and the longest, period was between 1900 and 1954. The timespan coincides with the founding of the NAACP and significant Supreme Court decisions in 1954. A fundamental objective of that earlier civil rights period was to end discrimination and inequality through the court system. The NAACP leadership went into court filing brief after brief until 1954 when a decision did point out that any form of segregation was, in fact, unconstitutional. Rustin notes that in this period the lawyer going to court was the symbol of civil rights activity.

The second period of civil rights was from 1955 to 1965. This era is symbolized by people marching in the street. A basic relationship exists between the two periods because no fundamental activity could have been undertaken if it had not been for the Supreme Court decision in 1954. The Supreme Court also assured the Negro of his right to protest.

The third and the most recent period of civil rights activity started in 1965 and has continued to the present. The year 1965 was the beginning of a period of political activity by civil rights groups. Rustin argues that during the first period, and perhaps during the second period, the Negro required or demanded only a philosophy of faith.[15]

In regard to the current strategy for eliminating slums or creating adequate schools and new jobs, the older philosophy of faith is inadequate. An analysis of society's economic structures and the sociology of social change, as well as a philosophy of history, must be added to the philosophy of faith.

Most of the leadership that provided perseverance and courage dominated in the older periods of the civil rights movement. Perhaps now, disillusionment dominates. "From 1955 to 1965 the federal government did not expend one penny, except for police protection, for basic Negro objectives won in that period."[16] Now the federal government must spend in those areas where the Negro has not been able to advance. True freedom, according to Rustin, must first be conceived in economic categories.

The economy is the bone. The social institutions are the flesh, and the political institutions are the skin, which grows on that flesh and bone. Ultimately all human freedom is determined by economic structures of institutions.[17]

Current Economic Emphasis

The current period of civil rights activity is oriented toward a very complex issue. It is basically an economic as well as a political struggle to deal with the foundations of poverty, inferior schools, and bad housing. Rustin concludes that if the civil rights movement does not concentrate basically on economic issues, freedom for Negroes will never be achieved in our time. Thus, Rustin indicates that the Negro is concerned now with economic problems only because he has moved successfully through the establishment of the permissive legal conditions within which attention can now be turned to the obvious symptoms of his impoverished condition.

The Negro's evolution within the industrial system is also significant in regard to the manner in which he reacted to the economic deprivation. In a discussion of the civil rights evolution, James Boggs, the black theorist from Detroit, assumes that the movement really began with relatively few concepts other than that of integration and that blacks could live in the same manner as whites.[18] The economic environment of the Negro actually began to change in the 1930's because the Great Depression accelerated Negro movement to northern cities. The North treated the black immigrant as "immigrant laborer." During the decades of immigration blacks became numerous enough to be a force in the industrial process. The black immigrant laborer in the North began to focus on economic activity or practices in 1963, after the economic boycotts in the South. This activity of the southern Negro gave the northern black a sense of direction as to how he might effectively deal with economic problems. The movement, which started out as a civil rights movement in the South, changed when it moved to the industrial North. Boggs believes that the idea of community control was translated into economic control, but he is quick to point out that control of the community is not necessarily economic control.

The black movement is only sixteen years old. The economic focus of the black is just five years old. It is a relatively short period, in the lifetime of the average Negro, for maturity to have occurred in regard to the direction and the focus of the movement.

The ways in which the black believes that their economic ills can be attacked reflects a great diversity of ideas. But civil rights activities since 1967 have emphasized an economic dimension. The national Negro organizations have attempted to implement a variety of programs to improve the economic status of the American Negro, a significant expansion of the past emphasis on legal action in the courts.

Profile of Black Economic Programs. Although all the economic programs advocated by black militants and nonmilitants are characterized by diversity, there are now three basic solution-oriented alternatives advanced. The first is a skills-training and employment-access emphasis. The NAACP and the Urban League are active in attempting to improve the employment opportunities, both through job placement and skills training, in new industrial firms in the ghettos and in established businesses. (The primary group in the jobs-oriented approach, however, is the private-sector white corporation.) A second general approach to the solution of the economic plight of the Negro is black economic development, or the black-capitalism approach. Within this orientation one course of action would establish Negro businesses within the existing community. Negro businesses and capitalists would face competition across the color line. The alternative course of action would establish an economic substructure for the blacks. In this environment, newly formed black businesses would operate in a market composed of blacks. In extreme form, the latter alternative has a geographical or spatial dimension of a separate black economic system. The Congress of Racial Equality, the Black Muslims, and the Black Panthers have already given evidence of a preference for a black-capitalism approach that leads to a separate black economy.

Negro moderates in the National Business League, A. Philip Randolph Institute, and the NAACP, as well as the Urban League, have formulated programs that permit the Negroes to establish businesses, but within the existing institutional type of framework.

These two types of programs are not inconsistent with the preservation of the pattern of black residence in the ghetto. The programs are predicated on the assumption that the ghetto will continue to exist and only minor changes will occur in its physical environment. The evaluation of the potential success of the various types of programs is reserved for later sections of this text, but there are several issues relating to the choice or strategy that become significant. The issues relating to black economic development are complex simply because the problem is complex. The dimensions of the problem are obviously characterized in economic terms, but they include social, cultural, and other institutional elements.

The strategy that is now receiving priority among Negro leaders and organizations of all ideological postures is black economic development. They have identified control over resources as a major source of more power and now believe that the existing status of economic conditions and related ideological tenets are the central obstacles to the emancipation of the Negro.

From the moderate National Urban League and the National Business League to the militant Congress of Racial Equality, organizations and leaders now assume that the Negro must participate in the economic machinery of this country. If they are blocked in this effort by the present institutional structure, they believe that the economic system must be restructured. Many organizations have already prepared to achieve economic power outside existing economic institutions. Some civil rights organizations, such as the NAACP and the Urban League, maintain the older and traditional interest in job and skills training, but most organizations have abandoned this approach. This rejection is found in the current policies of the conservative organizations as well as the black militants. Economic integration through jobs and skills training is no longer the focus of Negro actions for economic and social equality. The primary and current orientation is the quest for economic participation and the drive for black control of resources.

The black programs do emphasize metropolitan problems and disparities between the central city and the suburbs. The central city crisis represents a complex of nationwide social problems reflected in the black in his life in the cities. State and other local governments have not been able to provide an adequate level of municipal services for the central-city areas. Thus, the Negro and other minority groups living in central-city areas have been abandoned by the government closest to home. The federal government has not yet provided programs well-enough designed or financed to make significant inroads into the hard-core employment in these areas. The white-dominated free enterprise-capitalistic system has supported resource allocation in a way that has perpetuated the deprivation of minority groups living in metropolitan areas.

The Economic Problem—
Black Focus

The Negro organizations and Negro leaders have undertaken an attack on long-term, massive problems through their economic programs. It is trite to say that the particular programs advocated for the economic improvement of the Negro by the Negro are products of the conditions of the past that have excluded him from the sources of economic power and control over economic resources. It is teleological to note that the recommendations and the formats of the programs advocated by Negro groups reflect future as well as current needs. Most of the programs are narrow in scope because they do not deal with general poverty, nor do they deal *per se* with all the elements of the urban crisis in America.

Increasing concentration of population in large urban centers will make public and private consumption more costly. The increased size of these urban centers and the resulting congestion will also produce a psychological and social crisis in urban living conditions. The concentrated Negro population in the central city will add to the syndrome of factors referred to as "incendiary conditions" in central city ghettos.[19]

The advocates and designers of these economic development programs have focused on economic conditions which are symptoms of much larger problems of imperfection in the market mechanism, discrimination and racial bias, malallocation of resources, and control of political and social activity by individuals or institutions who are insensitive to the needs of the black population. The focus of most black economic development and employment programs is on attempts to deal with the dependent variables within a larger system of causal factors. All programs call for a process of optimizing Negro economic conditions, but within a larger institutional framework that is suboptimal in and of itself.

Black organizations in their economic programs have undertaken a commitment to some type of growth of black economic institutions stemming from more jobs, more black business opportunity, and improved physical environment of the ghetto. Many black development programs illustrate a concept of a unilateral, upward development and improvement in these economic indicators that will permit the black to enjoy a higher socio-economic status and will eliminate the problems that make life disadvantaged for the central city Negro.

However, there are a series of factors that relate to strategy that are highly significant in any effort to positively change the status of economic deprivation and discrimination. Any program designed for long-term success, undertaken by the black community or the majority white community, must attack the total syndrome of institutional problems or the independent variables in this schema of urban and social ills. If the black programs as types of action are an isolated effort to improve only the obvious economic conditions, none of the black programs can be successful. An alternative strategy would be to attempt to influence a longer term process of change aimed at making the larger institutional environment more optimal for the black and other disenfranchised groups, which seems more rational than enduring suboptimality. Isolated action on economic suboptimality symptoms will have no repercussion on the total syndrome of causal factors that perpetuate the undesirable conditions. There is a need in the American system for major societal changes including a reallocation of resources and a fundamental restructuring of the market allocation mechanisms that adversely affect the Negro.

Provided that the black intends to participate as a pressure group to build up the economic and political power to change the institutional structure system, he may be able to force long term and massive changes within the system. The problems of the larger institutional malfunctions are currently reflected in actions by other disenchanted citizens in the majority white community. The syndrome of problems is the same. Efforts are directed to democratize our economic, political, and social institutions, or to re-establish the concepts of earlier free-enterprise individualism within all, not merely some, selected sectors of the community.

The Negro interested in overall institutional and structural change will find ready allies among the other disenfranchised whites in the community. The black should look to the activity of American college youth and other white liberals who attack the inequities in the institutional structure as a significant symbol of commitment by the white to deal with the fundamental problems that have plagued the black for the last 100 years.

In regard to the specific programs advanced, the Negroes responsible for the design of these programs reflect a compulsion to have overt and symbolic action occur immediately. But the need for immediate action must be tempered by an evaluation and assessment of the design of the black programs to solve the dilemma for the individual Negro. The issues in evaluating these programs are whether or not the programs are feasible in their design. Will the programs affect those individuals who are actually disadvantaged in a manner that will bring about long-term improvements? Will the programs allocate resources on a short-term basis consistent with a long-term evolutionary change in the institutional factors that will permit fuller participation in the mainstream of American economic life? Will the cost of funding these programs, including money costs and the opportunity costs of the real resources sacrificed (money and real costs), be justified by the results produced for the Negro himself and for the nation as a whole in terms of alternative programs advanced for the same purpose? Will these programs be supported by blacks? Are the programs acceptable to white policymakers and not inconsistent with the humane orientation of the socially responsible white?

An issue in program success is whether the ghetto reflects distortions and disparities in the pattern of economic life of blacks or whether the ghetto itself is the causal factor. Does the restriction of the Negro population to a particular area really underlie all aspects of the problem?

Most action advocated by black organizations is oriented toward problems which imply that the ghetto reflects but is not the cause of economic distortions and disparities. This orientation is critical to the successful design of problem-solving programs.

CHAPTER 2

Black
Economic
Philosophies:
Historical
Antecedents

The Report of the National Advisory Commission on Civil Disorders (the Kerner Report) has proffered the thesis that

The black power advocates of today consciously feel that they are the most militant group of the Negro protest movement. Yet they have retreated from a direct confrontation with American society on the issue of integration and, by preaching separatism, unconsciously function as an accommodation to white racism. Much of their economic program, as well as their interest in Negro history, self-help, racial solidarity and separation, is reminiscent of Booker T. Washington. The rhetoric is different, but the programs are remarkably similar.[1]

The laboratory of history can be utilized in evaluating con-

For Notes to Chapter 2 see pages 334–336.

temporary black economic development programs. Historical or antecedent models that have proven historically successful should be emphasized. Earlier models that have been demonstrated to be dead ends or based on false hopes should be eliminated. However, in this evaluative process the variability of social and economic institutions in which contemporary movements are being implemented should be recognized. A new environment may produce a fertile ground for economic development models that failed because of an earlier incompatible environment.

Utopian Experiments

In the pre-Civil War period of the nineteenth century attempts were made to establish separate Negro communities in the United States and Canada.[2] During this time approximately one hundred and seventy-eight communities were initiated. The movement to establish these experimental settlements was the outgrowth of three factors: First, this period in the history of the United States offered such permissive conditions as the existence of a frontier, for the establishment of utopian communal experiments. Second, the program of the American Colonization Society to resettle Negroes in Liberia contained no well-planned design for the social and economic structure of new African societies. The lack of structure in colonization schemes encouraged the communitarian theorists to examine the possibilities of implementing their programs within Negro utopian experiments in the United States and Canada.[3] Third, Negro communal experiments proffered an alternative to colonization in Africa or Latin America or continued legal, social, and economic discrimination toward the freedman within American society.

In Negro communal settlements, utopian idealism was tempered by a pragmatic reality of Negro circumstances. In general, the form of organization was not communistic nor socialistic as in nonblack utopian communities.[4] The new settlements reflected the political, social, and economic philosophy of the American middle class and engendered the qualities of self-reliance, individualism, and economic self-sufficiency. The economic structure of these communities was capitalistic. Programs were designed to provide economic and skills training that would allow settlers to compete in a capitalistic society. The reasons for gathering together on a communal basis were for mutual assistance, the pooling of resources, and to present a common front to a hostile environment. For most Negroes membership in these communities was not permanent. The temporary educational experience provided training for economic self-sufficiency and a process of acculturation prior to assimilation into the larger society.

The economic training received in these communities was primarily in agricultural skills.

. . . . Here, too, the philosophy of the organized community reflected the attitudes of the day. Much of the American Dream was a Jeffersonian Arcadianism, a love of the soil, a belief in the inherent virtues of the agricultural life. Evil were the ways of the big city, pure the air and life of the rural community.[5]

The significance of these "black utopias" was not great. Many collapsed soon after their inception. Others flourished briefly and then declined because of scarcity of capital and inept or dishonest leadership. All failed before the end of the Civil War. But in these communities, perhaps for the first time in the Negro struggle, the philosophies of economic self-sufficiency and separation from the dominant society were advocated and implemented, albeit with discouraging results.

Half a century had gone by. The organized Negro communities had run their course. The settlers, their leaders, and their supporters had fought a good fight. Here indeed were men of good hope. Let this be their epitaph. For their vision was unrealistic; their practice, at last, unfruitful.[6]

A prominent characteristic of the contemporary black civil rights movement is the rejection of traditional techniques for achieving social and political integration. Emphasis is now on economic development as a technique of obtaining social and political power. This current focus is not new. Economic independence and economic security was a unique element in Booker T. Washington's theory, which emphasized the economic improvement of the Negro.[7] Washington's emphasis was on keeping the door of economic opportunity open to the Negro and was based on the premise that economic opportunity was more essential than political and social equality to the Negro at that time.[8] This emphasis on economic development was criticized by other Negro leaders who advocated political activities to obtain acceptances into American society.

The radical and conservative tendencies cannot be better described than by comparing, or rather contrasting, the two superlative colored men in whom we find our highest embodiment—Frederick Douglass and Booker T. Washington. The two men are in part products of their times, but are also natural antipodes. Douglass lived in the day of moral giants; Washington in the era of merchant princes. The contemporaries of Douglass emphasized the rights of man; those of Washington his productive capacity. The age of Douglass acknowledged the sanction of the Golden Rule; that of Washington worshiped the rule of gold. The quality of man was constantly dimmed into Douglass' ears; Washington hears nothing but the inferiority of the Negro and the dominance of the Saxon. Douglass could hardly receive a hearing today; Washington would have been hooted off the stage a generation ago. Thus all truly useful men must become in some measure, time servers; for unless they serve their time, they can scarcely serve at all. . . . Douglass had no limited copyrighted program for his race, but appealed to the Decalog, the Golden Rule, The Declaration of Independence, The Constitution of the United States; Washington, holding these great principles in a shadowy background, presents a practical expedient, applicable to present needs. Douglass was a moralist, insisting upon the application of righteousness to public affairs; Washington is a practical statesman, accepting the best terms which he thinks are possible to secure.[9]

Washington recognized the needs of his time as reflected in the social and economic environment in which he lived. His philosophy was pro-capitalistic. He wanted to bring the Negro into the economy as a productive element. Participant economic power would be the leverage to obtain political and social power. He argued that "the man who has learned to do something better than anyone else, has learned to do a common thing in an uncommon manner, is a man who has a power and influence that no adverse circumstances can take from him."[10]

The individual or race that owns the property, pays the taxes, possesses the intelligence and substantial character, is the one which is going to exercise the greatest control in government whether he lives in the North or whether he lives in the South.[11]

Washington believed that the Negro, because of the indispensable value of his services to the economic sector, could achieve equality of status and win the respect from his neighbors. "Nothing else so soon brings about right relations between the two races in the South as the commercial progress of the Negro."[12]

Washington's program for the economic development of the Negro was directed towards the South. He believed that the opportunities for advancement for the Negro in this region were greater than in the urbanizing North, because of the underdeveloped nature of this region relative to its material resources and potential for further development.

The South is still an underdeveloped and unsettled country, and for the next half-century and more, the greater part of the energy of the masses will be needed to develop its material resources. Any force that brings the rank and file of the people to have a greater love of industry is therefore especially valuable.

This result industrialization is surely bringing about. It stimulates production and increases trade—trade between the races; and in this new engrossing relation both forget the past. The white man respects the vote of a colored man who does $10,000 worth of business; and the more business the colored man has the more careful he is how he votes.[13]

Booker T. Washington's economic philosophy took form at Hampton Institute and was applied in industrial education programs while he was president of Tuskegee Institute. His economic approach received national attention in the now famous Atlanta Exposition Address of July 4, 1881. His remarks contained the essential elements of his philosophy, namely that the Negro in the South would be willing to accept a subordinate position without social equality if given the opportunity to develop economically. Through self-help and self-development the Negro could win respect in the South, then mutual economic progress would break down racial barriers. To the Negro Washington admonished:

. . . . To those of my race who depend on bettering their condition in a foreign land or who underestimate the importance of cultivating friendly relations with the southern white man who is their next-door neighbor, I would say: Cast down your bucket where you are—cast it down in making friends . . . of people of all races by whom we are surrounded.
    Cast it down in agriculture, mechanics, in commerce, in domestic service and in the professions. And in this connection it is well to bear in mind that whatever other sins the South may be called to bear, when it comes to business, pure and simple, it is in the South that the Negro is given a man's chance in the commercial world. . . .

Washington appealed to the southern whites.

. . . . Cast down your bucket where you are; cast it down among the 8 million Negroes whose habits you know, whose fidelity and love you have tested. . . . Cast down your bucket among my people, helping and encouraging them as you are doing on these grounds, and to education of head, hand, and heart, you will find that they will buy your surplus land, make blossom the waste places in your field, and run your factories.

In talking to both blacks and whites Washington commented:

. . . . In all things that are purely social we can be as separate as the fingers yet one as the hand in all things essential to mutual progress. . . . The wisest among my race understand that the agitation of questions of social equality is the extremist folly, and that progress and the enjoyment of all the privileges that will come to us must be the result of severe and constant struggle rather than artificial forcing. No race that has anything to contribute to the markets of the world is long in any degrees ostracized.[14]

This speech brought Washington nationwide attention and acclaim. As a preeminent leader of the Negro in the United States, this approach on the process of social and economic integration prevailed in white attitudes.

Washington thought that the South offered unique opportunity to the Negro because of the relatively underdeveloped agricultural and industrial resources. Thus, education at Tuskegee Institute was oriented towards basic industrial and agricultural vocational training. Despite this rationale for industrial training, Washington did exhibit an agrarian bias. "We are living in a country where, if we are going to succeed at all, we are going to do so largely by what we raise out of the soil."[15]

Washington argued that industrial education would make "an intelligent producer of the Negro who becomes of immediate value to the community rather than one who yields to the temptation to living merely by politics or other parasitical employments."[16] Industrial education was a technique that would secure the cooperation of whites and accomplish the most that is possible for the blacks.[17]

In response to the criticism that industrial education would deprive the Negro of a professional class, Washington argued that the best way for the Negro race to move into professional positions was through the basic occupations.

This will give him a foundation upon which to stand while securing what is called the more exalted positions. The Negro has the right to study law; but success will come to the race sooner if it produces intelligent, thrifty farmers, mechanics, and house-keepers to support the lawyers.[18]

Washington's influence was pervasive, both in the Negro community and in shaping white attitudes towards Negro economic, political, and social development. Because of his dominant position within the Negro community, Washington fell prey to the criticism of other aspiring Negro leaders. W. E. B. DuBois, one of Washington's most vehement critics, criticized both his position and his philosophy.

> Mr. Washington represents in the Negro thought the old attitude of adjustment and submission; but adjustment at such a peculiar time as to make his program unique. This is the age of unusual economic development and Mr. Washington's program naturally takes an economic cast, becoming a gospel of work and money to such an extent to almost completely overshadow the higher aims in life. . . . Mr. Washington's program practically accepts the alleged inferiority of the Negro races. . . . Mr. Washington withdraws many of the high demands of Negroes as men and American citizens. . . . Mr. Washington distinctly asks the black people to give up at least for the present three things,—first, political power; second, insistence on civil rights; third, higher education for Negro youths,—and concentrate all their energies on industrial education, the accumulation of wealth, and the conciliation of the south . . . . as a result of this tender of the palm branch, what has been returned? In these years there have occurred: one, the disfranchisement of the Negro. Two, the legal creation of a distinct status of civil inferiority for the Negro. Three, the steady withdrawal of aid from institutions for higher training of the Negro.[19]

Both in his philosophical orientation and in the opposition he aroused in other Negroes, Booker T. Washington shaped the philosophy of the Negro in the United States. He was the original advocate of black capitalism. "The businessmen's gospel of free enterprise, competition, and laissez-faire never had a more loyal exponent than the master of Tuskegee."[20]

C. Vann Woodward has criticized Washington's anachronistic economic philosophy because he did not take into account the realities of mass production, industrial integration, financial combinations, and monopoly.

The shortcomings of the Atlanta Compromise, whether in education, labor, or business, were the shortcomings of a philosophy which dealt with the present in terms of the past. Not that a certain realism was lacking in Washington's approach. It is indeed hard to see how he could have preached or his people practice a radically different philosophy in his time and place. The fact remains that Washington's training school, and the many other schools he inspired, taught crafts and attitudes more congenial to the pre-machine age than to the 20th century; that his labor doctrine was a compound of individualism, paternalism, and anti-unionism in an age of collective labor action; and that his business philosophy was an anachronism.[21]

The Economic Vision of W. E. B. DuBois

With the death of Booker T. Washington, William Edward Burghardt DuBois became the spokesman for the American Negro. DuBois' life was spent in preparation for this task. While in college at Fisk University and Harvard, he accepted as duty the leadership role and dedicated himself to the redemption of the Negro. His education was in the social sciences. He believed that these areas were most germane to the study of the Negro in America. At Harvard he studied political economy and history under tutors who emphasized institutions and historical development as a means to achieve an understanding of the present. This orientation was further reinforced by study in Germany under two of the leaders of the historical school of economics, Gustav Schmoller and Adolph Wagner. This education uniquely prepared him to research and interpret the Negroes' relationships to the political, social, and economic institutions.

DuBois' interpretation of the Negro and American society remained in transition throughout most of his lifetime. It is thus difficult to extract a composite picture of his overall economic views. An economic orientation was only a part of his total view of the influences on the future of the Negro. His interpretation of economic possibilities altered with his progressive disillusionment with the prevailing American institutions. Initially, he advocated integration into the industrial system. But later in his life he was critical of capitalism and the profit motive, and espoused a system of industrial democracy and qualified socialism.

DuBois attacked Booker T. Washington's advocacy of industrial education and his accommodation and conciliation to southern racial attitudes. This criticism was most carefully articulated in *The Souls of Black Folk.*

The black men of America have a duty to perform, a duty stern and delicate—a forward movement to oppose a part of the work of their greatest leader. So far as Mr. Washington preaches Thrift, Patience, and Industrial Training for the masses, we must hold up his hands and strive with him, rejoicing in his honors and glorying in the strength of this Joshua called of God and of man to lead the headless host. But so far as Mr. Washington apologizes for injustice, North or South, does not rightly value the privilege and duty of voting, belittles the emasculating effects of caste distinctions, and opposes the higher training and ambition of our brighter minds—so far as he, the South, or the Nation, does this, —we must firmly oppose them.[22]

DuBois refused to accept injustice in order to obtain white support for Negro industrial education. Although not opposed to industrial education per se he was concerned that emphasis on this goal dissipated resources available for liberal arts institutions such as Fisk, Atlanta, and Howard. Liberal arts education would create a vanguard of leaders for the redemption of the Negro race, or the Negro intellectual élite, the "talented tenth." Throughout his lifetime DuBois retained his faith in the ability of an intellectual aristocracy to redeem the masses.

The Negro race, like all races, is going to be saved by its exceptional men. The problem of education, then, among Negroes must first of all deal with the Talented Tenth; it is the problem of developing the Best of this race that they may guide the Mass away from the contamination and death of the Worst in their own and other races. . . .

. . . . The Talented Tenth of the Negro race must be made leaders of thought and missionaries of culture among their people. No others can do this work and Negro colleges must train men for it. . . .[23]

DuBois' program for the economic emancipation of the Negro centered around three complementary concepts: separatism, cooperation, and socialism. Francis Broderick, a biographer of DuBois, relates that over a period of years DuBois realized the dilemma of Negro separatism. The aims of integration, the long-range goal, and security, a short-range goal, were in conflict and pulled in different directions.[24] This conflict was expressed in *The Souls of Black Folk*.

One feels ever his two-ness—an American, a Negro; two souls, two thoughts, two unreconciled strivings; two warring ideals in one dark body, whose dogged strength alone keeps it from being torn asunder.[25]

Repeated rebuffs in efforts to enlist support of white groups to assist the Negro led DuBois to the conclusion that separation would be necessary to permit the development of the race. The separatism advocated was not physical or geographical, but cultural, social, and economic—that is, a self-sufficient Negro culture exclusive of state and cultural lines.[26]

Harold Cruse in *The Crisis of the Negro Intellectual* argues that this rejection of nationalism was the great weakness of DuBois —the only real flaw in the man's intellect. Cruse contends that "It seems not to have occurred to DuBois that any thorough economic reorganization of Negro Existence imposed from above, will not be supported by the popular masses unless an appeal is made to their nationalism."[27] He argued that segregation and discrimination do not necessarily go together. Opposition to segregation should arise only when there is discrimination. Although DuBois believed that, in the long run, the greatest human development would occur in a system permissive of wider contact, the racial barriers confronting the Negro made this wider contact improbable.

. . . . It is impossible, therefore, to wait for the millennium of free and normal intercourse before we unite, to cooperate among ourselves in groups of like-minded people and in groups of people suffering from the same disadvantages and hatreds.

. . . It is the conscious black man cooperating together in his own institutions and movements who will eventually emancipate the colored race. . . .[28]

DuBois accepted an economic segregation when separation resulted in economic benefits for the Negro. In referring to the existence of Negro businesses, he noted that newspapers, barbers, and morticians catering to Negro clientele existed only because of segregated business patterns. In industry Negroes held only unskilled low-income jobs and competed with white labor, creating racial animosities. In small retail stores Negroes were not competing with large chain stores. In the service sector they received insufficient wages to support themselves and their families, and in agriculture blacks faced the general decline of the industry.[29] In 1928, when DuBois argued for "intensive economic organization of the Negro market behind a tariff wall of racial pride,"[30] he believed that Negroes must organize on a cooperative basis.

We see more and more clearly that economic survival for the Negro in America means . . . that he must employ labor, that he must organize industry, that he must enter American industrial development as a group, capable of offensive and defensive action, and not simply as an individual, liable to be made the victim of the white employer and of such of the white labor unions as dare.[31]

Within this cooperative movement a new sense of values would be operative that contrasted with the individualism of the private competitive system.

Under economic cooperation we must strive to spread the idea among colored people that the accumulation of wealth is for social rather than individual ends. We must avoid, in the advancement of the Negro race, the mistakes of ruthless exploitation which have marked modern economic history. To this end we must seek not simple home ownership, small landholding and savings accounts, but also all forms of cooperation, both in production and distribution, profit-sharing, building and loan association, systematic charity for definite, practical ends. . . .[32]

If carefully organized cooperatives would lead to economic prosperity, Negro labor and entrepreneurs would control each successive stage of production. Negro cooperative stores would obtain their goods from Negro producers, which were supplied raw materials from Negro farmers. Intermediate stages of productions, such as extractive industries and transportation, were to be Negro controlled. Final products would be purchased by Negro consumers who patronized only black stores.

The profits derived would remain in the system and benefit everyone who shared in the cooperatives. This economic structure would provide for the Negro's economic independence and eventually lead to cooperation between the American Negro and the West Indies, South America, and Africa.[33]

DuBois was critical of capitalism as an economic system because of its exploitation and constraint of the Negro. The Great Depression revealed the structural weaknesses of capitalism, and he had believed that this disaster would move the United States away from its faith in private capitalism. The system, according to DuBois, was based on the fallacious concept that the pursuit of private profit would produce the best social results with no external interference in the market.[34] His alternative was a system in which distribution was based on social ethics, and where an "industrial democracy" had much greater control of labor and the fruits of the industrial process.

Although he never fully endorsed socialism, he accepted many socialist tenets. Writing in *Horizon* in 1907, he stated:

I am a Socialist of the Path. I do not believe in the complete socialization of the means of production—the entire abolition of private property in capital—but the Path of Progress and common sense certainly leads to a far greater ownership of the public wealth for the public good than is now the case. I do not believe that government can carry on private business as well as private concerns, but I do believe that most of the human business called private is no more private than God's blue sky, and that we are approaching a time when railroads, coal mines, and many factories can and ought to be run by the public for the public. . . .

In the socialist trend thus indicated lies the one great hope of the Negro American. We have been thrown by strange historic reasons into the hands of the capitalists hitherto. We have been made tools of oppression against the workingman's cause—the puppets and playthings of the idle rich. Fools! We must awake! Not in a renaissance among ourselves of the evils of Get and Grab—not in private hoarding, squeezing and cheating, lies our salvation, but rather in that larger ideal of human brotherhood, equality of opportunity and work not for wealth but for Weal— here lies our shining goal.[35]

Although DuBois continuously questioned the tactics of the American Communist Party, he approved of the Russian revolution. He maintained that communism embraced the "goals of every unselfish thinker of the previous century; abolition of poverty and illiteracy, production for consumption, not profit, social control of nature's riches, and abolition of unemployment. Against this statement of the ideal, mortal men in capitalist nations were hard pressed to compete."[36]

In his autobiography, *Dusk of Dawn*, in the chapter entitled "Revolution," DuBois set forth an economic program for the Negro. This program was designed to achieve a "cooperative commonwealth." The cooperative commonwealth constitutes his ultimate state of thought on economics and the Negro.

☐ **1** We American Negroes are threatened today with lack of opportunity to work according to gifts and training and lack of income sufficient to support healthy families according to standards demanded by modern culture.

☐ **2** In industry, we are a labor reservoir, fitfully employed and paid a wage below subsistence; in agriculture, we are largely

disfranchised peons; in public education, we tend to be disinherited illiterates; in higher education, we are the parasites of
reluctant and hesitant philanthropy.

☐ **3** In the current reorganization of industry, there is no adequate effort to secure us a place in industry, to open opportunity
for Negro ability, or to give us security in age or unemployment.

☐ **4** Not by the development of upper classes anxious to exploit
the workers, nor by the escape of individual genius into the white
world, can we effect the salvation of our group in America. And
the salvation of this group carries with it the emancipation not
only of the darker races of men who make the vast majority of
mankind, but of all men of all races. We, therefore, propose this:

Basic American Negro Creed

☐ **A** As American Negroes, we believe in unity of racial effort, so
far as this is necessary for self-defense and self-expression, leading
ultimately to the goal of a united humanity and the abolition of
all racial distinctions.

☐ **B** We repudiate all artificial and hate-engendering deification
of race separation as such; but just as sternly, we repudiate an en-
nervating philosophy of Negro escape into an artificially privileged
white race which has long sought to enslave, exploit and tyrannize
over all mankind.

☐ **C** We believe that the Talented Tenth among American
Negroes, fitted by education and character to think and do, should
find primary employment in determining by study and measure-
ment the present field and demand for racial action and the
method by which the masses may be guided along this path.

☐ **D** We believe that the problems which now call for such racial
planning are Employment, Education and Health; these three: but
the greatest of these is Employment.

☐ **E** We believe that the labor force and intelligence of twelve
million people is more than sufficient to supply their own wants
and make their advancement secure. Therefore, we believe that,
if carefully and intelligently planned, a co-operative Negro industrial system in America can be established in the midst of and in
conjunction with the surrounding national industrial organization
and in intelligent accord with that reconstruction of the economic
basis of the nation which must sooner or later be accomplished.

☐ **F** We believe that Negro workers should join the labor movement and affiliate with such trade unions as welcome them and
treat them fairly. We believe that Workers' Councils organized by

Negroes for interracial understanding should strive to fight race prejudice in the working class.

☐ **G** We believe in the ultimate triumph of some form of Socialism the world over; that is, common ownership and control of the means of production and equality of income.

☐ **H** We do not believe in lynching as a cure for crime; nor in war as a necessary defense of culture; nor in violence as the only path to economic revolution. Whatever may have been true in other times and places, we believe that today in America we can abolish poverty by reason and the intelligent use of the ballot, and above all by the dynamic discipline of soul and sacrifice of comfort which, revolution or no revolution, must ever be the only real path to economic justice and world peace.

☐ **I** We conceive this matter of work and equality of adequate income as not the end of our effort, but the beginning of the rise of the Negro race in this land and the world over, in power, learning and accomplishment.

☐ **J** We believe in the use of our vote for equalizing wealth through taxation, for vesting the ultimate power of the state in the hands of the workers; and as an integral part of the working class, we demand our proportionate share in administration and public expenditure.

☐ **K** This is and is designed to be a program of racial effort and this narrowed goal is forced upon us today by the unyielding determination of the mass of the white race to enslave, exploit and insult Negroes; but to this vision of work, organization and service, we welcome all men of all colors so long as their subscription to this basic creed is sincere and is proven by their deeds.[37]

DuBois' advocacy of black cultural separatism and nationalism was carried to the extreme by Marcus Garvey who emphasized separatism and black cultural economic and social development outside of the existing institutions of the United States. In contrast to DuBois, Garvey did not believe that there would be, at some time in the future, a coming together of the races after the Negro had developed a racial and cultural identity.

Marcus Garvey:
The Universal Negro
Improvement Association

A new dimension was introduced into black thinking in the United States by Marcus Garvey and the advent of the Universal Negro Improvement Association. The dynamic force of black nationalism could have supplied the motivating ideology lacking in the programs and philosophies of other Negro leaders in the post-Civil War period. Garvey, a Jamaican by birth, established the Universal Negro Improvement Association first in that country. Its purpose was to conduct a crusade for the rehabilitation of the Negro race. The stated objectives of the association were:

... to establish a universal Confraternity among the race; to promote the spirit of race pride and love; to reclaim the fallen of the race; to administer and assist the needy; to assist in civilizing the backward tribes of Africa; to strengthen the imperialism of the independent African states; to establish commissionaries or agencies in the principal countries of the world for the protection of all Negroes, irrespective of nationality; to promote a conscientious Christian worship among the native tribes of Africa; to establish universities, colleges, and secondary schools for the further education and culture of the boys and girls of the race; to conduct a worldwide commercial and industrial intercourse.[38]

Garvey was greatly influenced by Booker T. Washington. He became convinced of his destiny as a leader of his race upon reading Washington's *Up from Slavery*. In 1916 he came to the United States to meet with Washington and to promote interest in the work of the UNIA in Jamaica. Before he arrived Washington had died. Although failing in his specified purposes, Garvey's travels had a tremendous impact upon the Negro race in the United States.

The disillusionment arising from the realization that the Negroes' participation in World War I had done little to achieve any rights for himself, and the increasing concentration of the Negro in urban areas, created a psychological climate that caused the Negro to look for a leader capable of providing a sense of racial identity and dignity. This new mood, along with the vacuum in black leadership created by the death of Booker T. Washington, produced circumstances uniquely receptive to the personal charisma of the dynamic Jamaican. Garvey remained in the United States and established a branch of the Universal Negro Improvement Association in Harlem. This office ultimately became the headquarters of a worldwide organization.

The message that Garvey espoused spoke directly to the needs of the disillusioned urban Negro. He proclaimed that through racial unity and racial cooperation the Negro could achieve respect and dignity. The Negro must be "one race" and have "one God and one destiny." He attempted to mobilize the urban black behind the rallying cry, "Up you mighty race, you can accomplish what you will." The Negro responded to this message. It "brought to the Negro people for the first time a sense of pride in being black. Black pride is the core of Marcus Garvey's philosophy. Around this ideal he centered his life."[39]

The New York *Amsterdam News* stated that "... it was because Marcus Garvey made black people proud of their race. In a world where black is despised, he taught them that black is beautiful. He taught them to admire and praise black people and black things. They rallied to him because he heard and responded to the heartbeat of his race."[40]

Garvey's program for the attainment of racial pride contained two complementary dimensions: geographical separatism and economic self-sufficiency. Separation was the only practical manner in which the Negro could obtain release from subjugation. This belief was based on the premise that white cultures could not permit the assimilation of the black because assimilation was a form of racial suicide. He argued for complete separation and particularly against miscegenation.

I believe that white men should be white, yellow men should be yellow, and black men should be black in the great panorama of races, until each and every race by its own initiative lifts itself up to a common standard of humanity, as to compel the respect and appreciation of all, and so make it possible for each one to stretch out the hand of welcome without being able to be prejudiced against the other because of any inferior or unfortunate condition.[41]

For Garvey, no race could ever be free as long as it was subjugated to another culture. Thus, the Negro must break all cultural ties with the dominant white society.

No Negro . . . shall be truly respected until the race as a whole has emancipated itself, through self-achievement and progress, from universal prejudice. The Negro will have to build its own government, industry, art, science, literature and culture, before the world will stop to consider him. Until then we are but wards of a superior race and civilization, and outcasts of a standard social system.[42]

To achieve these ends the Negro must have a nation and a country of his own where he can demonstrate to the world his "own ability in the art of human progress."[43] This position is perhaps posited most strongly in the statement concerning "What We Believe" of the Universal Negro Improvement Association.

It believes in the social, political and physical separation of all peoples to the extent that they promote their own ideals and civilization with the privilege of trading and doing business with each other. It believes in the promotion of a strong and powerful Negro nation in Africa.[44]

For Garvey the return-to-Africa or pan-African movement was no visionary or utopian concept. He vigorously sought to implement such a concept throughout his lifetime. A governmental structure was organized, and titles of nobility were established. Garvey was the chief executive. Representatives were sent to Liberia to locate sites for Negro colonies, which were to house Negroes from around the world. Blacks could return to their historical and cultural homeland. Garvey thought that "The other races have countries of their own and it is time for the four hundred million to claim Africa for themselves."[45]

White America, in Garvey's view, had an obligation to assist the Negro to return to Africa. "Let white America help us for 50 years honestly, as we have helped her for 300 years, and before the expiration of many decades there will be no more race problem. Help us to gradually go home, America. Help us as you helped the Jews. Help us as you have helped the Irish. Help us as you have helped the Poles, Russians, Germans, and Armenians."[46]

It is possible that this return-to-Africa program would have become a reality. But Garvey's statements on a united Africa for the Africans induced a strong opposition to his program from the European colonial powers in Africa. Colonial powers brought pressure on the government of Liberia, which resulted in fear within the Liberian government that the rapid influx of American Negroes would be prejudicial to Liberian interests and autonomy.

It was only after Garvey saw his African dream shattered that he turned his attention to political action within the United States. In 1924, he organized the Negro Political Union, designed to "consolidate the political forces of the Negro through which the race will express its political opinions."[47] This organization attempted to elect candidates to public office in order to assist the Negro in his cause.

Garvey believed that the Negro would ultimately demonstrate his capacity for initiative and self-sufficiency.

Lagging behind in the band of civilization will not prove our higher abilities. Being subservient to the will and caprice of our progressive races will not prove anything superior in us. Being satisfied to drink the dregs from the cup of human progress will not demonstrate our fitness as a people to exist alongside of others, but when of our own initiative we strike out to build industries, governments, and ultimately empires, then and only then will we as a race prove to our creator and to man in general that we are fit to survive and capable of shaping our own destiny.[48]

Garvey's attitude on economic self-sufficiency was attributable

to Washington's philosophy that the Negro must become independent of white capital and operate his own business activities.[49]

Garvey recognized that the economic system in the United
States was designed to exploit the Negro. The white man's solution
for the Negro problem in this country was to utilize the black
population to build up the country to the point when black labor
was no longer needed and then "throw them off and let them starve
economically and die of themselves or emigrate elsewhere, we care
not where. Then no one can accuse him of being inhuman to the
Negro as we have not massacred him."[50] In addition, Garvey argued that in this country increased wealth of the Negro or the
Negro vote could never force the government to recognize Negro
needs. The government is dictated by the majority of the people.
In the United States when the majority are against something
"then the government is impotent to protect that measure, thing
or race."[51]

However, the system of capitalism was necessary to the progress of the world. Anyone who opposed this economic system was
an enemy of human advancement. Garvey opposed socialism and
even labor unionism. In "Capitalism in the State," Garvey argued
that there should be strict limitations on the income or wealth
that any individual or corporation could hold. The state should use
and invest the money above specified limitations. He also argued
that warfare was inherent in modern capitalistic systems and was
the product of conflicts that arose as a result of the colonialism
of capitalists throughout the world.

Garvey intended to use capitalism to supply the means to
achieve economic self-sufficiency for the Negro. No race in the
world was so just that it would be willing to provide a "square deal
in things economic, political and social."[52] The only protection
against injustice is physical, financial, and scientific power. It was
necessary for the Negro to construct a strong economic base from
which to seek his other political and social objectives. Only
through material achievement gained by the force of their own
effort and initiative would the Negro be recognized. Thus, the

Negro must establish an economic organization to achieve effective economic cooperation in the world.

Garvey's goal was to initiate this economic organization within the framework of the Universal Negro Improvement Association. The purpose of this organization was to construct black-owned and black-operated businesses that would provide sources of incomes for Negroes within the United States. The most prodigious effort to establish black enterprise was the Black Star Steamship Line. Money was raised through contributions and stock subscriptions from Negroes to purchase several steamships to engage in foreign and domestic trade and ostensibly to provide a means of transportation for repatriation to Africa. Several steamships were actually purchased and did make abortive efforts in oceanic trade. The Black Star Steamship Line ultimately failed because Garvey and the Universal Negro Improvement Association were defrauded in the purchase of the ships. There was also evidence of dishonesty and duplicity of some of the Black Star Line executives.

Garvey's unique talent was in his ability to mobilize people and initiate projects. He had little knowledge of financial affairs, however, and lacked the organizational and structural acumen necessary for large ventures. The fact that the Black Star Line failed did not minimize the significance of this venture. It was the first large-scale attempt to establish a black business corporation financed by contributions of the masses of the Negroes, to be managed by black entrepreneurial talent. The Black Star Line was a landmark in Negro history and provides a valuable illustration for contemporary "black-capitalism" programs.

A second type of economic enterprise was organized under the auspices of the Universal Negro Improvement Association. The Negro Factories Corporation was designed to "build and operate factories in the big industrial centers of the United States, Central America, the West Indies and Africa to manufacture every marketable commodity."[53] The corporation was capitalized at one million dollars. Common stock was sold to blacks at $5 a share. Several types of businesses were established by this enterprise: a chain of cooperative grocery stores, a restaurant, a steam laundry, a tailoring-dressmaking shop, a millinery store, and a publishing house.[54] Other related efforts were made to encourage Negro entrepreneurs to start businesses of their own. The Negro Factories Corporation was to supply initial investment capital and organizational, executive, and technical guidance. These enterprises were less than a complete success. However, their significance is not in their economic impact, but as an illustration of Negro operation and entrepreneurship.

Garvey served a prison sentence for supposed malfinance in the operation of the Black Star Steamship Line. He was deported after his release. Although he attempted to keep his movement alive from Jamaica and from London, his business activities never retained the scope and force they possessed prior to his imprisonment. But the impact of Garvey's enterprise was unique. He was the first to mobilize and hold the allegiance of the masses of urban blacks. He was able to direct Negroes toward the goal of rehabilitation and improvement of the Negro race through black programs of pan-Africanism and economic self-sufficiency. Most of the bases of the potential achievement of economic self-sufficiency and economic separation are found in Garvey's philosophy and work. W. E. B. DuBois, although an enemy of Garvey, provided this assessment of the Garvey enterprises.

It was a grandiose and bombastic scheme, utterly impractical as a whole, but it was sincere and had some practical features; and Garvey proved not only an astonishing popular leader, but a master propagandist. Within a few years, news of his movement, promises and plans, reached Europe and Asia and penetrated every corner of Africa.[55]

Many contemporary economic philosophies and development programs of Negro moderates and militants were contained in the economic philosophies of earlier black leaders such as Booker T. Washington, W. E. B. DuBois, and Marcus Garvey. The black utopian movement and the philosophies of W. E. B. DuBois and Marcus Garvey displayed antecedents of the modern economic separatist movement and the contemporary emphasis on black economic development. Washington and Garvey, in particular, were outspoken advocates of black capitalism and black entrepreneurship. The arguments of DuBois are a nucleus for the concept of black nationalism and cultural separatism, and the modern emphasis on cooperatives as an efficient vehicle for economic development. DuBois' philosophy contained the concept that a black economic system could evolve as a moral system that was more desirable and more ethical than the capitalism of the United States. Marcus Garvey's plan for black capitalism was the most useful contribution to black economic development. Many black militants emulate Garvey's model as the best means for the black to achieve social and economic development. Garvey's ill-fated enterprises represent the essential procedural and conceptual elements of militant nationalism and black capitalism.

CHAPTER 3

Moderate and Militant—Diversity in Ideology

There is a wide spectrum of attitudes in the Negro community toward the social institutions of American society and particularly the institution of capitalism as an economic system. Many blacks are now pessimistic about the possibility of ever achieving successful integration in American society or of employing capitalistic means of achieving economic development. Thus, they argue that the only alternative remaining is to separate from this system and its institutions and to attempt economic and social development outside its institutional structure. Other Negroes, both moderate and militant, accept the existing social institutions and believe that working through the system they may obtain material progress. This disparity in attitudes about institutional structures creates

For Notes to Chapter 3 see pages 336–339.

45

difficulties in determining which developmental approaches within the black movement may be successful in achieving rapid economic advancement.

Acceptance of the
Institutional Structure

Negro educator Kenneth B. Clark has noted that the urban-racial crisis in America stems from the fact that America "believes that it is possible to have an affluent, healthy, capable society in general with pockets of despair, pockets of desperation, pockets within the city of large numbers of people who are excluded from the general affluence and who are relegated to the status of menials and inferiors. The belief that these pockets can coexist with urban stability is a self-deluding belief."[1]

Historical Views   The means by which the black can be raised from a menial and inferior status have an economic dimension. Many Negro leaders have assumed that the institutional structure of our United States economy does contain the mechanisms necessary for developing a total affluence that will include the Negro. The Negro must participate in a competitive manner, be trained, be educated, and move into a position of economic control of resources as a businessman or move into high-paid positions that will provide an independent source of income. The route out of the pockets of impoverishment and discrimination may be upward mobility through existing white economic institutions. A large number of blacks can be accommodated or may in fact join the white in entrepreneurial roles or as highly skilled well-paid employees. Thus, for some Negroes the free-enterprise capitalistic framework is an acceptable one that the black can manipulate for his own and thus the economy's benefit.

The acceptance of the upward-movement route is neither a new nor unique alternative for the contemporary black. There is a well-developed historical frame of reference for accepting and using the capitalistic framework, even though the Negro slave had been capitalism's most exploited victim.

For example, John Hope, a teacher at Atlanta University, urged blacks in 1898 to start their own businesses and to patronize them rather than white businesses. John Hope's views were that neither industrial education nor unions could really aid the Negroes' economic advancement. It was the establishment of a capitalistic class with Negro-owned and operated businesses that would provide employment that provided a solution to the Negroes' problems.[2]

The National Urban League was founded in 1910 with the principle task of improving the Negroes' advancement in industry. The League was then and is now concerned with the opportunity of the Negro to obtain work on the basis of his efficiency, to be promoted on the job, and to receive equal pay for equal work. In his book, *Black Bourgeoisie,* E. Franklin Frazier shows that a number of blacks connected with Negro business have advocated the establishment and operation of many black businesses as the best way for the race to win equality of opportunity.

A clear statement of black acceptance of the free-enterprise system as a base from which to achieve economic success was articulated by John Merrick, founder of the largest Negro business, the North Carolina Mutual Insurance Company. Merrick stated that even in the South "We [Negroes] have the same privileges that other people have. Every avenue is open to us to do business as it is to any other people."[3] Merrick's views are an extreme example of the assessment of the capacity of the capitalistic mechanism to be effective in facilitating solutions to economic discrimination and exclusion.

Contemporary Advocates   Today the Negro lives within two kinds of economic systems: (1) a white-dominated, free-enterprise, *laissez-faire* capitalistic system, and (2) a government-administered economy characterized by welfare support and antipoverty programs. For the Negro both economies have the same organizational features of being administered from the top down. For many Negroes, free-enterprise capitalism has a potential for producing economic democracy, or a pattern for sharing in the income and production. The leadership of many black activist organizations are pro-capitalistic. Leaders of the NAACP, the National Business League, and the National Urban League continue to accept the capitalistic economic institutions as an appropriate base through which their constituency may end impoverishment. Although the members in these organizations may be participants in the "welfare" economy, they accept the tenets of capitalism and rely on the mechanisms provided by the free-enterprise economy to propel them into the mainstream of American economic life.

F. Naylor Fitzhugh, the head of the Advisory Group for the Small Business Development and Guidance Center, confirms the black commitment to capitalism.

If you divide the American population into Blacks and Whites, there is as much commitment to the capitalistic framework among Blacks, other things equal, as among whites. . . . We definitely accepted American standards, American goals; we wanted to achieve within the American frame of reference. . . . I still think that despite all the setbacks we have had in this system that there are few Blacks who do not believe that in the long run their participation in the capitalistic system will have some important results in the community.[4]

Fitzhugh also points out that what the black community is looking for in the way of modification in capitalistic institutions is a greater emphasis upon the social and human concern by business and by government as it applies to opportunities for the black. One of the great problems of the capitalistic system is not its organizational base, but the newly institutionalized attempts to apply contemporary egalitarian standards to blacks. If the system applies the same rules to blacks and whites in economic processes such as hiring or firing, the black will never move up the competitive ladder. The enterprise system must look for qualifiable blacks, not qualified blacks. What the black community is saying to the leaders of the enterprise institutions is, "Don't give us your excuses, don't give us your explanations, don't even contend that you are being completely fair."[5]

In the area of economic goals of the system, Fitzhugh contends that the black objectives have not been spelled out in any theoretical sense. He further noted that spelling out quantitative economic goals makes little sense. "We have been at such a low level of participation in this whole field that anything that we accomplish becomes close to 100% improvement."[6] Fitzhugh has implied that a long-term evolutionary pattern of black participation within the white-dominated economic system will permit Negroes to move into the middle class in large numbers. Fitzhugh places the burden of the economic improvement of the black within the system squarely on the white. He stresses that "the tactics of Black America are actually being dictated by White communities. . . . What is going to turn out to be a sound strategy for the bulk of America's Black people is largely determined by the behavior of the White community."[7] The appropriate positive reaction from the black community will follow when and if the white community works for a coalition that has short- as well as long-term purposes. Thus, the white community or institutional groups have only to create a positive environment that permits upward mobility in order to reaffirm the blacks preconception that the capitalist system can, in fact, pose a panacea for economically disenfranchised blacks.

The same general thesis that the capitalistic system needs a more humanistic orientation and procedural reforms to obtain more complete acceptance by the Negro is voiced by representatives of the NAACP. William Morris, Housing Director, has posited that it is impossible to operate successfully an isolated black economic system. "Regardless of how far we go with the concept of black control, somewhere down the line there is going to be an interrelationship, and an interaction with the white community and the power structure, the financial structure, if it's going to have any success."[8] Morris' concept of economic development and improvement for the Negro runs counter to the black isolated-economy approach.

Economic development means the development of Negro entrepreneurs and the development of Negro businesses where they have some degree of economic independence. The upward mobility of Negroes must open into the general level of management and submanagement positions where they can participate fully in the mainstream of business and economic activity.[9]

For Morris, the Negro cannot succeed outside the system if he hopes to achieve the economic support or stature that will permit him to be autonomous and independent. Black economic independence comes from successful performance within the traditional business establishment that provides financial reward in amounts large enough to achieve financial and thus personal independence. Thus, Morris supports programs—black or white—that provide financial aid and technical training in the use of financial aid. Morris believes that the private sector, not the government, should be instrumental in getting development programs underway. The private business sector is less bureaucratic, not encumbered by tight regulations, and can move faster and more freely and make its own decisions. Business participation is essential if any economic development program for blacks is to be successful.

The role and type of action of the white business community that aids the black is concomitant with Morris' ideas on the manner in which blacks should focus on the "acquisitive business ethic" of work and achievement. "I am not as interested in making people comfortable in their poverty as I am in providing them with the tools to rise up and out of the poverty situation. Guaranteed annual wages and dole are programs that should be used to provide emergency temporary help to those that are in need. It should not be a permanent thing. Generation after generation may rely upon them. I think that our major emphasis has to be in terms of helping people to attain self-dependence financially where they can provide for their own needs and also provide for the needs of their children as they are coming up to properly prepare for them to take their place in a competitive society."[10]

Traditional Black Capitalism   Morris attributed the sources of his ideas and inspiration on these issues to Fitzhugh and

Burkeley Burrell, as well as to Clark College president Vivian Henderson. Burkeley Burrell is the current president of the National Business League based in Washington, D.C. The National Business League, since its founding in 1900 by Booker T. Washington, has advocated and encouraged the development of black capitalism. In *The Negro in American Business*, Kinzer and Sagarin identified the historical significance and rationale for the aim of Negroes to become businessmen:

From the moment that the American Negro first breathed the air of this country as a free man, up to the protests and struggles of the present day, the leadership of the race has turned its attention to the role of the Negro in American business. The Negro as a businessman, it was hoped, could provide sources for employment; could offer services to a people otherwise denied or cheated; could amass capital and exercise influence on the community; and develop a structure independent of the white dominated economy.[11]

In one view, what black business must do now during the urban crisis is exactly the same thing that it was charged to do by Booker Washington. For a black community to grow and to remain strong, Washington believed that it had to produce and trade in the marketplace. It had to learn the rules and acquire the skills and tools of the game to become and remain competitive.[12] Burrell articulates the pattern of action expected by the black business community from the majority white society.

. . . . It is an article of faith with us that the free entrepreneuring system that is an American trademark is directly and indirectly responsible for all of the good things that have inured to our citizenry. *We want to become a truly meaningful part of that system.* We do not want a *hand out,* but we need and seek the warm right hand of fellowship that only our white contemporaries can provide us. *Give* us nothing but loan us what we need. Money, guidance, counseling, know-how, are all professional commodities that should be available for a price. We ask only that the price be reasonable and equitable.[13]

In the same speech Burrell pointed out that in the field of

economics the National Business League has stood alone as the
sole advocate of minority entrepreneurship. Burrell has also noted
that there is probably no source in this country that has a keener
perception of the nature of the solution to urban tranquility
than the National Business League.[14]

The NBL is convinced that the development of a broadly
based, successful, ethnic minority business class is the single
catalyst essential to the establishment of urban peace.

A dispassionate look at our society tells us that all of the good
things our citizenry enjoys, all of the mores and standards of
citizen behavior, all of the elements of both the "Good life" and
the bad, are functional results of the profit process. There is
no more motivating element in our existence than the process of
profit-making. The profit-making process in and of itself imputes
to the individual citizen-at-once an attitude of mastery and control
of himself and his own destiny. It imbues him with a posture of
personal worth and significant social worth in terms of his controlling the destiny of others through his control of jobs.[15] It is President Burrell's view that the absence of a broad base of black
businesses within the subculture of the ghettos is the main cause
of mistrust, frustration, and hatred of those who control the
economic facets of the deprived urban existence.

The policy logically evolving from these views is the establishment of business opportunities in the urban cores as a basis of
eliminating the sources of black-white friction. This is in fact
what several NBL programs, discussed in a later chapter, have
been designed to accomplish. In terms of the NBL philosophy and
approach, what is wrong with the capitalistic system is that there
are too few black capitalists. Burrell called attention to this failing
of the enterprise system in these terms:

. . . as hard driving as we Americans are, as dedicated to progress
and profits as we are, we seem to totally miss the point of the dire
need for black, brown, yellow and red entrepreneurship. The
vigorous pursuit of profits in this country continues to wear a white
label, and the assimilation of minority citizens into the profit-
making process is an imperceptibly slow process and appears to
occur only on a person-to-person basis.[16]

Early in 1969, the NBL published a statement on "Black Capitalism and Social Justice." This statement noted that there can be no single solution to the complex urban problems. "Certainly, black ownership and management are not going to solve the moral and psychological aspects of the problem."

NBL now notes two basic categories of the problems of social and economic injustice. One problem category concerns the inequities that exist because of racism. The NBL's objective here is equal access to all resources with the concomitant opportunities to develop talents and abilities on an equitable basis. The second area of difficulty involves capital diffusion and income distribution. Thus, solutions will require changes in the economic system to get equitable distribution of income and wealth and eliminate poverty. Black capitalism becomes a means by which black people will qualify for "equitable inclusion" into the society as it is today.

The problems associated with racism are virtually insurmountable for the black entrepreneur, but black capitalism can be an implement to attack capital diffusion and income-distribution problems. Given this more reasonable context, black-owned and ghetto-based business and industry can perform the following useful functions:

☐ **1**   Make available on-the-job training opportunities to develop management talent.

☐ **2**   Become visible evidence of personal achievement resulting from study and industry.

☐ **3**   Provide job opportunities.

☐ **4**   Increase the inner-city tax base.

☐ **5**   Generally exert forces to improve the inner-city economy.

In terms of the ideas reflected by the NBL, capitalists provide the real leadership in our country. Capitalists direct and control our government institutions. Thus, if black people hope to acquire real influence, they must acquire the tools of influence—that is, land, labor, capital, and business enterprise.

Employment Emphasis   The Reverend Leon Sullivan, a Philadelphia minister and the dynamic leader of the Opportunity

Industrial Center Programs, is an outspoken advocate of the benefits of the capitalistic framework. When Sullivan started his program in 1964, few industries had liberalized hiring procedures and were practicing a kind of economic integration tokenism. But in the Delaware River Valley industries indicated that if blacks were trained or possessed a skill, jobs might be made available. Sullivan's answer to this dilemma was the creation of job-training centers in Philadelphia. For Sullivan, then as now, integration is the accepted pattern of economic improvement for the black. But integration without preparation is a source of frustration for the black. Sullivan is basically arguing that the black must be competitive with the white in order to make it in the system, and skills training is a suitable competitive base. He also recognizes the need to have employment options for newly trained blacks. The necessity for job creation was stressed in his 1968 testimony before the Joint Economic Committee.

. . . . Black people can create jobs where they are in their own communities. Help us develop skills, and we will rebuild our own inner cities. . . . We can create economic development ourselves for the good of all Americans. Not just for Black men, but for all Americans.[17]

The justification or rationale for the participation within the capitalistic framework is that blacks want to be productive, creative and earn more. Sullivan describes the "within-the-system" upward-migration orientation in the following comments:

I don't want to shine shoes. I want to make shoes. I want to make dresses, not buy them. My people want not just to be consumers, the beggar, we want to be producers. . . . The thing I am saying is there is a movement on foot here, a massive movement of self-habilitation in America; black men are saying—the cry is not "Burn, Baby, Burn," but "Build, Brothers, Build."[18]

The OIC programs are not dependent upon Federal government financial support. In fact, the government has failed to provide aid in cases of program development deemed essential by Sullivan. The pro-private business attitudes of Sullivan are reflected in guidelines provided for the participation of the government in urban communities. ". . . . I think the only support that can be feasible, even in making the government employer of the last resort—it should be counted as a temporary measure. My community, my people, cannot afford to be dependent on Government for their livelihood."[19] He wants his people to end their dependence on the white community and become more independent. Government programs and outright government aid for education and for jobs make the blacks dependent instead of independent of the white-dominated political and economic institutions.

On the matter of economics, the OIC programs are pointing the way and creating the means by which blacks can develop economically. Sullivan's personal commentary on this development is as follows:

. . . . So I get a dollar in a man's pocket, that is an independent dollar, and not a government dollar to keep him quiet. It is an independent dollar, so he can be independent as a man can be in America—so they can move out and buy a house there, where he is not permitted to buy because he does not have the kind of economic essentials to get it. I want him to have economic credentials. That is what I am working for.[20]

All the comments about capitalism and the acceptance of free-enterprise economic institutions noted in the previous sections are attributable to men who are overtly committed to the integration of the blacks into the white economic structure. It may be instructive to add the comments of a black writer who has a more radical viewpoint. Daniel Watts, editor of the militant monthly, *The Liberator*, has an objective evaluation of the capitalistic framework *vis à vis* the Negro's efforts to improve his economic status.

It should be noted at the outset, that Watts believes that whites and blacks will ultimately fight at the barricades in the streets, because the white power structure will not give up the control over management, ownership, and the productive and distribution activities. The juxtaposition of economic control must occur if the blacks are to avoid the necessity for violent confrontation. On the question of whether or not blacks accept capitalism, Watts indicated:

. . . . I take the position that we, the black community, would bring a new dimension in terms of human wealth, and human values, into the white capitalistic system in terms of how we view human life and the value that we place on it opposed to the whites, who, I think, look upon human life as something secondary, something to be bargained for with dollars. I don't think that coming out of the black experience black people would view human beings in the same light as whites do. I think that it is still possible for black people to get involved in the capitalist structure. Whether you like it or not, the basic fact of life is that the capitalistic system in America does produce. There is no question about it, the system works, it produces. Basically, I guess what we are speaking about is how to expand the base in terms of distribution of the goods that the system produces.[21]

The Rejection of the Institutional Structure

The failure of the capitalistic system to permit the Negro to achieve his own economic objectives, or to permit him to share in the massive productivity and unparalleled wealth has led to the position that only through the elimination—not reform—of capitalistic institutional structure can the Negro ever hope to become a vital economic participant. The positions and views of blacks who advocate reversing the basic American approach to economics, or socialism, cooperatives, and a black economic system completely separated from white-dominated capitalism are reviewed in the following sections.

James Boggs   Daniel Watts has identified James Boggs as one of the two leading theoreticians of the Negro movement.[22] Boggs, who worked in the auto plants of Detroit from World War II until his recent retirement, has published many articles appearing in radical and foreign journals and is the author of *The American Revolution: Pages from a Negro Worker's Notebook.*[23] His work has been directed towards making "black power" a scientific concept that can serve as a motivating ideology for a black nationalistic revolution. His thinking is reputed to have played a major role in the development of the ideology of the concept of black power and the black revolution.[24]

The conceptual framework utilized by Boggs is that of the stages of economic and social development of a society and the movement of social groups through these stages, which are relative to one another within each stage. Within this theoretical framework, Boggs has identified three stages of development: (1) the agrarian, (2) the industrial, and (3) the age of cybernation, which is the stage that the United States is approaching. He asserts that in the agrarian and industrial stages capitalistic development took place only through the exploitation of some segment of the population. Historically, the exploited segment has been the black populace. Other minority groups have progressed in relation to the Negro by climbing over his back and exploiting him to obtain capitalistic development. For this reason, Boggs emphatically rejects capitalism as an economic institution. Capitalism has no possibilities of resolving the questions and problems confronting the black peoples. Capitalism is exploitive and survives only because of its abilities to subjugate people nationally or internationally through some system of colonialism.

But in the present phase of capitalistic development the labor power of the Negro has become economically and socially unnecessary. Automation and cybernation have eliminated the necessity of having a cheap, exploitable source of labor. The blacks are now expendable, having no place in the industrial system. Negroes are no longer needed by the capitalistic system as producers, but they are still exploited as consumers.[25]

However, having been rejected from and by the economic system, the Negro is now himself free to reject the system. "Pushed out of the system by the system itself, they have become outlaws at war with all the values and legalities of white America. It is this rejection of the values and legalities of white America, objectively rooted in the separation of these black youth from the system, which invests the slogan black power with such revolutionary potential."[26]

It is not the institution of capitalism alone that Boggs rejects, but the entire institutional structure of the society. The dynamics of his plan for the rejection of the system is not to separate geographically, but to bring about a revolutionary restructuring of these social institutions so that they may provide for and be compatible with a just and humane society. He argues that "at this juncture in history the system cannot, will not, resolve the problems that have been created by centuries of exploitation of black people. It remains for the Negro not only to change the system but to arrive at the kind of social system fitting to our time in relation to the development of this country."[27]

Any serious improvement in the condition of the black peoples must depend upon their ridding themselves of the whole parasitical white structure. "These institutions and enterprises, now occupied by the white oppressor, must be liberated."[28]

To implement this movement the Black Revolutionary Party must devise strategies that will lead to the radical transformation of American institutions. In the initial stages these strategies should be designed to achieve parallel power structures within the system and to create liberated areas out of what are presently occupied areas. His reference is to the inner cities of the urban areas of the United States, which will provide the power base for the Black Revolutionary Party. He is, initially then, advocating self-determination within the ghetto areas. But, the ultimate aim is revolution. A goal of black power is to "turn over or overturn the society of human beings, liberating both society and man from the barbarism and subjugation to inhumane forces into which they have been plunged by capitalism and racism. . . ."[29] To accomplish the end of "overturning the society" Boggs contends that there must be expropriation of the means of production and distribution and communications within the system.[30]

The concept of an instant revolution, although as American as apple pie, is an illusion for the black. "For this must be substituted a concept of a long-range strategy to mobilize the masses of the blacks in a revolutionary struggle."[31] Even though this revolutionary concept is not invested with a sense of immediacy in its execution, the existence of a black revolutionary party within the society is in fundamental antagonism to it and thus makes conflict and violence inevitable.[32] He unequivocally states that he possesses no illusions that such a great change can come about peacefully.[33]

The Muslims: Separation from a House Doomed to Fail
The Black Muslim rejection of American society and their program for social, economic, political, and ultimately geographic separation from the institutions of this society is predicated on a conglomeration of religious, social, racial, and economic factors.

The religious cause for separation is based upon the prophecy of Elijah Muhammad, designated as the "Messenger of Allah, Leader and Teacher to the American So-called Negro,"[34] of the apocalypse of the western world, a cataclysm in which western governments, institutions, and culture will be destroyed; and the divine promise that the Muslim is preordained to be the inheritor of the heavens and earth. In the Black Muslim doctrine, Allah, through his messenger Elijah Muhammad, has decreed the breakup of the old world. It was given to the white man to rule the world for 6,000 years, a tenure which is now at an end.[35]

Today America's doom is set like a die. She cannot escape; it is impossible . . .[36]

. . . . .

In Muslim terms, the white race exhibits a long history of causing wars and generating crisis conditions. Thus "the God of the righteous" must find the whites so disagreeable and troublesome that they will be removed from the face of the earth. Because of the historical pattern of white domination of the black race, the black victims can certify the troublemaking characteristics of the whites. It will be the American Negroes who have endured the brunt of bad white conduct who will be Allah's choice to survive the calamity of white destruction, and to be "put on top of civilization".[37]

The economic and social cause for separation is based on the contention that in four hundred years of slavery the Negro helped to build this society and its material abundance. Yet in this time he has received neither economic nor social justice; rather he has been excluded from participating in the fruits of the system to whose affluence he contributed. Elijah Muhammad now argues that the black man will never receive justice in this society, and the white should no longer desire to hold the black in bondage because the necessity of his labor is being eliminated through increased automation.

It was black men who built white railroads, plowed plantations, and cut the trees and underbrush in the development of American agriculture. But today, the black laborer has been replaced with machinery. In plaintive terms, E. Muhammad notes that now two or three men can cultivate hundreds of acres of farm land. Cotton picking is now mechanized. Thus the old artisan and labor role of the black has been eliminated by machines. The whites have elected to replace the black by substitution of their human motive power with mechanical means. Given this inexorable economic disenfranchisement, why shouldn't the whites permit the black freedom to resume his old labor specialization? According to Muhammad, it is natural that the blacks want land where they can start building a political and economic system for their future. In a black economy, labor will not be subject to brutal treatment and economic conditions will exist where the black can enjoy the benefits of his labor status.[38]

In addition the Muslims indicate that they do not believe that the United States will ever be able to solve the problem of white unemployment and thus will never be able to provide employment for the black populace.[39]

Therefore the attitude of the Muslims is that the offer of integration into white society is hypocritical and an attempt to deceive the black man. It is an attempt to keep from the black the realization that time for separation from the white society is at hand.[40] They argue that the final solution must be physical and geographical separation from American society and its repressive institutions; that they must have some "good earth" on which they can build their own nation and produce for their people's needs.

They can not succeed unless they are within their own social structure. Anything outside this structure is alien and they want no part of it. Their hopes and dreams for this structure have no boundaries.[41]

．　．　．　．　．

They shall always cherish the principal of freedom from persecution. They will demand their own nation and have the freedom to sustain themselves.[42]

C. Eric Lincoln, in *The Black Muslims in America,* notes that the quantity of land indicated by the Muslims to be sufficient to their needs has varied. Usually it is two or three states, but the figure is sometimes larger.

If they don't want us to mix with them in their equality, give us a place in America. Set it aside . . . give us three, four or more states. We have well earned whatever they give us; if they give us twenty-five states, we have well earned them. Give us a territory. Give the same instrument that they had to start a civilization in that territory. Take care of us. Give us what we ask them for, for the next twenty-five years until we are able to go for ourselves. Demand something. Don't demand a job. Demand some earth. We have come to the point we must have a home on this earth that we can call our own.[43]

The concept of land or territory receives unique emphasis by the Muslims in their thrust for social and economic development. They assert a nation or a sense of nationhood cannot be developed without land.

Today, the international conception of honor, pride and dignity is not concerned with individuals within a country but is rather concerned with your work and value as a part of an established nation.

In order to be recognized today you must represent your nation. We must understand the importance of land to our nation.[44]

However, Lincoln concludes from his study that Muhammad does not believe that geographical separation of the races is a viable issue. He has not articulated any substantive proposals for achieving such a separation or partitioning of the United States.[45]

But the Muslims believe that there must be complete social, economic, and political separation of the races. They argued that in reality they have become a "nation within a nation" deprived of the freedom and opportunities which justice would demand of a society. The response to this exclusion must be for black men to come together and present a united front to the external society. They assert that in black unity lies the "blackman's one hope of freedom."[46] This process of physical separation is to be accomplished in stages. Social separation is immediate when all non-essential social contacts with the white are avoided. Economic separation is underway through the creation of black businesses and farms, but this goal can only be obtained through time. Political separation, the rejection of the last vestige of white dominance, will be last and the most difficult to achieve. But absolute separation and rejection of existing institutions is the ultimate goal.[47]

Malcolm X and the Organization for Afro-American Unity Malcolm X was converted to the nation of Islam while in prison. Upon his release in 1952 he became active in the Black Muslim movement, ultimately becoming a major spokesman for the organization before his dismissal from the movement. While serving with the Muslims, Malcolm X advocated separatism in accordance with the doctrine of Elijah Muhammad. In his final speech as a Black Muslim on December 1, 1963, he stated:

The honorable Elijah Muhammad teaches us that a desegregated theater or lunch counter won't solve our problems. Better jobs won't even solve our problem. An integrated cup of coffee isn't sufficient pay for four hundred years of slave labor, and a better job in the white man's factory or position in his business is, at best, only a temporary solution. The only lasting or permanent solution is complete separation on some land that we can call our own.

The honorable Elijah Muhammad teaches us that the race problem can easily be solved, just by sending these 22 million ex-slaves back to our own homeland where we can live in peace and harmony with our own kind. . . .

We want fertile productive land on which we can farm and provide our own people with sufficient food, clothing and shelter. The government must supply us with machinery and other tools needed to dig into the earth. Give us everything we need for them from 20 to 25 years, until we can produce and supply our own needs. . . .

We want no integration with this wicked race that enslaved us. We want complete separation from this race of devils. We should not be expected to go back to our own homeland empty-handed. After 400 years of slave labor, we have some "back pay" coming, a bill owed us that must be collected.[48]

In Breitman's interpretive study of the evolution of the philosophy of Malcolm X, he states that between Malcolm's split with the Black Muslims and his death in 1965, the last year of his life, his philosophy was in a state of rapid transition, and within this philosophy his concept of separatism was changing. Soon after his separation from the Muslims, Malcolm argued that the return to Africa or the separate state was still the most realistic solution to the problem, but that it must be viewed as a long-range goal; the plight of the Negro in America was immediate and short-run programs to improve this position were critical. This short-run surrogate for separatism was to be black nationalism. "Our political philosophy will be Black Nationalism. Our economic and social philosophy will be Black Nationalism. Our cultural emphasis will be Black Nationalism."[49] The implication of this position is that separatism and black nationalism are capable of being differentiated. A separatist must be a black nationalist but black nationalism does not necessarily infer a separatist philosophy.

By April of that year the transition was complete. Malcolm no longer advocated physical separation.

All of our people have the same goals, the same objective. That objective is freedom, justice, equality. All of us want recognition and respect as human beings. We don't want to be integrationists. Nor do we want to be separationists. We want to be human beings. Integration is only a method that is used by some groups to obtain freedom, justice, equality, and respect as human beings. Separation is only a method that is used by other groups to obtain freedom, justice, equality or human dignity.

. . . We have to keep in mind at all times that we are not fighting for integration, nor are we fighting for separation. We are fighting for recognition as human beings. We are fighting for the right to live as free humans in this society.[50]

Even though he had rejected geographical separation he contended that the Negro should maintain his identification with Africa in the manner of the Jews with Israel. He believed that the Negro should migrate to Africa culturally, philosophically, psychologically, while remaining within the United States physically.[51]

Just before his death Malcolm X was beginning to question even the application of the term *black nationalism* to the program that he espoused. He was coming to believe that his program was something more, that it was black nationalism plus a revolutionary emphasis on fundamental social change.[52]

Malcolm X's views on the acceptance or rejection of the economic institution of capitalism, however, were not in transition. He did not believe that there was hope for the Negro in America under the present political and economic system. He argued that the economic system was exploitive, forcing the Negro to pay inflated rentals for substandard tenements, food, clothing, insurance rates, etc.

But more than simply believing that there was no promise for the Negro under the present institutional framework, he argued that it was only a matter of time before capitalism would collapse completely.[53]

. . . You can't operate a capitalistic system unless you're vulturistic; you have to have someone else's blood to suck to be a capitalist. You show me a capitalist, I'll show you a blood-sucker. He cannot be anything but a blood-sucker if he's going to be a capitalist. He's got to get it from somewhere other than himself, and that's where he gets it—from somewhere or someone other than himself. So, when we look at the African continent, when we look at the trouble that's going on between East and West, we find that the nations in Africa are developing socialistic systems to solve their problems.[54]

It is evident that Malcolm X believed that the long-run solution for the economic underdevelopment of the Negro was some form of socialism. However, as a more immediate solution he accepted the Black-Muslim position that Negroes should pool their resources and establish small business enterprises.[55]

The economic philosophy of Black Nationalism only means that our people need to be re-educated into the importance of controlling the economy of our community, controlling the economy of the community in which we live. And controlling the economy of the community in which we live means that we have to learn how to own and operate the businesses of our community and develop them into some type of industry that will enable us to create employment for the people of our community. . . .

Also, in line with this economic philosophy of Black Nationalism, in order for us to control the economy of our own community, we have to learn the importance of spending our money in the community where we live. Anyone who knows the basic principles of economics must be aware of the fact that when you take money out of the neighborhood in which you live and spend it in an integrated neighborhood—or rather, in your effort to integrate, you spend it in a neighborhood in which you don't live—the neighborhood in which you spend your money becomes wealthier and wealthier, and the neighborhood out of which you take your money becomes poorer and poorer and this is one of the reasons why wherever you find Negroes, a slum condition usually develops, or we have to live in a ghetto—because all of our wealth is spent elsewhere.

And even when we try to spend the money in the neighborhood where we live, usually, because we haven't learned the importance of owning and operating businesses, the businesses of our community are usually also controlled by outsiders, the stores are controlled by people who don't even live in our community. So even when we try and spend our money in the neighborhood where we live, we're spending with someone who puts it in a basket and takes it out as soon as the sun goes down.

So the economic philosophy of Black Nationalism puts the burden upon the black man of learning how to control his own economy. . . .[56]

Breitman, however, contends that Malcolm did not even hold these ideas of economic separation before his death. The "Statement of Basic Aims and Objectives of the Organization of Afro-American Unity," issued in June, 1964, and the "Basic Unity Program of the Organization of Afro-American Unity," do not argue for the creation of black businesses.

In the Statement of Basic Aims the Organization of Afro-American Unity dedicates itself to the building of a political, economic, and social system of justice and peace. In the Basic Unity Program, under Section 4 entitled "Economic Security" appears the following statement:

The Organization of Afro-American Unity will take measures to free our people from economic slavery. One way of accomplishing this will be to maintain a technician pool: that is, a bank of technicians in the same manner that blood banks have been established to furnish blood to those who need it at a time when it is needed, we must establish a Technician Bank. We must do this so that the newly independent nations of Africa can turn to us who are their Afro-American brothers for the Technicians they will need now and in the future. Thereby, we will be developing an open market for the many skills we possess and at the same time we will be supplying Africa with the skills that she can best use. This project will, therefore, be one of mutual cooperation and mutual benefit.[57]

On February 21, 1965, Malcolm X was assassinated, one year after his dismissal from the Black Muslims. It is regrettable in the extreme that the black movement lost a man of Malcolm X's capacity and insight. Breitman believes that the assassination removed the man who was best equipped to build and lead the kind of movement that would meet the ultimate needs of black people and the ultimate needs of all working people.[58]

The Black Panthers It is difficult to determine the nature and thrust of the program of the Black Panthers. In their program entitled "What We Want Now! What We Believe," published in the *Black Panther,* they assert that "we want land, bread, housing, education, clothing, justice and peace."[59] However, it is apparent that this organization wants "freedom" and the "power" to determine the destiny of the Negro to be vested within the black community. Economic elements within this thrust for self-determination are decent housing, educational programs uniquely designed for the black, and full employment. The Panthers argue that the federal government is responsible for the provision of full employment or a guaranteed annual income. If full employment cannot be provided by the white business community, the means of production should be taken from the businessmen and placed in the community. The population of the community would then organize the business structure in such a way as to employ everyone in positions that will assure them of a decent standard of living.[60]

Because white landlords do not provide decent housing, property should be expropriated and a cooperative set up with government assistance to provide acceptable standards of housing. The Black Panthers also ask for a cash indemnity from the government. The payment is compensation for genocide of fifty million blacks by racist America. The total is based upon the overdue debt of forty acres and two mules promised to the blacks as retribution for slavery.

The separatist philosophy of the Black Panthers has been articulated by Eldridge Cleaver. He argues that black people are held in a colonial status in the United States and that integration is a deception which the white mother country attempts to perpetrate upon the colonized black people.[61] According to Cleaver there is a land hunger among the blacks of America, although, as he uses the term, *land* can be interpreted as a euphemism for *wealth.* The concept of black power is the central thrust in the effort to obtain this end.

Black power must be viewed as a projection of sovereignty, an embryonic sovereignty that the black people can focus on and through which they can make distinction between themselves and others, between themselves and their enemies—in short, between the white mother country of America and the black colony dispersed throughout the continent on absentee-owned land, making Afro-America a de-centralized colony. Black power says to black people that it is possible for them to build a national organization on someone else's land.[62]

The separatist thrust of the Black Panthers is motivated by the continuing injustices which the American Negro has suffered throughout his history in this country. The Panthers cite the following sections of the Declaration of Independence as justification for their separatist philosophy.

. . . . We hold these truths to be self-evident, that all men are created equal, that they are endowed by their creator with certain inalienable rights, that among these are life, liberty and the pursuit of happiness. That to secure these rights, governments are instituted among men, deriving their just powers from the consent of the governed, that whenever any form of government becomes destructive of these ends, it is the right of the people to alter or abolish it, and to institute new government, laying its foundation on such principles and organizing its powers in such a form as to them shall seem most likely to effect their safety and happiness.

Prudence, indeed, will dictate that governments long established should not be changed for light and transient causes; and accordingly all experience has shown, that mankind are more disposed to suffer, where evils are sufferable, than to right themselves by abolishing the forms to which they are accustomed. But when a long train of abuses and usurpations, pursuing invariably the same object, evidences a design to reduce them under absolute despotism, it is their right, it is their duty, to throw off such government, and provide new guards for their future security.[63]

Therefore, the Black Panthers call for a United Nations-supervised plebiscite in the black communities of America. The plebiscite would be designed to determine whether the Negro wished to remain a part of this country and its institutions or to separate, whether indeed they did consider themselves a nation, and whether they desired membership in the United Nations and the assistance and protections provided a nation under that institution.[64]

The Black Panthers refuse to accept capitalism as anything other than an economic system designed for the exploitation of the black. The capitalistic system, according to this organization, is "dominated by a few hundred white, monopolistic corporations. These corporations, owned, operated and controlled by "Big Chuck," control almost completely the entire economic life of North America, not to mention the world economy: this economic base forms the cornerstone for white power, which attempts to suppress all peoples of dark skin, in all parts of the world. Since the presence of economic monopolies can mean nothing else and that economic freedom has been whipped on back, it follows that there ain't no such thing as free enterprise within the borders of racist USA. Free enterprise died when monopoly capital took control of the White America's economic reins."[65]

The economic system that would be supported by the Panthers would be one of cooperative black businesses. This form of organization would insure that profits generated by these businesses would benefit the entire black community and would not fall into the hands of a few to be utilized for their own private benefit.

The economic dimension of the Black Panther program is viewed as a secondary level of effort, as a means to achieving the more pervasive end of black self-determination.

. . . . Within the context of the Afro-American struggle for survival and national liberation, black businesses must be viewed as an aid to that struggle, not an end in itself. There is no way to achieve liberation inside the framework of CHUCK's economic system; we can achieve a certain degree of autonomy in the economic sphere but in the final analysis black political independence must precede black economic independence! Black Power![66]

The Panthers reserved the right "to alter and abolish the system of government and institute a new form of government more consistent with the safety and happiness of indigenous peoples. It is assumed that military and/or other associated means would be used to overthrow the system.

The Republic of New Africa Movement   In the spring of 1968 two hundred black persons met in Detroit to organize the Republic of New Africa, a new nation within the United States with a separate government and its own elected officials. At this organizational meeting the delegates approved a Declaration of Independence which stated that the black peoples of America were "forever free and independent of the jurisdiction of the United States."[67] The reasoning behind the complete separation from the United States is clearly delineated.

We cannot exist side by side with white America, with her huge military, unless she changes. Therefore, we will have to depend upon internationalism for protection. But so long as we remain citizens of the United States of America no foreign government will come to our aid or even introduce our case to the U.N.[68]

This new republic proposes to establish a provisional capital in the State of Mississippi governed by its president in exile, Robert F. Williams. The first goal of the new government is to hold a plebiscite among the Negro population of the United States. The results of this plebiscite will be presented to the United Nations in an effort to enjoin this international body to establish a legal base for the state in accordance with international law.

The Republic of New Africa has also requested reparation payments and land from the United States government.

Reparations have never been paid to black people for the admitted wrongs of slavery (or since slavery) inflicted upon our ancestors with the sanction of the United States Constitution.... The principle of reparations for national wrongs, as for personal wrongs, is well established in international law. The West German government, for instance, has paid $850 million in equipment and credits in reparations to Israel for wrongs committed by the Nazis against the Jews of Europe. Demands for reparations, funneled through a united black power congress must include not only the demand for money and goods such as machinery, factories and laboratories, but a demand for land. And the land we want is the land where we are: Mississippi population 42% black, Louisiana 32%, Alabama 30%, Georgia 29%, and South Carolina 35%.[69]

Other than the demand for reparations, the Republic of New Africa movement appears to be mainly political in nature with little specifications as to the economic form or mode of the new state.

The Congress of Racial Equality The Congress of Racial Equality was established in 1942. At its inception it was composed of pacifistic idealists who were deeply committed to seeking admittance of the Negro into the mainstream of American society through peaceful and nonviolent techniques. It retained this emphasis until 1961 when James Farmer became its national director. At this time the emphasis shifted to direct action and confrontation while still retaining the tenet of nonviolence. The tactics of CORE during this period are illustrated by the following quote extracted from the pamphlet "All about CORE," published by the Congress of Racial Equality in 1963.

If negotiation over race over a length of time fails to desegregate an establishment, the CORE group resorts to the direct challenge. The form of the challenge depends upon the type of establishment to be desegregated. Sit-ins can be employed in restaurants and lunch counters, standing lines at theaters, wade-ins at beaches. Boycotts can be extremely effective. The businessman who refuses to desegregate for fear he will lose his business learns that he will lose much more business by persisting in his discriminatory policy.[70]

In 1966 James Farmer left CORE and Floyd McKissick became the new national director. During the period 1966–1968 CORE became an increasingly militant organization dedicated to the organization of ghetto communities into systems that could serve as an effective power base in the attempt to achieve social, economic, and political rights for the Negro in the United States. In 1968 the leadership of the Congress of Racial Equality was delegated to Roy Innis. Innis has rejected the traditional emphasis of CORE on integration into the institutions of American society and maintains that integration is "as much of a myth as the unicorn."[71] He now rejects any effort to achieve integration into the economic institutions of American society and instead seeks to develop an economic power base within the ghetto through the creation of "black capitalism." The emphasis upon economic separation is an element of the pervasive goal of self-contained Negro communities within the inner city. The current posture of the Congress of Racial Equality was stated by Innis at the Republican National Convention in 1968:

> Black people then find themselves in the untenable position of being powerless in a political state and culture that understands very little but power. The Black community sees the institutions that are charged with implementing programs for positive change in control of persons with diametrically opposing interests. . . .
> Blacks must manage and control the institutions that service their areas, as has always been for other interest groups. There is an immediate need in such institutions as education, health, social service, sanitation, protection, fire, housing, etc.
> Large or densely populated Black areas especially in urban centers, must have a change in status. They must become political sub-divisions of the state, instead of sub-colonial appendages of the city. They must become more autonomous of the existing urban centers. In short, Black people must be able to control basic societal instruments in the social, economic and political arenas.[72]

Innis further argues that the Constitution of the United States as a national contract for the people of this nation was never meant to include black people. He argues that a social contract or constitution designed for a particular group of people with distinct attributes and self-interests cannot serve as a contract for people with differing attributes and self-interests.

> . . . . Modifications and amendments serve only to postpone that time and place when both Black and White will be faced with the overwhelming need to forge a new contract which deals with white people and black people as two distinct groups occupying the same land at the same time.
> The obvious solution then is a new social contract (constitution). This contract will redefine the relationship between Blacks

and Whites. Black people must be recognized as a people—faction or interest group. This contract will then be between the major factions, blacks and whites. Ethnic groups will be sub-factions of the major factions. The contract must be defined pragmatically and in the mutual interest of both parties.[73]

Kermit Scott, Director of Chapter Development and Director of Community Relations for CORE, has further articulated the philosophical posture of the Congress of Racial Equality. He states that the present leadership of CORE has come to the realization that the Negroes and the whites comprise in fact two separate nations and two individual peoples possessing different kinds of attributes and different kinds of experiences. He further contends that in the period since slavery the thrust of all civil rights activities has been to minimize these differences, but differences do exist and they are nothing to be ashamed of. "We are two distinct people and we have two nation-like structures, not comparable in size or scope but in self-concept, within this country and to deal in the reality of this makes all the kinds of programs which we are now pushing viable and not only viable, but necessary."[74]

Other civil rights organizations, according to Scott, are still hoping that there will be a coming together of people without regard to race, creed, or color at some given time and place. He believes that this is possible, but that it is far beyond the scope of our times and that we must deal with the reality of this fact. This realization, then, leads Scott to accept a philosophy of black nationalism.

I conceive of the Black people as a nation. I conceive of them as a definite different group of people. I conceive of them as a group of people with a common experience and coming from a common origin, which is Africa, and having that kind of development and finding themselves in this kind of unfavorable situation in this country. Self-concept becomes a power that they can implement. It depends upon how you look at oneself. If you view yourself as a separate people, then you can view yourself as a nation-like entity. There are historical parallels. There were a number of people who didn't have any land for many years but who viewed themselves as a nation. And the nation-state might come of course, be in the future, but the nations could co-exist. Even Indians view themselves as a nation. The Jews moved around for some hundreds of years, but nevertheless considered themselves a peoplehood and a different nation. And now they have lit some place. They have moved much longer than we would hope to move. It is in this sense of a kind of self-concept that I am a Nationalist, not in the sense of a person who is suggesting that come Monday morning there will be a new nation waiting for me to take over.[75]

Scott believes that nationalism is a very powerful force within this country, that the United States is a strongly nationalistic society, and that this is the kind of drive that must be obtained by the Negro in order to achieve social, economic, and political self-development. The nationalism for which he argues has definite social, political, and economic dimensions, but no geographical dimension.

Many black activists do not feel the need to structure specific programs. They argue that the first step of destroying the institutional structure and removing themselves physically from it must occupy all their time and energy. Thus, there is a paucity of well-specified programs for social and economic development outside the institutional structure. However, some individuals and organizations have begun the process of translating their philosophies into specific programs, incorporating goals and techniques for their implementation. The nature of these programs exhibit wide diversity, but they illustrate what these individuals and organizations believe are the economic imperatives and techniques for developing an acceptable economic system.

CHAPTER 4

Economic Programs of Militant Separatists

Under capitalism, market forces and economic institutions shape the successful forms of economic behavior and the productive skills required and utilized. The pattern of economic activity dictated by the market and institutions determines the ways in which the returns or rewards for economic activity are distributed among the participants. The selection process within the market system has caused the rate of absorption of the Negro into the mainstream of the economy to be pathetically slow. The market mechanisms have discriminated inadvertently against the Negro worker and entrepreneur. Technical skill levels increasingly necessary in industries, cultural attitudes of aggressive acquisitiveness and material achievement which characterize much of western

For Notes to Chapter 4 see pages 339–342.

entrepreneurial behavior have not been acquired by the Negro. Specific industries and labor unions have discriminated to block the Negro from employment and skills training opportunities. The market and its supportive philosophies have worked to the detriment of the Negro as he has attempted economic advancement within the existing economic system.

The overtly discriminatory features of most economic institutions are eroding albeit at an excruciatingly slow rate in response to the pressures of legal fiat and the recognition of social imperatives. The black worker is being absorbed into the labor force at a faster rate than ever before with the possible exception of the World War II period in which the tight labor market of the industrialized North rapidly assimilated the immigrating Southern black. However many black leaders and ideologists are unwilling to wait until increasing economic prosperity and diminishing racial barriers permit members of their race entré into the economic system. They argue against this process on several ideological grounds. First, the trickling down process of economic prosperity is too slow. Several more generations would be sacrificed to economic destitution. Second, racism is now less overt, but thoroughly institutionalized. The larger white society is unable or unwilling to admit or accept the existence of racism. Some blacks argue that institutionalized racism will freeze the members of their race permanently outside of the economic system. Third, the nature of the capitalistic system in the United States is changing. The material promise of capitalism is beginning to be realized. Automation is rapidly displacing the laborer, particularly the black. The distributive share of physical labor is diminishing and that of capital increasing. Some Negroes, accepting this unsubstantiated argument, believe that this trend renders it unwise to direct major efforts within the black movement to achieve upward mobility through employment. They argue for some new system of distribution or sharing of the returns to the productive process. Fourth, the societal values engendered under capitalism are basically immoral and dehumanizing, and antithetical to the value system represented in the humanism of the Negro movement.

Fifth, economic and political power are not achieved through entrance into the labor force, but through the acquisition and control of the means of production.

Proponents of these views reject existing economic institutions and development models and seek economic development through radically restructuring the economic institutions of capitalism or by working outside of these established structures. The programs and objectives expounded are at once visionary and realistic, ideological and pragmatic. The basic design of the programs examined in this chapter exhibit this spectrum and blend of postures. Yet all have a unifying feature—a sharp contrast in philosophy and tactics with programs based on integration into the capitalistic economic system.

James Boggs:
A Just and Humane
Economic System

James Boggs is one of the few, if not the only, black theorist who, in rejecting the present institutional framework, structures his arguments against the system and his programs for a more humane and just system in terms of economic conditions and potentialities. He is perhaps the foremost economic thinker among the black militants.

Because of his rejection of capitalism as an economic institution, Boggs contends that black capitalism as a technique in the economic development for the Negro is a dream and a delusion and holds no possibilities for resolving the problems of the masses of the blacks. A system which through its operations and exploitive relationships, created the problem cannot be expected to resolve it. In addition, he argues that black capitalism could never become competitive with white capitalism. "It could only remain far behind, marginal, dependent, impermanent neo-colonial subjection to the enormous capital resources which American whites control and with which they can manipulate interest rates, commodity prices and wages, and destroy or sustain large or small enterprises at home and abroad."[1]

At the core of his economic theory rests the contention that the industrial system of the United States is in an advanced stage of automation and is pointing toward a fully cybernated system. He argues that the industrial system, and particularly the automotive industry, is capable of a much greater degree of automation than is presently utilized. Because of the national commitment to achieve full employment, many industries are not utilizing the capital intensive technologies available to them in order to provide employment for a greater number of laborers. This Boggs believes is wrong. He contends that the industrial system has now reached a stage in which men need no longer be captive to the machine but can be freed from the machine and the necessity of "productive" labor as defined in the current mores of our society. He asserts that the economic system is now capable of producing income to support the entire populace of this country. Therefore, as automation increases and cybernation is realized, the link between productive contribution and incomes must be broken. If men no longer can be productively employed, then they are, in a just and humane system, entitled to an income that is unrelated to their labor contribution. Man, in a highly industrialized system, is entitled to some form of guaranteed annual income.

But Boggs raises an issue similar to those raised by earlier institutionalists, that rapid technological progress has outstripped the politics and institutions of the society and the values inculcated within these institutions.

. . . . Today technology is ready for an era of plenty but our institutions are not. That is the blessing of the Negro revolution coming at this time—that it not only proclaims the right of all men to be equal but also poses the necessity for all men to have a right to a living regardless of whether they toil or not.[2]

. . . . .

A new reason for man's existence is in the making. His purpose in life can no longer be to live by the sweat of his brow. Freed from this compulsion to work, from forced labor, a whole new horizon lies before him. Whatever this may be, I am not the least afraid of it. The reason is very simple. I believe that if the changes are going to be made to utilize the full potential of cybernation, this in itself will demand the greatest revolution, the greatest social and political upheaval that man has ever gone through. Because those who have this perspective of cybernating and automating to the fullest to get rid of jobs will not only have to fight the capitalists' view. They will have to fight all the ways of life which society hitherto accepted as the epitome of man's destiny. I call this the revolution of and for the self-governing man, or the revolution by which man will make himself the decision-maker on how society is to be organized, who is to do and get what, when and why.[3]

James Boggs contends that the Bill of Rights and the Constitution of the United States were written to meet the needs of an agrarian society. Therefore, these fundamental documents defining the social contract among members of this society must be rewritten to conform to the new stage of development that the United States is entering, the cyber-cultural age. The basic elements of the economic program advocated by Boggs is contained within his ideas concerning the reformulation of the Bill of Rights.

☐ **1** Every individual adult should be entitled to a guaranteed income, working or not, which is adequate for his livelihood.

☐ **2** Government funds should be utilized to automate and cybernate industrial production as rapidly as possible: government should take over production.

☐ **3** Production should be for use with a margin of profit for further technological development.

☐ **4** Higher education should be completely free and public. Going to college should be considered a full-time job and those going to school should be guaranteed an income while doing so.

☐ **5** Educational institutions with full pay for those attending should be organized for those not interested in academic learning.

☐ **6** On the basis of seniority those working in industries should be steadily released from the need to work.

☐ **7** A national draft system with occupational codes, etc. should be set up to do the work that is still needed.[4]

Rewriting the Constitution has also been considered by Boggs.

Four elements of the suggested components of this new constitution relate directly to the relationship between the individual and the economic means of production. First, a new value would be established which recognized every man's inherent right to live well, whether he is employed or unemployed. This right would be based upon the technological and scientific development of the productive resources of this country. Second, there would be a complete restructuring of the intergovernmental relationships between the federal government, the states, and the cities. This reorganization would be in response to the recognition that the present federal-state relationships were designed for an agricultural area and are now obsolete because of the Industrial Revolution and the problems of the cities. Third, there would be a total reorganization of the relationship between man and property. Man would no longer be controlled by property, but man would come to control property. Fourth, the principle of the fullest utilization of all scientific, technological, and medical development for the use of man would be established.[5]

The particular elements of Boggs' economic program are posited in the *Manifesto for a Black Revolutionary Party*. In general, he argues that the black revolution would guarantee every individual a decent living. Control over the means of production would be given to those who worked in that enterprise, in order to create humane conditions in the work environment. A national crash housing program on a scale similar to that of mobilization for war would be undertaken to provide housing for those presently living in substandard dwellings. Free medical care would be guaranteed to every individual from birth. Public transportation would be made a free public service available to all. In sum man would be guaranteed his economic independence free to pursue the higher goals of life.

Because of his contention that the industrial system of the United States is now capable of providing a viable standard of living for all members of the society, Boggs believes that the issues for the black must be the acquisition of political power, and not economic power.

The organization for black power must concentrate on the issue of political power and refuse to re-define and explain away black power as black everything except black political power. The development of technology in the United States has made it impossible for blacks to achieve economic power in the USA by the old means of capitalist development. The ability of the US capitalists today to produce an abundance not only makes competition with them on an economic capitalist basis absurd but has already brought the USA technologically to the threshold of a society where each can have according to his needs. This black political power, coming at this juncture in the economically advanced USA, is the key not only to black liberation but to the introduction of a new society to emancipate economically the masses of people in general. For black political power will have to decide on the kind of economy and the aims and direction of the economy for the people.[6]

It is quite difficult to evaluate such a program. Obviously it is visionary and futuristic, and exhibits an uncritical optimism found in many of the nineteenth-century utopian socialist writers. There is little critical analysis in Boggs' work concerning the capacity of the industrial system to support the programs that he proposes or the cost of real resources necessary to implement these programs. There is no accepted conclusion that the United States is moving into a cybernated society. A study undertaken by the President's commission on automation and technology concluded that there is no concrete evidence that this euphoric state can be realized in the foreseeable future.[7] However, there are many sincere scholars who do believe that this state in the industrial process can be realized.

The contention that the United States could afford to provide a guaranteed income for those presently living in poverty could probably be substantiated. The cost of the guaranteed annual income is estimated to vary from $8 to $25 billion, depending upon the rate of active income tax utilized and the type of plan undertaken. The magnitude of these figures can easily be compared with the cost of such undertakings as the Vietnam War, the space program, and the agricultural subsidy programs. The problem here then becomes the establishment of new national priorities in some systematic manner. This is a process not presently being undertaken as a formal and institutionalized procedure.

The Black Muslims

The economic program of the Black Muslims is an integral element of their overall program for the advancement of the black race. The philosophy through which they approach economic development reflects insight into the problem of economic growth and the constraints that inhibit the acquisition of material wealth. Perhaps the most effective point of contact between the Black Muslims and other Negroes is through their economic operations and the success of their undertakings.[8] Therefore, the relative prosperity of the movement, its economic undertakings, and its individual members are a potent enticement for recruitment into the Muslims.

Elijah Muhammad recognizes that the economic problem of the Negro is critical. The economic plight of the black people has been neglected for so long that few Negro leaders understand its very basic importance to the development of the race. "Our economic position remains at the bottom of the ladder because of this ineffective leadership and because so many of our people ignore the basic rules of a healthy economic life. We fail to develop self-leadership in economics."[9] There are also indications that the Muslims possess a keen insight into the relationship between economic independence and self-sufficiency and human freedom. Eric Lincoln in his study of the Muslims indicates that when a minister of the movement addresses an audience he asserts that the white man owns the material means of production necessary to survival and through his control the white obtains dominance over the black. All he needs to do is to deny the Negro a job, and he will soon be . . . dead.[10] The Negro (in order to insure himself from exclusion from participation in the economic sector by the white) adopts an attitude of servility. Thus, the Negro cannot be free until he obtains economic independence from the exclusive control of the white man's means of production.

The economic orientation and approach of the Black Muslims are contained in two basic programs of the movement, the overall twelve-point program for the development of the black race and the three-year economic program. The twelve-point program was articulated by Elijah Muhammad in his "A Program for Self-Development," and these points were defended by him in article "What Is Un-American?"[11] written in response to the California State Senate Fact-Finding Subcommittee on Un-American Activities, which charged the Black Muslims with being un-American and operating a school for the indoctrination of Negroes with race hatred.[12] The following statement of the twelve-point program is a compilation of these two sources, the latter of which is addressed to white America:

☐ **1** Separate yourselves from the "slave-master." You had us segregated for 400 years and now say that we are free, is it being un-American to leave you or separate from you, a people who have enslaved and destroyed us as human beings? Have you not separated yourselves from us?

☐ **2** Pool your resources, education and qualification for independence. Is pooling our resources, education and qualifications for self-independence, as you and other nations have done and since you say we are free, what do you call un-American?[sic]

☐ **3** Stop forcing yourselves into places where you are not wanted. Should we not stop forcing ourselves, our presence, on you in places of yours where you forbid us and tell us we are not wanted? Is this what you call un-American—keeping away from that of yours that you forbade us?

☐ **4** Make your own neighborhood a decent place to live. Making our own neighborhoods a decent place to live and seeking a place in your neighborhood just because yours looks better and cleaner; making wherever we live a nice and clean place to live and making a decent life among ourselves if you and yours can do it, so can we . . .

☐ **5** Rid yourselves of the lust for wine and drink and learn to love self and your kind before loving others. If we want to rid ourselves of the lust of wine and other intoxicating drinks and learn to love ourselves first before loving you or others, is this what you call un-American?

☐ **6** Unite to create a future for yourself. Have you given us anything in the way of your past and present treatment of us that we can believe that it will not be "hell" on "hell"?

☐ **7** Build your own homes, schools, hospitals, and factories. Is it un-American for us to build our own homes, and schools, hospitals and factories while we are suffering and being turned away from many of yours?

☐ **8** Do not seek to mix your blood through racial integration. Is it un-American for us to want to keep our blood pure from being mixed with yours, our enemies?

☐ **9** Stop buying expensive cars, fine clothes and shoes before being able to live in a fine home. Is it un-American to stop wasting our money. . . .

☐ **10** Spend your money among yourselves.

☐ **11** Build an economic system among yourselves.

☐ **12** Protect your women.[13]

Within this twelve-point program are contained all the major elements that dictate the conceptual approach of the Black Muslims to economic development. The "economic blueprint"[14] and "three-year economic program"[15] of the organization are specifications of the techniques for implementing the more general philosophical concepts of the catholic program. Muhammad states that it is difficult for an economist to formulate a wise plan and implement it because of the economic circumstances of the Negro and because of the economic dominance of the white society. ". . . it is difficult to plan an economic program for a dependent people who, for all their lives, have tried to live like the white man."[16]

The essential elements of this economic program are separatism and black unity. The Black Muslim is urged to spend his money with his own kind at black businesses, to build through the Muslim nation black enterprises, and to utilize his profits for the further expansion of business investments. Muhammad exhorts his followers to emulate the white man in his economic behavior. The white is thrifty, he saves his money, and works hard. These are principles that are inculcated into all Muslims. "Observe the operations of the white man. He is successful. He makes no excuses for his failures. He works hard in a collective manner. You do the same. If there are six or eight Muslims with knowledge and experience of the grocery business—pool your knowledge, open a grocery store—and you work collectively and harmoniously, Allah will bless you with success."[17] The command to "buy black" is emphatic.

It is as natural for the black man to patronize black businesses as it is for the whites to spend money with their own kind. E. Muhammad argues that by spending black money at black businesses, new jobs for blacks will be created. He points to the Chinese and Japanese experience of helping their "own kind" when they are in need. Elijah Muhammad admonishes Muslims to defend and support their brothers, and to break away from their established practices of deliberately walking past the place of business of one of their own kind, that is, a black man, and spending black dollars with the blacks' natural enemy—the whites. Because the American black has never boycotted or criticized the white man as effectively as their own kind, Muhammad uses this as the basis for arguing that the black shows love for his enemy and hatred for other blacks.[18]

The form of economic organization of the Black Muslims is described by Muhammad as "communalism."[19] Under this organization members are expected to contribute a portion of their incomes, as a 10 per cent tithe, to the nation to be used for the establishment of businesses. The businesses thus established are owned by the central organization and not by the individual contributors in individual shares. The profit derived from these operations accrue to the Muslim temples. Disposition is decided by the temple officers. Before 1957 profits were invested in new businesses, but since that time approximately 75 per cent of the profits have been used to support the operations of the temples and to provide for the sick, unemployed, and aged. The remaining 25 per cent goes to the University of Islam operated by the Muslims.[20]

The communalism advocated by Muhammad is designed to instill three related values in the Negro: (1) to engender habits of

saving and a sense of responsibility for economic self-development; (2) to provide a channel for investments through the collective business enterprises owned by the Temple; and (3) to create a
sense of responsibility for the welfare of the Muslim community.[21]
Muhammad contends that these values are lacking in the American Negro and must be encouraged to achieve economic and social
development.

The businesses owned and operated by this group are small
and in the service sector—that is restaurants, clothing stores, gas
stations, barber shops, and apartment houses. Muslims hope to
expand the scale of operations into industrial enterprises. The
implication of their approach, however, is that economic growth
and development should begin from an agricultural base and
proceed through stages of economic growth similar to those
described by W. W. Rostow.[22]

Elijah Muhammad argues that the best way for the Negro
race to develop is to first buy farmland and to produce their own
food, to buy timberland and clayland, to produce those basic
necessities that would make their nation self-sustaining.

According to Muhammad, blacks have thousands of dollars
deposited in white banks. These moneys are not helping the black
man and should be put to work to promote black economic independence. By buying land with these deposits, blacks can
produce cotton, grains, and livestock. The cattle and sheep would
be used for food, leather products, and wool; cotton would be
the basic stable fiber. Agricultural production would be accompanied by handicraft industry that would provide numerous
dry goods. In terminology reminiscent of Booker Washington,
Muhammad recommends that Muslims first go to the soil, work
the earth, and produce needed food and fiber. Warehouses should
be built to store food and retail outlets established to serve black
customers. Not only will the blacks gain monetary and economic
independence, but an autonomous black economy will carry the
black man through the future exigencies of economic collapse
of the white system.[23]

Through this program the Muslim is taught that they can obtain the necessary savings to build a national savings bank and to purchase the necessary goods and services for their nation. The lack of savings is identified as a critical factor in the Black Muslim program for economic development. To alleviate this lack of savings Muhammad calls upon his followers to make sacrifices for a period of three years. He argues that too much money is wasted through the acquisition of luxuries that could be foregone. The Muslim is told that by cutting down on his extravagances and by letting the nation sacrifice for three years, his people can be rid of poverty and want.

Using concepts illustrated in Russian and Pakistanian economic planning, E. Muhammad generalizes on the need for foresight in carefully structuring economic development. Blacks and particularly Muslims must forego current consumption and become more oriented to the productive use of planned invest-ment as a principal means to fight poverty. Three year Economic Savings Programs facilitate the accumulation of funds necessary to create economic conditions which can make blacks happier and generate a spirit of independence necessary for a successful black nation. [24]

The goal of this program was to raise at least 500-million dollars to purchase the land.

E. U. Essien-Udom indicates that the income of the Nation of Islam is a well-kept secret. Estimates of the annual income from all sources range from $300,000 to $500,000.[25] He does not believe that Muhammad is receiving aid from foreign sources, as has been alleged. A speech by Muhammad in Washington, D.C., on May 31, 1959, is relevant.

I have been charged, because of the continued progress that I am making towards uniting my people, I am now being charged indirectly of receiving outside aid which is absolutely false. There is not one dime that has come to us from any source other than ourselves. . . . I will not walk around Capitol Hill or go to the

White House begging the President or the Congress for anything of America. I have no need to do so.[26]

The Muslims realize that their program can only be implemented over a significant span of time. In the interim, specific demands are asked of white America as part of their natural right. In addition to social goals such as freedom, equal justice under the law, and equal opportunity, Muslims believe that former slave masters are obligated to provide fertile land for them. These former slave masters are obligated to maintain the people of this new nation in separate territory for the next twenty to fifty years, or until they are able to become economically self-sufficient.[27] As long as Muslims are not allowed to establish this territory they demand equal opportunity now. They ask the government of the United States to exempt the Negro race from all taxation as long as they are deprived of equal justice under the laws of this land.[28]

It appears that the Muslims do possess an economic program of substance that has been relatively successful in bringing prosperity to members of the Muslim nation. The priorities established to achieve economic development are those which many underdeveloped countries have delineated as the most efficient techniques of approaching this goal. Religiously connative nationalism is used as a means for mobilizing the indigenous population. Communalism is utilized as a means of achieving economies in the collection and allocation of savings. The emphasis on agricultural self-sufficiency is a coherent thrust if the Muslim nation is indeed establishing itself in a separate and virgin territory. However, this emphasis does not appear to be economically feasible in the environment in which the Muslims now operate, or in the industrial system of the United States. However, this goal can be justified on religious and social grounds by the Muslim. It may well be that a religious minority such as the Black Muslims, with emphasis on black nationalism, may prove to be a focal point for the economic development of the Negro race. Kurt Samuelsson, a Swedish economic historian, has suggested that economic development is less associated with a dominant religion such as Protestantism, as Weber suggested, and more related to the activities of religious minority groups.[29]

The Congress of Racial Equality—Economic Development

The philosophy for economic development and the specific program of CORE are well formulated. It is the only carefully designed program for economic development advocated by the black militants. No other militant organization has progressed as far as CORE in setting forth the operational aspects of the steps necessary to establish ghetto autonomy. The economic philosophy and conceptualizations under which CORE operates are clearly set forth in a program and fund appeal presented to possible funding sources in Cleveland, Ohio.[30]

This program was presented to the City Council of Cleveland; other governmental agencies in the state of Ohio, both state and municipal; relevant agencies of the federal government; and interested charitable foundations, corporations, firms, and individuals in the business economy of the Cleveland area. The philosophy contained within this document is based upon the work of Lewis Kelso and Mortimer Adler in their analysis of contemporary capitalism.[31]

These authors believe that to be truly free, man must have economic security and independence. Only if he is released from the necessity of constant striving to obtain the material means of subsistence does he have the chance to become truly free in the pursuit of the fullest perfection of himself as a human being and of the civilization in which he lives. Kelso and Adler contend that every man has a natural right to life and thus a right to obtain their subsistence by participating in the production of wealth. They argue that in the current phase of the Industrial Revolution the promise of capitalism may be fulfilled. This promise is that a whole society of men may be economically free and that all men of that society may have the opportunity to live their lives as dignified human beings. They base this argument on the fact that over a period of history since the Industrial Revolution human labor has become a diminishing source of productive power, and capital equipment an increasingly major source of productive power. In the industrial society, in advanced stages of automation, it will be possible for all men to have a share of the income derived from capital, which will permit them to become economically free.

On the basis of this philosophy CORE argues that there must be a basic change in the attitude towards work in this society, the the so-called Protestant ethic, that man should only receive income in proportion to the contribution of his physical labor to the production process. They argue that it must be realized that man now does not produce through his physical labor alone, but mainly through his ownership of capital equipment and other factors of production.

To insist that man continue to legitimate his income through symbolic toil is to negate the achievements of science, engineering, management and labor itself in shifting the burden of economic production from man to the forces of nature harnessed in non-human labor. It is a unique advantage of the CORE program that it conserves the puritan ethic as a moral principle, but adapts it to the industrial age.[32]

CORE then assumes that there are only two possible techniques of distribution in an advanced industrial system, and that these are differentiated in the extreme. One technique is to break the link between productive contribution and income and to base the system of distribution upon the need of the individual. This is the philosophy that underlies the proposals for forms of guaranteed annual income, such as the negative income tax and the conventional welfare programs. CORE contends that this system of distribution is "foreign to and incompatible with human dignity, with economic motivation, and with the production of general affluence. It destroys civil liberties and political freedom."[33]

The second alternative basis of the distribution system is as follows: Income is allocated on the basis of productive contribution of the individual's labor power and the productive energy of the capital equipment to which he holds title, or the basic principle of distribution of a capitalistic society. It is implicit in the philosophy of CORE, given the structural changes in the pattern of ownership of productive wealth, that distribution based upon productivity would result in distributive justice.

The structural changes which CORE believes must occur are related to the wide discrepancy between those living in poverty and those possessing concentrations of wealth and productive power. Institutional changes must be brought about that will increase the productive power of low-income households so they will "legitimately" receive sufficient income to meet their "reasonable needs and desires." CORE proposes to undertake these changes by establishing a series of economic institutions that would facilitate the acquisition of capital by Negroes. They believe this technique of alleviating poverty has yet to be tried in any economy. It is compatible with the tenets of the capitalistic system and would tend to protect the institution of private property.

Based upon this supportive philosophy, the Economic Development Program of the Congress of Racial Equality is designed to achieve the following general goals:

☐ **1** To raise the power to produce wealth (and thus receive income) of individuals of low or no economic productive power by enabling them legitimately to buy, pay for, and become the owners of productive capital.

☐ **2** To so structure the financing of the second economy[34] that its ownership can be legitimately acquired, in moderate size and diversified holdings, by the great majority of families and individuals . . . and most urgently by the poverty-stricken black families and individuals who live in the ghetto area.

☐ **3** To enable the smooth expansion of the production of useful goods and services of the . . . economy and the commensurate expansion of the ability of all of its citizens to consume, free of the distortion of prices, and the demotivating influences of all the time-worn and discredited techniques of attempting to distribute the income produced primarily by capital through labor and welfare.[35]

The dominant thesis of this program is that economic freedom in an advanced industrial society requires ownership of property; or, to insure the Negro freedom he must obtain the control of productive property. The goal of CORE is to create new black-owned and black-controlled economic institutions and to employ the principles and techniques that have fostered white business success.[36] The economic program of CORE is designed to present an alternative to the present concentration of wealth in the hands of a few individuals, and to suggest techniques by which newly created wealth and existing wealth might be redistributed to make the productive process available to the widest number of people.[37]

The objective of the CORE development program is to establish the power to produce wealth for low-income individuals by financing a second or ghetto economy in which ownership can be acquired by indigenous black families. CORE has proposed that a corporation or a group of corporations establish plant location and industry selection partnerships with CORE. Under this arrangement the corporate partners would agree to contribute partnership capital based upon a given time schedule. The partnership would then determine industries that are interested in locating industrial plants within the ghetto area. The partnership would establish an arrangement with this firm whereby the partnership would locate and purchase a plant site that met the specifications of the firm and construct the physical facilities necessary for the operation of that industrial enterprise. The property and physical facilities would then be made available to the firm on a long-term lease basis. The rental income derived from this leasing arrangement would be used to repay the corporate partners the capital contribution plus interest at a prime rate. When this contribution plus interest has been fully repaid, the corporation's partnership interest would be terminated. The advantage to the corporate partner in this arrangement is that all tax losses and deductions during the early stages of this development process would accrue to them.

CORE would establish a community development corporation which would hold CORE's partnership interest. The ownership of this development corporation would be stock/shares held by persons who met given specifications of CORE. The specifications are designed to achieve a broad base of black participation and would be limited to ghetto residences whose net worth was below some specified minimum.[38] In the long run, as rental payments exceed the amount necessary to repay the debt to the corporate partner, these excess funds would be distributed to ghetto shareholders along with the equity ownership of the land, building, and capital equipment.

CORE suggests that in the negotiations for the lease it might be stipulated that the firm set aside some portion of its stock to be used in an equity-sharing plan for its ghetto residence employees. Under this arrangement the corporation would pay part of its wage bill through an equity-sharing or bonus program, which would eventually place a significant share of the ownership of that firm in the hands of the ghetto residents. Then, advantage of this procedure to the corporation is the allowable tax deduction of the value of the stock contributed.[39]

CORE contends that the Homestead Act and the Federal Housing Act help to build America by making it possible for people who do not own land and homes to acquire real property in these forms.

As these programs were new in their time, America now needs a new institution for the automative industrial society. This institution should give to people who own no interest in the structures and equipment of this society the opportunity to build an interest in them.[40]

A Special Guarantee Fund is proposed by CORE which would provide sources of loans to persons and firms for property. The sources of capital for this special fund would be wealthy individuals, foundations, charities, corporations, and, at some point, the funds from its economic development group CORENCO.

On an institutional level the CORE thrust for economic development is implemented by the introduction into the House of Representatives two bills, the Community Self-Development Act and the Rural Development Incentive Act of 1968.[41]

The Community Self-Development Act is described as a bill "to establish a community self-determination program, to aid the people of urban and rural communities in securing gainful employment, achieving ownership and control of the resources of their community, expanding opportunity, stability, and self-determination, and making maximum contribution to the strength and well-being of the nation."[42]

The bill is designed to promote the establishment of community development corporations which would enable the communities in depressed areas to organize for responsible action and insure optimum use of the community resources. A community development corporation is defined as "a corporation established by the people of an urban or rural community to expand their economic and educational opportunities, increase their ownership of productive capital and property, improve their living conditions, enhance their personal dignity and independence, expand their opportunities for meaningful decision-making, and secure economic development, social well-being, and stability in their communities. . . ."[43]

Under this bill an agency of the United States government designated as a National Community Corporation Certification board would be established. This board, under the supervision of the President of the United States, would be independent of all agencies and departments. The role of this new agency would be to encourage the development of local community corporations and to oversee the procedural and organizational aspects of their inception and to charter these organizations. It would also serve as a coordinating agency for other federal-government activities directed toward the local communities and would be a source of funding to local community development corporations.

Local community development corporations would be organized in communities that have no fewer than 5,000 residents of 16 years of age and over and no more than 300,000 residents. The criterion for eligibility for establishment of a community development corporation would be based upon "the development index" for that community. These development indices would be computed in the following manner: (1) The ratio of (a) the percentage of the labor force unemployed on a national basis or within the relevant standard metropolitan statistical area, whichever is lower, to (b) the percentage of the labor force unemployed in the appropriate community area. (2) The ratio of (a) median family income in the appropriate community area to (b) the median family income on a national basis, or within the relevant standard metropolitan statistical area, whichever is greater. The development index that would be applied would be the lesser of the two ratios computed in this manner.[44]

The ownership of a community development corporation would be represented by the shares of stock that it had outstanding. The shares would be in one class and would have a par value of 5 dollars. The ownership of these shares of stock would be restricted to residents within the community development corporation area of 16 years of age or over. The stock could be purchased either in the form of monetary payments or in the form of labor or services performed for the development corporation. The net income of the corporation would be used for working capital for the corporation itself and for the payment of dividends. No less than 20 per cent and no more than 80 per cent of this income can be allocated to a working capital fund. This money would then be used "to extend the business operations of the corporations, or to purchase shares, or interests in, or obligations of other corporations."[45]

The initial funding for the establishment of the national development corporations would consist of federal appropriations. These would amount to $50 million for the fiscal year 1970, $75 million for the fiscal year 1971, and $125 million for the fiscal year 1972.

To facilitate capital funding and organizational and technical advice, CORE would use a United States Community Development Bank and its subsidiaries in the local community development corporation areas. The United States Community Development Bank would "serve as a secondary financial institution and as a source of technical, managerial, and financial expertise to community development banks as established by the act, and to promote the economic development of the communities and areas where no community development bank has been established. . ."[46] The specific functions of this bank would be to provide the capital for the establishment and expansion of business and commercial facilities and supporting public development facilities in community areas, to provide a source of management training and technical and other supportive assistants, to aid in other economic development, to encourage people in these communities to acquire ownership and management of profit-making abilities within their community areas, and to bring together public and private capital, investment opportunities, and capable management to effect such economic development.[47]

The National Community Development Banks, within the Community Development Corporation areas, would provide the banking functions for this community. The function of these banks would be credit creation within the local communities. Consumer credit could be extended to any stockholder of the corporation or to other eligible borrowers.

The CORE bill also contains extensive proposals for the provision of tax incentives to attract industry into the community. These proposals are described in Chapter 8 dealing with sources of capital funding.

The companion Rural Development Incentive Act of 1968 is designed to "encourage national development by providing incentives for the establishment of new or job-producing industrial and commercial facilities in rural areas having high proportions of persons with low incomes. . . ."[48] These incentives are built into the program through a system of investment tax credits and rebates.[49]

The community development corporation model advocated by CORE has been implemented successfully in underdeveloped countries. As in the case of the Muslim economic development program and the thrust for economic cooperatives (discussed below), this model provides a vehicle for mobilizing resources which are most scarce within the black community—risk capital and entrepreneurial ability. It is imperative that developmental programs within the black community be designed to economize on these factors and insure their allocation to activities in which they are most productive.

It is argued subsequently (Chapters 9 and 10) that programs designed to establish black businesses within the ghetto environment possess an inordinately high risk of failure because of the inadequacies of the ghetto marketplace. Successful black businesses must concentrate on advancing sectors of the economy and not the declining sectors such as small retail or service proprietorships and partnerships which presently characterize the ghetto economy.[50] Business opportunities in advancing sectors do not exist in adequate numbers to sustain a "black economy." Thus, although the CORE program is based upon a successful development model, the attempt to contain its economic endeavors within the ghetto context well may prove self-defeating. The potential for successful implementation of program would be significantly enhanced by establishing black industry and businesses within a bi-racial context in which they capitalize on positive locational factors and compete for white purchasing power.

Thrust for Cooperative Economic Organization

As early as 1928, W. E. B. DuBois argued for Negro economic organization on a cooperative basis. He believed that this form of cooperation was necessary for the Negro to survive in the larger white-dominated system. He envisioned that this form of economic organization could inculcate a more humanistic sense of values than those operative under the individualism of the private competitive system. Central to his thesis was the contention that carefully organized Negro cooperatives lead to economic prosperity. In his later life, DuBois followed this line of thought to its logical conclusion, by advocating a system of socialism. He argued that the one great hope of the Negro American lay in socialism.

The cooperative form of organization as a means to achieve economic development for the Negro is again receiving current emphasis. Varieties of community action programs such as the City-Wide Citizens Action Committee, promote plans for Negro co-operatives as a working force within the ghetto. The Reverend Albert Cleage, Jr., of the Black Madonna Central United Church of Christ in Detroit, emphasizes the possibility of endeavors of this nature. Cleage has criticized the basic concepts of black capitalism because "it just continues the exploitive pattern." The cooperative economy is a logical and acceptable alternative to the structure of black economics. Cleage noted that "there doesn't seem to be any other way to avoid the exploitation that is going to creep in just by sheer ponderance of control of the money." The cooperative economy would prevent the drain of economic power to selected groups, make inroads into the basic capital shortage problem, and prevent this form of organization from being used in economic and non-economic activities to assure local control. In the development process it is assumed that black cooperatives would first be substituted for existing retail and service outlays and then be extended forward to manufacturing, then back to the farmer, agriculture, and then through the entire economic system. Cleage knows and has made use of the Swedish experiments in co-ops. His interest in that country's experience continues to be a source of knowledge and motivation for those militants following Reverend Cleage. The cooperative thrust is consistent with the militant concept, that "black people, more and more, recognize the fact that their identification with the total structure has been broken. Most black people are willing to do the sacrificial thing necessary in order to help black people to build some kind of economic position in American life."[51]

One technique of implementing the cooperative form of organization is through the community action corporations. In Detroit the corporate structure of the City-Wide Citizens Action Committee is controlled by blacks who invest in black economic cooperatives.

... we don't have concentrations of capital that are easily available. When we go outside we actually lose control of the thing.
The co-op principle of a lot of people putting in little bits of
money is very practical for us.[52]

Harold Cruse, in *The Crisis of the Negro Intellectual,* conceives
of the utilization of the co-op form of economic organization as
the most effective way to bring about positive change for ghetto
residents. Capitalism does not offer such a mechanism.

Black ghettos today, especially Harlem, subsist on two kinds of
economics: laissez-faire, free enterprise, capitalism, and welfare
state, anti-poverty economics. Are either of these schools of
economic method compatible with racial equality? They are not,
therefore, logic demands that the movement of social change must
be motivated by some other school of economic thought, or else,
it is foolish itself and wasting people's time. This is especially
true in view of the fact that both free enterprise capitalism and
welfare state economics are administered and controlled from the
top down.[53]

Cruse argues that the change for the Negro must come from
the bottom up, whereby black group consciousness can find a
viable outlet. He advocates the formation of communitywide
citizens' planning groups and business cooperatives to buy, sell,
and distribute within Harlem. Cooperative self-help on every level
of human experience in industrial societies is seen as the best
technique of ethnic group survival within a generally capitalistic
society.[54]

The model set forth in the nineteenth century by Robert
Owen, English utopian socialist, for a cooperative form of social
and economic organization has been recognized within the black
community. One Negro writer has argued that the cooperative
society has created a strong new class in the social order of white
communities, and that cooperative organizations are successfully
breaking into such areas as banking, stores, mills, factories, real
estate firms, and unions.[55]

He argues that the success of these enterprises has indicated
that it can be the working model for black economic development.

. . . . Now after years and years of procrastination, we need to become attuned to the cooperative business line which has already brought security and protection to millions of white families around the world. We need to face up to the current economic revolution initiated by the development of automation and united cooperative action to insure us a solid foundation on which to build and live a good life.

. . . . In this day and age, when automation is speedily snatching away jobs from all Americans, cooperative business action is the most important step black people can take in order to achieve belated self sufficiency. Owning and operating small, independent businesses is no longer a viable alternative. . . . cooperative business action can take black people out of the orbit of mental confusion. Cooperative business action can help black people to make the challenge of this electronic-automation age.[56]

National Black Economic Conference

The first National Black Economic Conference was held in Detroit in April of 1969. The widely publicized result of this meeting was the "Manifesto" directed to the white Christian churches and Jewish synagogues and all other racist institutions in the United States. This declaration, initially presented by James Forman, states that these religious institutions are part and parcel of the capitalism, the most vicious and racist system in the world. Therefore, because of this historical complicity between economic and religious institutions, the Manifesto demands reparation payments of $500,000,000 from the churches and synagogues.

Lost in the furor over the disruption of church services as a technique of delivering the manifesto was the emphatic rejection of the capitalistic system contained therein. The introduction, entitled "Total Control as the Only Solution to the Economic Problems of Black Peoples" states:

Brothers and sisters:
We have come from all over the country, burning with anger and despair not only with the miserable economic plight of our people,

but fully aware that the racism on which the Western World was built dominates our lives. There can be no separation of the problems of racism from the problems of our economic, political, and cultural degradation. To any black man, this is clear.

But there are still some of our people who are clinging to the rhetoric of the Negro and we must separate ourselves from those Negroes who go around the country promoting all types of schemes for Black Capitalism.

Ironically, some of the most militant Black nationalists, as they call themselves, have been the first to jump on the bandwagon of black capitalism. They are pimps, Black Power pimps and fraudulent leaders and the people must be educated to understand that any black man or Negro who is advocating a perpetuation of capitalism inside the United States is in fact seeking not only his ultimate destruction and death, but is contributing to the continuous exploitation of black people all around the world. For it is the power of the United States government, this racist, imperialist government that is choking the life of all people around the world.[57]

The economic system advocated by the conference is

a socialist society inside the United States where the total means of production and distribution are in the hands of the State and that must be led by black people, by revolutionary blacks who are concerned about the total humanity of this world. And, therefore, we obviously are different from some of those who seek a black nation in the United States, for there is no way for that nation to be viable if in fact the United States remains in the hands of white racists. Then too, let us deal with some arguments that we should share power with whites. We say that there must be a revolutionary Black Vanguard and that white people in this country must be willing to accept black leadership, for that is the only protection that black people have to protect ourselves from racism rising again in this country.[58]

To accomplish this end a revolution and long years of guerilla warfare within the United States is threatened. A supportive action would be a crippling of the economy by sabotage of the chief industries which are worked by blacks.

However the immediate thrust of the Manifesto is for the half-billion dollars. These funds are to be utilized in the following manner.[59]

In the United States is only a beginning of the reparations due us as people who have been exploited and degraded, brutalized, killed and persecuted. Underneath all of this exploitation, the racism of this country has produced a psychological effect upon us that we are beginning to shake off. We are no longer afraid to demand our full rights as a people in this decadent society.

We are demanding $500,000,000 to be spent in the following way:

☐ **1** We call for the establishment of a Southern land bank to help our brothers and sisters who have to leave their land because of racist pressure for people who want to establish cooperative farms, but who have no funds. We have seen too many farmers evicted from their homes because they have dared to defy the white racism of this country. We need money for land. We must fight for massive sums of money for this Southern Land Bank. We call for $200,000,000 to implement this program.

☐ **2** We call for the establishment of four major publishing and printing industries in the United States to be funded with ten million dollars each. These publishing houses are to be located in Detroit, Atlanta, Los Angeles, and New York. They will help to generate capital for further cooperative investments in the black community, provide jobs and an alternative to the white-dominated and controlled printing field.

☐ **3** We call for the establishment of four of the most advanced scientific and futuristic audio-visual networks to be located in Detroit, Chicago, Cleveland and Washington, D.C. These TV networks will provide an alternative to the racist propaganda that fills the current television networks. Each of these TV networks will be funded by ten million dollars each.

☐ **4** We call for a research skills center which will provide research on the problems of black people. This center must be funded with no less than 30 million dollars.

☐ **5** We call for the establishment of a training center for the teaching of skills in community organization, photography, movie making, television making and repair, radio building and repair and all other skills needed in communication. This training center shall be funded with no less than ten million dollars.

☐ **6** We recognize the role of the National Welfare Rights Organization and we intend to work with them. We call for ten million dollars to assist in the organization of welfare recipients. We want to organize the welfare workers in this country so that they may demand more money from the government and better administration of the welfare system of this country.

☐ **7** We call for $20,000,000 to establish a National Black Labor Strike and Defense Fund. This is necessary for the protection of black workers and their families who are fighting racist working conditions in this country.

☐ **8** We call for the establishment of the International Black Appeal (IBA). This International Black Appeal will be funded with no less than $20,000,000. The IBA is charged with producing more capital for the establishment of cooperative businesses in the United States and in Africa, our Motherland. The International Black Appeal is one of the most important demands that we are making for we know that it can generate and raise funds throughout the United States and help our African brothers. The IBA is charged with three functions and shall be headed by James Forman:

(a) Raising money for the program of the National Black Economic Conference.

(b) The developments of cooperatives in African countries and support of African Liberation movements.

(c) Establishment of a Black Anti-Defamation League which will protect our African image.

☐ **9** We call for the establishment of a Black University to be funded with $130,000,000 to be located in the South. Negotiations are presently under way with a Southern University.

Summary

Diversity exists in the economic development thrusts of those organizations which advocate the establishment of an economic structure outside of existing economic institutions, or restructuring these institutions. James Boggs and those who support cooperative ventures seek to develop economic forms which contrast to existing economic organizations. Boggs envisions a form of humanistic socialism to supplant capitalism as the predominant economic system in the United States. The evolution or destruction of existing economic institutions and many social institutions is necessary. The cooperative form of economic organization could and does exist within present economic framework. In terms of the present cultural and economic circumstances of a significant segment of the black populace, the cooperative form of economic organization appears to be an excellent means to develop programs for economic advancement.

The programs of the Muslims and the Congress of Racial Equality ostensibly are based on the capitalistic model and have been widely displayed under the euphemism of "black capitalism." The Muslim program is communal in nature and does not fit in the conceptual designation of "capitalism." The CORE program employs a corporate model in order to acquire investment funds. CORE has designed a program to utilize capitalistic mechanisms in order to establish new institutional structures. The program provides an economically feasible technique to raise venture capital and to distribute ownership shares to ghetto residents. However, it should be emphasized that the anarchistic conditions of the ghetto economy are not a workable environment for development efforts of this kind, particularly in a time span acceptable to black separatists. The same goals could be achieved within a bi-racial economy with a significantly greater potential for success. There is nothing in the nature of CORE model to preclude its use in a bi-racial environment. The short-run employment impact on ghetto residents might be smaller under the bi-racial approach, but the flow of income into the ghetto would be greater in the short-run, and in the long-run, when market forces will determine the success or failure of the embryo black businesses.

CHAPTER 5 *Development Programs Within the Institutional Framework*

The capitalistic system in the United States has evolved an economic structure that mal-allocates resources but produces a large volume of goods and services. The labor and management performers, who are within the institutional framework, are rewarded on the bases of their bargaining power, or asset ownership and control of processes. The control of resources or ownership focus is the basis by which the self-interested person shares in the income and wealth of the existing system. American blacks in moderate organizations have established an orientation for emulating the acquisitive white as a strategy for improving the economic conditions of their constituency.

Negro organizations have identified the tactics and programs

For Notes to Chapter 5 see pages 342–343.

for economic betterment in terms of the traditional evolutionary success pattern existing for many citizens in the American system. Moderate Negro organizations stress the ideas that hard work, education, skills training, property ownership, and business operation are potentially the most advantageous means by which the black can obtain an equitable share of the benefits of a highly productive capitalist system. The specific economic programs identified with the moderate organizations have been structured to provide guidance and aid in imitating the success pattern of whites and selected minorities. The programs are diverse, but are directed to improve the basic capacity of the Negro to enter the white economic structure on a competitive basis, either through ownership and/or through higher-paying jobs.

The concept that underlies and influences the design of particular programs of the moderates is essentially an individualistic, evolutionary, upward migration to high rewards. Basic to this evolutionary process is the idea that an economic man acting in his own self-interest can be or is driven to improve his material condition. He is propelled by a universal trait of self-interest which identifies and unites all men, both black and white. For the individual Negro, this approach means that he "makes it in the system" by fulfilling the necessary conditions of specialization in a productive skill, or as a resource owner by operating and/or owning a business. Given the control over resource use by ownership or operation of businesses, the black can guide his own economic destiny and share in personal economic improvement. Productive work in a skill or high-paying job may permit the black to be rewarded on the same basis as the equally productive white. This route permits long-term income improvement and wealth accretion. From within this economic structure, the black shares in personal economic growth that is aggregative for the economy as a whole. Inherent in this evolutionary improvement in the personal competitive position of the black is the assumption that the institutional structure of our economic system can accommodate the more successfully and effectively competitive black.

The National
Business League

The emphasis on black entrepreneurship and improved skill level has long been an integral element in programs of the moderate Negro organizations. The organization that has been the most vigorous and persistent advocate of the "within-the-systems" business route is the National Business League. Founded as the National Negro Business League in 1900 by Booker T. Washington it was the parent organization for eighteen national Negro trade associations.

Although Washington played an instrumental role in the organizational activity, his financing came from the white corporate community, that is, from John D. Rockefeller of Standard Oil and Julius Rosenwald of Sears. NBL continues to rely on the white corporate community for aid in its "partnership-not-plantation" orientation.

Although the name of the organization was changed in 1956, the intent and program design of the agency has changed little since the days of Washington. The recurring theme of Washington that the "black man who has succeeded in business, who was a taxpayer, and who possessed intelligence and high character . . . was treated with the highest respect by members of the white race"[1] still pervades the programs advocated and implemented by the modern National Business League.

Berkeley G. Burrell, the president of NBL, continues the tradition of the need for an organization through which the principles of good business practice and mutual business aid can be disseminated among Negroes. The organization's current programs are well formulated, professionally developed, and formally structured.

The National Business League believes that the right to participate fully in the free-enterprise system is one of the most important fundamental rights of American citizenship. The barriers that restrict business participation by the Negroes represent some of the most important obstacles to solving the nation's growing racial unrest. Negroes do not now possess the economic base or business leadership required either for assimilation for elimination of existing economic disparities between blacks and white. "For this reason the NBL is dedicated to the development of this required economic base and the entrepreneurial leadership essential for the achievement of economic, political and social equality."[2]

The methods to achieve these objectives and to implement the philosophy are not utopian schemes for an egalitarian society. The NBL does not require any massive expansion of welfare or "private handouts." The NBL does focus on the need for and access to the capital required to supplement the initiative of persons with limited entrepreneurial experience in a partnership with government and private enterprise.

The current blueprint for economic action is a three-stage or sequential program designated (1) Outreach, (2) Uplift, and (3) Mainstream. Outreach I, the first phase, has attempted to identify training needs, profit potential, and technical assistance requirements of small business. Outreach has utilized and developed local community resources to assist, train, and improve the latent potential in small-business operators. This first phase project, now underway, will continue programs of "outreach" to the small business operator in urban areas. Outreach was funded by the NBL and the federal government and is now in Stage II of implementation. Some of the key priorities for local chapters of the NBL under Outreach II are listed below:

☐ **1** Building the chapter through implementation of a strong, appealing local program geared to tackle the needs of the community, and to gain moral and financial support of local business and power structures. This will involve active, continuous efforts to get financial support from the corporate community, both in the form of corporate memberships in NBL, or contributions, or major funding grants.

☐ **2** Recruiting of membership from the ranks of the disadvan-

taged and affluent *minority* business communities. Both groups
are needed for success of our program.

☐ **3** Defining the exact nature and scope of management problems and needs confronting disadvantaged small business owners
and aspirants, continuing and strengthening the organizational
efforts begun under Outreach I, geared to span the disadvantaged
and affluent business communities and encouraging these groups
in joint efforts to develop practical answers to these problems and
needs.

☐ **4** Overtly seeking modifications in national and local policies
and practices which influence success potentials of small businesses.

☐ **5** Strengthening and broadening the training program already
set up under Outreach I.

☐ **6** Refining, broadening and making more effective the counseling and technical assistance services already established under
Outreach I. This involves bringing in of additional resources into
the program and streamlining the process of establishing contact
between client and counselor.

☐ **7** Increasing efforts in the area of procurement—to provide additional outlets to Outreach clients for contracts, subcontracts and
business-allowing for planned, healthy growth and expansion.

Outreach I and II are examples of the self-help, personal
initiative and individual effort that permeates all NBL programs.
Outreach has been and continues to be directed toward the
most disadvantaged owners of small businesses located within
impoverished communities. Services of management training,
business counseling, and the preparation of basic financial record-
keeping systems are provided to the individual owners of small
businesses. The management assistance program is the most
important feature of the Outreach project. "The most obvious
reason is that the major problem confronting small business
operators is their own management deficiencies."[3] The management assistance program is designed to attack these deficiencies
by developing and implementing orderly and rational approaches
to small-business problem solving. The NBL also continues to try
to organize more small businesses, to establish alternative forms
of business organization, and to foster cooperative business

activities for small inefficient firms. For example, the first stage of Outreach also contained a pilot program, initiated in its local chapters, to find persons interested in going into business and to provide preliminary training and technical training and advise them how to get into business.

The other feature of the pilot effort was work in twelve pilot cities to locate and help 40 persons capable of holding management training jobs, 250 persons to open sound new businesses, and 500 existing entrepreneurs whose business activities have shown measurable improvement. These basic pilot programs have been successful.

As early as May, 1968, Project Outreach programs in NBL cities were producing significant results. For example, a Local Development Company has been formed in Atlanta. The LDC was composed of forty paid members and was seeking projects in Atlanta ghetto areas. Classes in business administration management were begun in May, and firm commitments from the citizens and Southern Bank of Atlanta for a $1,000 cash contribution plus office equipment and manpower for the seminars and counseling were obtained.

In Cleveland, twenty Negro retail electronic businesses, all members of the NBL, were merged into a wholesale supply-and-distribution corporation through the efforts of the local project director and chapter president. The Columbus, Ohio, chapter had a kick-off program for Operation Project Outreach attended by almost 500 people. The Ohio State University helped to establish business-management seminars with twenty-five local businessmen enrolled. In Columbus two $15,000 loans were secured through Outreach efforts, to build a grocery store and to finance an automotive center and car-wash operation. The car-wash operation was opened in the late winter of 1969.

Detroit, Michigan, Durham, Jackson, Los Angeles, New York, Richmond, Virginia, Chicago, Seattle, Washington, Norfolk, and Memphis were also cities where local chapters of NBL reported significant progress in establishing either local Negro businesses or establishing training programs or advisory services for members of NBL groups.

In the case of the Memphis chapter organization, franchise and dealership opportunities were explored. In May of 1968, the Memphis chapter members were working to initiate a national franchise for Mahalia Jackson Soul Chicken carry-outs.

The franchise program is a particularly interesting development. The franchise and business opportunity analysts of the Washington office of NBL are responsible for locating and identifying viable franchise opportunities and establishing the reputability of the originators. The Washington office has been working closely with A. W. Willis and Judge Benjamin Hooks and others to develop a variety of franchise packages. The franchise concept is a particularly constructive tool because it can provide complete advice and operational details on all services as well as skills necessary to establish and operate the enterprise. The franchise provides for standardization of physical facilities, inventory control, accounting, and other functions. By the end of the first quarter of 1969, the Mahalia Jackson Soul Chicken franchises were being established throughout the Midwest. The successful implementation of the first stage of Project Outreach has permitted the staff of the NBL to deal with the larger and more significant Mainstream Program.

Project Mainstream is a composite five-point program that coordinates existing government programs to foster economic growth and development for the Negro communities. The program was designed to make local citizens an integral part of the urban development process through:

☐ **1** The creation of Small Business Investment Companies to provide equity capital resources for indigenous businesses.

☐ **2** The creation of local or state Development Companies to facilitate the evolvement of physical plants and equipment for the local enterprisers.

☐ **3** The establishment of Urban Development Foundations that seek community organizations' participation in the development process.

☐ **4** Providing basic training for entrepreneurship as a pre-requisite for more advanced training.

☐ **5** Setting up and operating data-processing business reporting and accounting control systems to bring to the local businessman these services which he could not afford.

The NBL description of Mainstream points out:

The principle of Self-help is and must always be paramount in all our efforts. While the deprived entrepreneur must receive reasonable assistance from the total community it must clearly be understood and fully appreciated that neither Mainstream nor any other program aims at replacing individual's own initiative, diligence, physical exertion, and financial sacrifice.[4]

Project Mainstream is designed to serve as a catalyst for rapid urban development in the twelve NBL regions. In each area a Small Business Investment Company has been set up by using sources of funds procured from the majority white businesses in the area. Loans were not sought. Sale of ownership through preferred or common stock, or bonds of the SBIC, rather than loans are the sources of capital. Given the resources provided by corporations and interested white citizens, the SBIC's use the capital to combine and amalgamate individual small businesses into larger business entities that foster the kind of economic growth conducive to reduction of hard-core unemployment. The Local or State Development Companies will make use of Section 502 of the Small Business Act, which provides for financing of plant and equipment in shopping centers and small industrial parks. Businesses financed in this manner will hire the local hard-core unemployed. These firms will provide job opportunities because shopping centers and the industrial parks are designed in such a way to provide not only local services in convenient and attractive facilities, but to provide simplified production techniques or fractionalize otherwise complex techniques so that they are easily mastered by the urban poor.[5] The NBL visualizes the plants as simple assembly and manufacturing firms than can use the skill capacity of the indigenous workers. One of the subsidiary aims is to help welfare recipients to become more self-sufficient by trying these local low-skill level jobs.

The third element of Mainstream is the Urban Development Foundation. The UDF is established to provide promotion and planning of urban development. Local charitable and service organizations and agencies will be asked to go into ghetto areas to motivate the population to undertake physical and social development. Emphasis will be placed on encouraging rehabilitation, conservation, and redevelopment of the physical environment of the ghetto. It is assumed that out of the physically renewed or revitalized areas will flow the incentive to motivate the local resident population. There is only one UDF pilot program. In the Los Angeles NBL chapter a 100-page proposal has been prepared for a local UDF effort. The scope of the NBL's programs includes housing and urban development as well as economic and entrepreneurial assistance. The "modular-core" concept is a $75-million housing and business development plan to be undertaken in every ghetto in the NBL's fifty chapter cities. The modular core plan is one type of overall blueprint for the physical revitalization of any given tract of urban blighted areas. A housing, business, and public service mix of facilities is planned. On the periphery of the "cores" light industry such as light manufacturing and warehousing will be established.

Within this new core we would create a new economically stratified housing environment, a new diversified shopping environment, and a new governmental services or civic environment. During the process of physically erecting the core, we would involve every element in the moving and vibrant community. We would train the able bodied in skills that are marketable as they rebuild an area they can identify as their own. We would create a class of entrepreneurs by the merging of white resources with minority capability. We would maximize the benefits of government social programs by making them productive of meaningful social benefits.[6]

The modular core will create new employment opportunities which will increase local capital injections and stimulate continued cash flow. The "core," through basic economic processes, will create a buffer against further blight in the future. The local jobs should cut down travel time to employment and permit families to spend more time together. The modular core attacks the basic problems of the inner city, that is, high-density population concentration, shortages of housing, high rates of unemployment, increasing cost of crime prevention, and the exodus of industries and jobs to the suburbs. Social amenities and community protection must be provided so that the central cities will be desirable places for employers to locate, for employees to work, and for everyone to live.[7]

The NBL has undertaken a direct attack upon the more visible ghetto economic problems and has provided a series of programs that aim at making the ghetto or urban cores more attractive places in which to work and live. It has also undertaken entrepreneurship training programs which it is hoped will provide a pool of available and talented businessmen to operate the newly created business in the revitalized urban areas. The spirit for development "within the system" using the capitalistic institutional structure is evident implicitly and explicitly in all NBL programs.

The persistent challenge faced by the NBL is to "take what we have and make of it what we want, without becoming involved in the quicksands of "civil rights" advocacy that others are possibly more capable of advancing. Our interest must always be purely "profit oriented," as are the interests of the majority business community, while maintaining a keen sense of social responsibility. Black and white—together—we can forge a new urban society that is wholesome, vibrant and economically viable. Ethnic minorities are destined to dominate our urban environs, and it is our responsibility and our challenge to make our urban centers enriched cultural environments."[8]

In terms of pathways to proceed, the NBL assumes that if black people hope to acquire real influence or to assure relevant responses to their needs, the Negro must acquire the tools of influence. These tools are land, labor, capital, and business enterprise, or economic control vested in the hands of black capitalists.

Urban League Programs

A "within-the-system" approach is also advocated by the National Urban League. Although the NBL's historic thrust has been Negro entrepreneurship, the Urban League has been the preeminent organization in the effort to improve skill level, jobs placement, and occupational training. The economic objectives of the Urban League are not fundamentally different from the National Business League—that is, to improve the Negro's opportunity to find jobs on the basis of training and productivity, and to improve chances of promotion to higher-paying jobs and assurance of equal pay for equal work.

The Urban League now offers a more comprehensive general policy of improving urban conditions, although it continues to promote skills training, job placement, and Negro advancement in business and industry.[9] The Urban League has carried the major responsibility for program development and planning of on-the-job training programs funded by the Department of Labor and implemented by Urban League affiliates. If the number of people participating is used to evaluate programs, the Urban League's activities are the most significant of all Negro organizations. In the mid-sixties, the annual rate of participation in skills training programs was about 4,000, and over 40,000 people took advantage of the Urban League's job-placement services.[10]

Within the last two years the Urban League has added significantly larger dimensions to its economic programs. Statements in the spring of 1969 made clear the broad-gauged interests of the Urban League and its explicit reliance on the federal government to establish clear and enforceable national standards to alleviate the problems central to the urban-racial crisis.

In 1966, Whitney Young, the Executive Director, appealed to the Congress for a guaranteed annual wage and the use of the government as an employer of the last resort. He also supported the A. Philip Randolph proposal called the Freedom Budget as a source of federal funds to finance massive programs in housing, education, health, and employment improvement.[11] Young's earlier recommendations were expanded in the 1969 Urban League program referred to as "A Call to Action."

The "Call to Action" is an omnibus program encompassing renewed and enlarged federal responsibility in manpower policy, welfare, education, housing, health, youth, armed services returnees, and other areas. The multistructure recommendations are oriented to permit the Negro to compete more effectively for jobs, and to permit him more fully to enjoy participation in the mainstream of American economic, social, and political life. The Urban League's 1969 call for action reflected a new urgency in implementing a variety of long-overdue recommendations. Immediate implementation of the recommendations in the following reports was urged: the Kerner Report (Report of the National Advisory Commission on Civil Disorders); the Kaiser Committee Report (the President's Commission on Urban Housing); the Office of Economic Opportunity Advisory Commission Report; the Report of the National Advisory Council on Economic Opportunity; the Report of the President's Commission on Automation, Technology and Economic Progress; and the Report on the Commission of Law Enforcement and the Administration of Justice.

The omnidirectional recommendations of these reports signal the complexity and magnitude of solutions to the problems facing the Negro. Some details of the Urban League's immediate concern with economic conditions within the overall problem syndrome are stated below:

☐ *Manpower development.* Calls for a vast expansion of currently successful manpower training programs (On-Job-Training, Neighborhood Youth Corps, and Special Impact Programs) on a scale calculated to meet the nation's total need.

☐ *Minimum wage.* Recommends a minimum wage of $2 per hour with automatic increases consistent with the cost of living, extended to everyone who works; inclusion of protection for both employer and employee through a subsidy for hiring the marginal worker.

☐ *Role of the Small Business Administration.* Urges a full-scale review of the agency's administrative regulations and the procedure established to implement its mandate.

☐ *The JOBS program of NAB.* More data and analysis are necessary before a conclusion about the JOBS program can be reached. It has demonstrated clear gains and obvious problems. The fact that so many employers have become involved and express a commitment to employing the hard-core unemployed is an impressive achievement.

☐ *The Job Corps.* It should be required to assume at least some responsibility for follow-up services and placement now in the hands of the employment services.

☐ *Rural economic development.* Emphasis should be placed on the establishment of black-owned cooperative farms with the full support of trained agronomists and other specialists, and the establishment of food-processing plants and similar enterprises indigenous to a rural environment.

☐ *Inner-city economic development.* Advocates the establishment of opportunities for black entrepreneurship designed to render the Negro immune to further exploitation even by black people. A comprehensive plan for the economic development of the ghettos should draw on the full tax, credit, and subsidy powers of the federal government to induce the participation of private industry and should allow full ownership by blacks once a given enterprise has become competitive. The federal government should also conduct an extensive program of encouraging private industry to spin off branch operations (retail outlets, small parts manufacture, etc.) in the ghetto.

☐ *Welfare.* Public assistance programs are so low and so unevenly distributed that the government is, by its own standards, a major source of continuing poverty. Public assistance should be based upon a single criterion need. The affidavit system for establishing eligibility should go into effect immediately. Use of the affidavit would also permit immediate emergency aid as required in individual instances.

☐ *Income maintenance.* The one prompt, effective, and certain solution to the poverty problem in an affluent society is to provide everyone with a minimum income.

☐ *Housing.* ". . . the 1968 Housing Act expands the potential for dealing with the housing problems. Urban Renewal and Model Cities programs should be funded at least at the level requested by the Johnson Administration. . . ."

☐ *Health.* Urge the establishment of a Presidential Commission to review and evaluate all federal health programs and institutions involved in the organization and delivery of health services.

Additional Urban League recommendations deal with youth, family planning, day-care centers, problems of returning veterans, more use of existing institutions to administer current and proposed programs, and improved education support. Another important recommendation is the establishment of a Council of Social Advisers. This Council, comparable in structure and responsibility to the President's Council of Economic Advisers, would provide an annual account of the state of our social health. Our system of economic accounting (national income accounts) provides a reliable system of warning signals whenever problems occur in the economy. Almost the opposite prevails in the social field where the lack of regular information fosters lethargy and irresponsibility.[12]

The Urban League recommendations suggest extension of existing federal programs, plus some unique suggestions for amending and supplementing operational aspects of on-going efforts. The Urban League's traditional emphasis on evolutionary upward mobility within the system is expressed in their prior recommendations. The pattern of potential success for the black in economic affairs must be established by the federal government to assure the black supplemental and compensatory assistance from the government. But existing economic institutions *per se* are not challenged. The supportive elements of the recommendations allude to the implication that the basic problems are reallocative within the existing framework and do not require a change in the economic system. The Urban League does note, however, that "we believe the urban-racial crisis confronting America represents a far more dangerous threat to the stability of the nation than any other problem—foreign or domestic. We believe that solutions to these problems must have the highest priority at all levels of government. . . . The major issue before us is not whether we can solve the urban and racial problems which threaten to engulf us, but whether we have the will to resolve them. Our technology, our social philosophy and our national resources, perhaps for the first time in the history of man, make it possible for us to do almost anything we set out to do. The question is one of national resolve."[13]

The solutions to the issues will not be arrived at by destroying the productive and innovative capacity of the economic system. The Urban League recognizes that it is precisely the results of functioning productivity that provide the system with the opportunity to deal effectively with black economic deprivation.

The National Association for the Advancement of Colored People

There are few other broad-based moderate national organizations in the United States that offer comprehensive alternatives to programs advocated by the National Business League and the National Urban League. Other national organizations with extensive membership roles have no unified program dealing with the specific economic issues. The NAACP, for example, does not have a well-developed economic program.

The NAACP has been vitally active in efforts to pass legislation to end various forms of discrimination in economic activities, including employment opportunities and union membership. Herbert Hill, the National Labor Secretary, has been particularly forceful in the NAACP's persistent efforts to identify and end unfair employment practices. Yet the NAACP economic development policy is more than a functional aspect of their long-term drive for civil rights.

Assuming that Hill's position reflects with reasonable accuracy that of the NAACP, the NAACP has recommended a comprehensive attack on ghetto problems. In 1966, a generalized program to end the ghetto was advanced by Hill. Elements of this program included a comprehensive ten-year overall housing plan; replacement of dilapidated housing; detailed planning of community needs for unused space outside ghetto boundaries as well as planning for needs within the revitalized ghetto areas for youth centers, nursery schools, health clinics, and adult community and recreation areas; fundamental expansion and reorganization of the nation's vocational and apprenticeship system to include additional occupational and on-the-job training with private business; upgrading and extending the educational systems at all levels in our country; and additional investment in big-city transport facilities and water supplies.[14] The annual investment of $50 billion required to implement these recommendations should be available as a result of revising the pattern of federal-local government tax structures. The federal government must free sources of tax revenue for use by localities. The central government must also reallocate its own spending priorities to support or participate in selected programs. Thus, federal responsibility was clearly assigned. Changing the financial resources of localities is an initial step to solving the extensive racial-urban problems.

The NAACP has not, however, vigorously pursued this ghetto improvement program. In more recent years, this leading moderate organization has not emphasized economic improvement or development programs. Nevertheless, William Morris, the Director of Housing Programs for NAACP, has worked to implement broader participation of Negro contractors in the implementation of the 1968 Housing Act. Several successful meetings were held in New York City to unite the talents, skills, and economic resources of black and white contractors who have a mutual interest in sharing to provide the weaker black contractor with the social and money capital prerequisites for competitive bidding on large residential and nonresidential construction projects.

Morris has noted that "it is not enough simply to provide jobs,

jobs, jobs, where people are being employed by someone else and perhaps limited as to how far they can go on the upward path. Economic development to me means the development of Negro entrepreneurship, the development of Negro businesses where they can have some degree of economic independence, and opening up the upward mobility of Negroes into the general level of management and submanagement positions where they can participate fully in the mainstream of economic life."[15]

The NAACP's stated emphasis on economic programs is consistent with that of a number of other civil rights groups and organizations with smaller constituencies. For example, the A. Philip Randolph Institute has published a program based on "A Freedom Budget," which calls on the Congress to undertake massive financial support for a program of domestic economic development. This program, like all others outlined in this chapter, is a product of black origin and is advocated by a great many blacks as consistent with their own views on economic development.

A Freedom Budget   The Freedom Budget established seven basic objectives:

☐ **1**   To provide employment for all willing to work.

☐ **2**   To assure decent and adequate wages for all who work.

☐ **3**   To assure a decent standard of living for those who cannot or should not work.

☐ **4**   To wipe out the slum ghettos and provide decent housing for all Americans.

☐ **5**   To provide decent medical care and adequate opportunities for all at a cost they can afford.

☐ **6**   To purify our air and water and develop our transportation and natural resources on a scale suitable to overall economic growth; and

☐ **7**   To unite sustained full employment with sustained full production and high economic growth.

These objectives represent a summary of steps necessary to bring a higher standard of living to all economic performers in the system. The massive financial and administrative requirements to achieve the objectives noted above are the responsibility of the public sector at the federal level. The programs of the Freedom Budget would be specified in a new section of the President's Economic Report. The Freedom Budget goals would be financed by a "national dividend" and allocated to existing federal agencies as increased authorizations for expanded and newly established programs. The "national dividend" would accrue to the economic system through the exercise of "prudent" monetary and fiscal policies. The size of the dividend is determined by the incremental change in gross national product for the period through 1975. Estimates by the Randolph Institute set the average annual "economic growth dividend" at $231.5 to $244.2 billion.[16]

Mr Randolph pointed out the need to rely on the federal government in any attack on urban and racial problems.

.... But the very nature of a total war against unemployment and poverty and all their manifestations calls for greatly increased emphasis upon adequate Federal programs and huge increases in Federal expenditures. Increases in private incomes alone, while necessary, cannot themselves at appreciable speed channel a large enough part of our resources into clearance of slums, the rebuilding of our cities, the construction of schools and hospitals, the recruitment and adequate pay of teachers and nurses . . . .[17]

For Randolph the federal government must be the catalyst to precipitate the necessary national development programs.

The Southern Christian Leadership Conference

The Southern Christian Leadership Conference, like many other moderate organizations, accepts the fact that the federal government must provide financial aid and leadership in developing programs geared to potential solutions of the racial-urban crisis. The SCLC leadership had offered inspired leadership to a large segment of the black community. In the period prior to his death, Martin Luther King had begun to structure an approach to economic problems. King's focus was on the "poor people" who were symbolized by those who participated in the Poor People's Campaign in Washington in 1968. The Poor People's Campaign was designed to attract national attention to the economic, social, and physical plight of minority groups. To the extent that publicity did result from the "campaign," the SCLC effort did direct significant national attention to selected economic needs of the poor. It is difficult, however, to determine overall goals or economic objectives of SCLC.

The Rev. Ralph Abernathy, President of SCLC, presented a series of "Goals of Poor People's Campaign" in June, 1968. The goals included passage of a jobs bill providing for public and private sector employment for minorities; passage of the 1968 housing bill; passage of collective bargaining legislation for farm workers; higher appropriations for school lunch and breakfast programs, poverty programs, and other social programs that help the poor; provision of food for every hungry person through the expanded food-stamp and commodity programs; provision of a guaranteed annual income as a matter of right for those who cannot or should not work, plus legislation that insures every American citizen a decent job at decent wages and a decent house at reasonable cost.

In testifying before the Subcommittee on Equal Opportunity in an Urban Society at the Republican National Convention in 1968, Abernathy re-affirmed the need for the federal government to expand existing programs, although SCLC originated no specific plans or programs. The SCLC approach includes elements of the older skills training and employment opportunities as well as economic development applied specifically to rural areas. Abernathy appealed to the Republican subcommittee to implement the recommendations in the Kerner Commission.

I will not pretend that our demands and proposals of the Kerner Commission are inexpensive, although in the long run it would be far more expensive to ignore the plight of the poor. I will not pretend that poverty can be ended without massive federal programs. . . . I suggest, however, that a key feature of many programs I am recommending is in keeping with the principles of the Republican Party: local control. In housing, in economic development, in anti-poverty projects, we in the Poor People's Campaign have insisted that there must be maximum citizen participation. Citizen participation really means local citizen control. It does not mean control by political bosses and Washington bureaucrats.[18]

Later pronouncements from SCLC indicated that Abernathy was not interested in making black individuals rich, but in helping groups. "We need to organize community owned development corporations where profits will be returned to building the community. . . . We want to share in the public sector of the economy through publicly controlled non-profit institutions. . . . I don't believe in Black Capitalism. I believe in black socialism."[19] Although considered a moderate and a "within-the-system" advocate of economic advancement, the black socialism statement by Abernathy reflects his frustration with the pattern of events in early 1969 that prevented implementation of the general demands of SCLC. For SCLC the traditional evolutionary economic development based on white experience of increasing income from better skills, more high-paying jobs, and asset accretion could not foster the necessary pace of economic advance. The socialism statement is vague, but denotes a desire to have a form of economic organization that returns to the black a larger share of the value added in productive processes. The earlier position of SCLC on rural economic development seemed to imply that a longer-term evolutionary pattern of development was acceptable for the poor in agricultural areas. The earlier acceptance of economic development stages, that is, moving through improved agriculture production techniques, was concomitant to improved and extended ownership, improved working conditions, and more equitable distribution of the fruits of productivity. This approach has been by-passed for more simplistic organization forms that assure direct participation of blacks in the control of production and distribution. The curious admixture of need for federal government responsibility in financing and initiative but local citizen control of programs, and the appeal to cooperative socialism, makes it difficult to characterize the thrusts or focus of SCLC's economic programs. But the extensive areas of concern also typify other moderate organizations, including the National Urban League and the National Business League.

SCLC's "Operation Breadbasket" "Operation Breadbasket," a program utilizing capitalistic institutions, has achieved limited success in promoting industry in the ghetto. As the economic arm of the Southern Christian Leadership Conference, Operation Breadbasket methods gained initial success in Chicago. For example, Jewel Tea Company agreed to buy products from Negro-owned companies to sell throughout its chain of stores. Jewel also agreed to hire a Negro contractor to build a store in the ghetto. The contract provided for deposit of company funds in Negro banks. Jewel agreed to hire fifteen Negro high-school students and to promote Negro employment.

SCLC has boycotted white-owned businesses that thrive on spending by blacks but which shun products made by blacks. Boycotts have been used against Chicago area A & P stores. As a result the chain promised 700 jobs, upgrading of black workers, placement of black products on store shelves, and the utilization of black services such as banking and construction. Operation Breadbasket, headed by the Reverend Jesse Jackson, assesses the overall gains of its operation at 3,000 jobs of $17 million total increase in Negro income.

Forty-two cities now have Breadbasket projects. Contracts with large firms to involve ghetto peoples within the ghetto are sought. Targets include General Motors Corporation, Pepsi-Cola, Kellogg Company, National Dairy Products (wholesaling in Kraft and Sealtest), and California Packing Company (Del Monte brand producers). If successful, it is estimated that some 60,000 new jobs could be generated each year in the slums. Increased money for Negro banking and saving institutions would also be realized. Boycotts are seen as the key to encouraging action. The Chicago boycott was successful, but results elsewhere are inconclusive.

**Specific Objective
Programs**

Other black moderates with somewhat isolated local influence have elected to stress more specific means to the attainment of selected economic objectives. The jobs-placement and skills-training emphasis dominates two localized but significant programs.

The Opportunities Industrial Center   The Reverend Leon Sullivan is a typical strong local leader who has effectively implemented a program designed to enhance employment options and opportunities. The Opportunities Industrial Center (OIC), inaugurated by Sullivan in Philadelphia in 1964, has been a prototype operation for similar programs in at least eighty-one other cities. The Centers are locally owned and black managed. The OIC program is based on self-help and self-motivation and trains adults in saleable skills to meet the needs of indigenous industries.

There are two phases of OIC programs. The first is skill development to provide Negroes with at least minimum skills. The other phase of the program is what Sullivan calls the more important—the process of self-habilitation, or prevocational training preparation.

For example, the Minneapolis OIC started a program in 1967 with 75 trainees. The OIC raised $80,000 from business to carry out the program. In early 1968 this local OIC had over 1,200 trainees in its programs and about 500 graduates on the job. Like other OIC's, about half of its training is devoted to skills, office and shop work, and the service trades; the other half to work habits, attitudes, grooming, and basic reading and arithmetic.[20] Following skills training the OIC aids in job placement by trying to emphasize the individual needs of both employee and employer. High job placement of trainees characterizes this program. In the five Philadelphia OIC's more than 12,000 people have been placed in jobs.

It is reported that the Philadelphia OIC's have added about $25 billion new purchasing power locally, and that the State of Pennsylvania has saved about $2.5 million in relief payments because of program effectiveness.

The OIC training and related programs are financed by business grants, bank loans, small local contributions, and some foundation support. They are not dependent upon government financial support although OEO has provided over $650,000. The self-help approach of the OIC has been attractive to white businessmen. Corporate executives from at least half a dozen major corporations provide guidance for the OIC's through a National Advisory Council.

In mid-1969 more than 80,000 people were participating in various OIC training programs. These OIC techniques can train a worker for about one third the cost of government job-training programs, and retention rates are longer. The self-help OIC approach has become firmly established as an effective skill training and job placement program administered almost exclusively by blacks, and has established several "progress corner" business including a shopping center in Philadelphia.

The OIC is a program created out of the black community, the leadership is provided by the black community, and the program is not related to the financing or administration of any federal program. In Sullivan's terms, it "is a program in the true American tradition—of the people, by the people, and for the people."

The OIC leadership is also interested in developing and operating business management programs similar to those provided by the National Business League.

I am going to train 200 men for business in Philadelphia . . . not only for our own creative businesses but for supermarkets, and other enterprises. Frankly it is my ambition to train a thousand entrepreneurs a year. And I will do it without the Government.[21]

The Small Business Development and Guidance Center Another small organization that directs its efforts at providing practical advice, counseling, and training for the new Negro entrepreneur is the Small Business Development and Guidance Center in Washington, D.C. Although the director of the program is not Negro, the assistant director is a very successful Negro businessman. The SBDGC obtains counsel from an Advisory Group currently headed by F. Naylor Fitzhugh, a Vice-President of Pepsi-Cola and former professor at Howard University.

The purpose of the Center is to expand small business opportunities by providing management assistance to businessmen located in metropolitan Washington, Baltimore, and Richmond. In discussing the programs of SBDGC, A. S. Venable makes explicit the within-the-system, moderate approach.

We strongly believe that economic organization of minority group owned businesses represents an effective means of setting in motion self-perpetuating machinery which will allow the Negro community, eventually, to function and grow on its own as a vital part of the total business community.[22]

Since 1964, the Center's assistance has been offered through two primary programs: (1) individual and (2) group counseling and training. Emphasis has been placed on administrative and operating problems such as record keeping, marketing, personnel, housekeeping, and location and relations with taxing and regulatory agencies. Financing and loans are not emphasized unless the needs of a business call for a loan and if the owner is qualified to manage the money successfully. Counseling efforts usually involve a few enterprisers and a leader meeting in an informal environment to discuss immediate problems encountered by the budding entrepreneurs. The scope of this program is limited by facilities and funds. During 1968 classes were held for seventeen organized groups with about 270 people enrolled. The number of people affected is relatively small compared with similar activities of white organizations, but the program is significant for several reasons. It is well managed. It relies on successful Negro businessmen to convey information and enthusiasm to potential black businessmen. Program designs are established on the basis of known need and reflect the institutional prohibitions that have restrained the Negro's entrepreneurship efforts. The programs are designed to provide the information necessary for a Negro to be a knowledgeable businessman.

Most whites enter the small-business route either through formal training or experience-related training. Historically, there has been limited opportunity for a black man to become the confidant of a white small businessman. It is through the relationship established by observing, assuming some responsibility, meeting customers, suppliers, bankers and manufacturer representatives that the white has been able to learn enough to start his own business. Negroes have not been able to build up the business contacts, clientel, or experience. The nuances of the white-black small business relationships have militated against the possibility of the Negro matching the white pattern of success in small business. The SBDGC is making a significant but modest effort to provide the potential black businessman with the very basic experience requirements necessary to launch his own enterprise.

Another significant feature of the SBDGC program is the commitment to the capitalistic system, and economic development within the system.

It has been my experience that as far as Black businessmen are concerned, they had a great deal more faith in business as a philosophy of life and as a means to salvation. As a matter of fact, I used to criticize black businessmen's associations. I used to say if you would stop trying to save the Negro race and start saving your businesses, the association would make more sense. . . . They are 110% committed. . . . I have had several people say to me, you keep talking about the Negro middle class. Why stay middle class? There's nothing wrong with our getting wealthy. If we have 10% of the population, let's have 10% of the multi-millionaires.[23]

A Ghetto Economic
Development Plan

Another unique black effort to end poverty by creating a strong locally owned economy is called the Ghetto Economic Development and Industrialization Plan. The "GHEDI plan" was developed by a Harlem-based, Negro economic consultant, Dr. Dunbar McLaurin. McLaurin views the ghetto as a unit and as an underdeveloped area. The plan seeks to remove the causes of poverty in the ghetto not only by creating or helping individual businesses, but by developing the entire community as an economic entity. The prime focus is not the small-service business, but large-scale business and industry that will have a larger productive economic impact. The plan would restructure and diversify the economic base of the ghetto by creating new businesses and industry. This plan, which establishes a manufacturing employment base, will use local resources productively. The goal is to establish a more balanced, diversified, and self-supporting economy that will generate capital and support a stable, friendly society.

The overall economic development orientation of McLaurin contrasts sharply with the activities and goals of the OIC's and the SBDGC. McLaurin criticizes these and similar methods of creating potential black economic mobility.

It is apparent that if every minority businessman was thoroughly trained in bookkeeping, inventory control, layout, etc., and if each was given a small loan, the economy of the ghetto would hardly move upward an inch. The result would be a community of clean, neat, tidy—but still marginal—shopkeepers with a minimum economic output.[24]

The GHEDI plan has two basic components—a source of funds for business in the ghetto and a guaranteed market for the ghetto business once established. In the particular plan, the City of New

York would provide the financing by depositing a portion of city funds in slum area banks, with the proviso that the banks make development loans to at least ten newly found corporations created to funnel the monies into local businesses. Five of these corporations would be nonprofit Local Development Corporations that attract new industry and try to stimulate economic activity in the ghetto in other ways. The remaining corporations would be Small Business Investment Companies, which would help convert the local government deposits into venture capital and loans.[25] Thus, under the plan the productivity of the ghetto's private sector could be increased and the city would more fully employ its under-utilized fiscal and purchasing resources. The city's interest-bearing bank accounts can be used as a lever to induce banks to finance community corporations. A portion of the city's purchasing power will constitute a guaranteed market for new business and industry in the ghetto. The plan would be administered and set up by an Office of Minority Economic Development within the Human Resources Administration. The ultimate goals, after successful implementation of the GHEDI plan, would be to turn all machinery over to private enterprise and dissolve the Minority Development Office. Ownership would be localized and represented by stock ownership or ownership of the productive facilities.

No action has been taken by the City of New York on this plan. It should be noted that the plan is operative with the resources of any governmental unit—local, state, or federal. New York's Commissioner of Manpower and Career Development stated that "The use of government procurement to provide a guaranteed market for ghetto businesses to start a business, or to expand one or to put a floor down is clearly a dynamic new use of our resources. We in New York believe it can work nationwide as well as locally."[26]

The plan can be implemented and made operational without the need to rationalize the approach by identifying the ghetto as an underdeveloped economy. This identification is the basis for the "nationalistic basis" of local ownership of the economy and control of its destiny.

McLaurin's position is that local control and ownership reflects

.... the universal feeling that dignity, opportunity and a sense of economic independence are vital energizing elements for the development of a young economy, whether in the ghetto or not.[27]

This rationale may be applied to either a strong drive for "making it within the system" or for a separate economic base of an isolated Negro socioeconomic system. The issues of importance relate to the willingness of the governments to cooperate in providing funding for initiation of this GHEDI plan.

The GHEDI plan assumes that urban problems can only be solved by making the ghettos productive and self-sustaining. The objectives of the plan relate specifically to the causes of urban poverty. The plan seeks to remove the lack of a productive economic activity and to increase the "poverty GNP," or "ghetto national product," by increasing the ghetto-owned industries that produce rather than merely distribute. The plan also includes machinery by which the ghetto can help itself by channeling aid through local leadership and control. The new economic base will be diversified and strengthened so that the ghetto may be a competitive factor in the larger economic activity. The plan stresses the fact that the ghetto is an entity and must be treated as such. The GHEDI plan is a feasible means by which the concept can be implemented.

The Negro Industrial and Economic Union

A unique and individualized illustration of succeeding in the system is epitomized by James Brown, former Cleveland Brown football player and now a Hollywood actor. Brown was responsible for establishing the Negro Industrial and Economic Union in 1965. The group's motto is "Green Power." The green stands for money that this group lends to aspiring black businessmen in the ghettos. The Brown operation is carried on now in six cities. Brown heads the largest organized black economic group in the country, according to statements by NIEU. NIEU has sponsored graduate training for eight black students at Harvard and four at the University of Chicago and University of California at Los Angeles. These graduate students will take jobs in the organization to provide business and economic expertise. The firm was financed in its early stages by Brown, but in 1967 NIEU received a grant of $250,000 from the Ford Foundation and an additional $250,000 from the Department of Commerce Economic Development Administration. NIEU operates a variety of companies, including Magnificent Hair Products and other cosmetic lines. There are several hundred employees working for the group, and their interests are in getting into business areas that are primarily service and that deal with basic needs such as food, clothing, shelter.

The "New Breed"

A significant illustration of small black business is the New Breed. This all-black "industrial-cultural development project" began in April, 1967, with the sale of stock to raise $20,000 for a clothing store specializing in products of African heritage. The store opened in Brooklyn in January, 1968. Shortly after, a corporation, the New Breed Industries, was formed with the cooperation of the Negro Industrial and Economics Union (NIEU). A black-owned shoe factory is underway, and plans for a black-owned shopping center in Brooklyn have been completed. The possibility of expanding the operation of the Afro-oriented manufacturing to exports and imports with African countries is being discussed.

Besides the NIEU, New Breed is supported and promoted by many. CORE backs its endeavors. The Reality House, which works for the rehabilitation of dope addicts, is investigating ways to channel Harlemites into New Breed. LeRoi Jones has helped in promotion campaigns. Bill Cosby, Sammy Davis, Jr., Milton Clark (New Breed Production Vice-President), Howard Davis (style designer for New Breed), and others are also active.

One of the principles underlying New Breed is black unity. New Breed seeks to cooperate and contribute to the economic development of all blacks. The attempt to make the black man a capitalist instead of a mere employee is the chosen means to realize black power. Today organizations such as New Breed, which are initiated, developed, and run by blacks, are one means of ghetto economic improvement. Encouraging forms of black capitalism is looked on as a meaningful way to promote Negro economics and the welfare.

Small-Business Initiative

There is increasing evidence of a current higher incidence of new small businesses formed by private owners. For example, in the Boston area Mr. Archer Williams is President of Freedom Enterprisers, Inc. This is a Negro conglomerate engaged in business activity in food, electronics, engineering, and advertising. The firm will probably branch into cable television, computers, and housing at some time in the future. Williams is an illustration of the growing number of Negroes in various parts of the country who are becoming more active in business. The firm's headquarters are in a rehabilitated fifth floor of a former flophouse on Dudley Street. The building was rehabilitated by the white owners and several other self-help enterprises, including the Boston Model Cities program and the Small Business Development Center. This building, which houses these black-oriented entrepreneural activities, is sometimes referred to as the black Rockefeller Center.[28]

Freedom Enterprisers was financed privately and based on the profit motive. Mr. Williams, who raised $40,000 of equity money, from his own savings and loans from friends, bought a supermarket from a white chain. The former white owners of the supermarket and John Hancock Life Insurance provided additional capital money through mortgages. Another of Williams' earlier enterprises was to set up a garage and automobile showroom in the slum.

The Freedom Industries, Inc., Freedom Enterprisers' food division, owns and operates two supermarkets in the Boston area and is negotiating for an increase in the number of those stores. The organization's total sales are expected to be about $7 million for the first year of operation. Future expansion will depend in part on whether or not stock is issued publicly. Freedom Electronics manufactures components under contractual arrangements with several industries along highway Route 128. The expansion plans of Freedom Industries are optimistic.

Several more examples of black entrepreneurship are found in the Chicago area. For example, Mrs. Marguerite Carter owns a corset shop at 4227 Madison Street. She is one of the many emerging merchants on Chicago's west side. She has raised capital from other business enterprises and has succeeded in the traditional route of accumulated earnings and investing in new shops. Her business seems to be good in the new area. It should be noted that her expectations are significant, since an earlier store was destroyed when violence disrupted in Chicago. The insurance money received, along with funds sought and obtained from the Small Business Administration, was the capital basis for her new business.

A dry-cleaning shop, also on Madison Street, is run by Mr. David Jones, whose shop was spared during the rioting. After the rioting he was undecided as to whether or not to continue. He decided to stay in business and obtained a $20,000 loan from SBA to modernize and expand his cleaning plant as well as to remodel his store. In both of these cases the SBA did provide some of the seed money. The SBA was active in this Madison Street area after the riots, and encouraged Negro businesses to get back into activity in their old locations. The SBA issued only twenty-three loans, totaling $704,000. The riot-damaged property and business in 1968 was estimated at over $5 million.

An example of a rapidly expanding black business is the

American Dream Soap Company. This organization is operated and owned by blacks. The products of the firm are marketed principally in Cleveland but will be sold in the New York area. The A & P Tea Company, as well as ShopRite and PastMark, will stock the products. The detergents have been sold in Cleveland since the spring of 1969. The firm hoped to gross more than a million dollars or show earnings of nearly $100,000 in the first three quarters of operation. This firm is an addition to the black businesses oriented toward the black ethnic market. Soul Brothers line of liquors, the Joe Louis Milk Company, the Supreme Beauty Products, subsidiary of Johnson Publications, which also publishes *Ebony* and *Jet* Magazines, are already well established. Progress Laboratories, a subsidiary of International Rectifier Corporation, although still unprofitable, markets pharmaceuticals primarily to Negroes under the name of Our Own Brand. This is a company that has headquarters in the Watts area of Los Angeles.[29]

An extended survey of such examples points up the typical characteristics of these black entrepreneurship cases. Almost all examples illustrate the fact that these businesses are small, have a limited market, are oriented toward serving blacks, have limited potential in expansion because of market and capital restrictions, and have developed in the services or retailing sector. Despite the excellent examples of initiative and personal drive, the black capitalism cases point to the problem of the individualist approach for "making it in the system." Financial and other aid is a necessity. The sources of strength, both resource and personal, are to be found in alliances or amalgamations with other similarly inclined blacks.

A form of organization that offers great potential for these needed types of cooperative efforts is the neighborhood corporation.

Community Corporations

One successful means of organizing and administering local areas in impoverished regions is the neighborhood (development) corporation. These local corporations have the authority to govern social services and economic development. Thus, the neighborhood corporation can become involved with all appropriate public and private agencies and organizations. It is an additional component of the organizations that provide public services in a city.

More formally, these corporations are legal entities within the ghetto and have tax-exempt status. The corporations are a structure within which the poor people in the ghetto can participate in the services of the community. The corporation is capable of potentially becoming a primary agent in local economic development. When the local corporation is contracting agency for state and federal funds under existing programs, the corporation can undertake a development role. Development may be initiated if the corporations purchase dilapidated housing for rehabilitation or new construction at federally subsidized interest rates. The corporation could then realize home ownership, subsidized funds for rehabilitation, reduced rents for its members, and perhaps surplus income for future investments. Through subsidiary profit organizations it can obtain loans for small business investment. The corporation may also use subsidiary corporations to finance consumer loans of members, obtain food and other distribution franchises, or obtain franchises for light assembly or manufacturing. The corporation can purchase real estate and start businesses outside the ghetto or anywhere in the city. The corporation thus may be a bank, producer, employer, or employee itself.[30] In all the activities the corporation invests its capital from outside sources in building a neighborhood economy.

The most successful neighborhood corporation is the East Central Citizens Organization in Columbus, Ohio. ECCO has a democratic structure in which 7,000 members participate. The one-man one-vote membership was founded through church transfer of its settlement agency to the corporation. "The success of ECCO over the last two years, in program, political life, and relationships to the city suggests the model value of the neighborhood corporation in other cities as a principal agent of rebuilding our slums from an oppressed community into independent corporate communities of decision and viable economy."[31]

The future success of the neighborhood corporation-organized format is dependent upon the flow of capital from private and public sources and the innovative management talent at the local level. The corporation format does provide local control and autonomy for programs that the neighborhood deems significant, or sources of styles. Neighborhood control of its destiny may be a necessary condition for creating a nonoppressive or non-antagonistic base from which other black-originated programs can improve the impoverished areas.

The neighborhood corporation may provide the organizational structure and *modus operandi* for attacks on social disintegration, poverty, and economic deprivation that exist in large urban ghettos. For example, a neighborhood corporation could meet most of the organizational requirements for Harold Cruse's revitalization of Harlem. Cruse points out the need for communitywide planning groups for an overhaul of Harlem's political, economic, and social life; to form a new, all-Negro, communitywide political party; for forming of business cooperatives of small businesses to take over buying, selling, and distributing basic commodities; for the establishment of tenants' cooperatives for ownership of housing; for the reorganization of Harlem's lines of communication from the community to departments and agencies in Washington; and for devising a new school of economics based on class and community.

Such a school should be predicated on the need to create a *new black middle class* organized on the principle of cooperative economic ownership and technical administration. Such a class would be more responsible to the community in social, political and cultural affairs than middle classes based on free enterprise and laissez-faire economics. Such a class development along co-operative lines must be, in part, federally financed.[32]

Cruse also notes that the "hour for Harlem is late, insofar as autonomous, self-directed social change from the *bottom up* is concerned. Under capitalism, the dynamics of time and tide wait for no one. Ghetto uprisings have alerted the power structure that ghettos need change, redevelopment, planned community rehabilitation and so forth."[33] Given the flexibility of the scope of areas on responsibility, plus additional financial support, the neighborhood corporation may be the most significant means through which indigenous ghetto residents may control their own development.

Summary

Although all the programs advocated by black moderates are characterized by diversity, there are two basic solutions-oriented alternatives. The first is the skills-training and employment emphasis. The Urban League, NAACP, and OIC are active in attempting to improve employment opportunities through job placement or skills training, either in new industrial firms in the ghetto or in established businesses. A second general approach is the black economic development or the black capitalism alternative, whereby Negro businesses will face competition with established businesses within the existing economic community.

The two alternatives are not inconsistent with the preservation of the ghetto. The programs are predicated upon the fact that blacks will continue to live in the central cities. Related programs of the A. Philip Randolph Institute, Urban League's "A Call to Action," and the NBL's "modular core" programs are designed to improve the livability of the existing ghetto areas. Thus, most of the moderate programs introduced in the preceding pages are designed to improve the social and economic environment of the ghetto, to make it a better place to live, but exclude direct incentives for emigration from these areas. This current emphasis on ghetto economic development implies that the ghetto can serve as a useful unit for economic development. Even McLaurin's GHEDI plan, which recognizes a concept of development, would have the restructuring of the economy a ghetto-related phenomenon. The issue of whether or not the ghetto is a logical and useful place for black economic development is a challenging aspect of the evaluation of the moderate-sourced programs. Before any evaluation is undertaken it is important to note other elemental features of these moderate programs.

Programs advocated by nonmilitant blacks are designed to help the Negro "make it" within the existing economic framework. There are no suggestions for a separate black state or other forms of economic segregation, *per se*. All the proposals referred to in this chapter are aimed at raising income, expanding business opportunities, and improving the economic well-being of the Negro through publicly- and privately-supported assistance programs.

It is difficult to evaluate these specific programs in terms of their probable success in eliminating the underprivileged and impoverished status of the American Negro. With the exception of the one or two job-oriented programs, all the other programs and positions are new or in developmental stages and remain untested. Cost-effectiveness studies and/or other comparative and evaluative information which could provide a basis for assessment of these programs are nonexistent. A useful frame of reference for evaluating the alternative general approaches such as jobs and entrepreneurship must include at least three elements of concern focusing on the moderate emphasis *vis à vis* the direction of overall social policy. For the black businessman or worker, economic development is but one technique for achieving social and political priorities. The effectiveness of economic development as an appropriate mechanism for obtaining these other nonmaterial goals must be evaluated. If it can be argued that economic development is a suitable means to obtain these noneconomic ends, the techniques being employed to augment development need to be evaluated. Then the consequences of the present orientation and applied methods should be investigated in terms of the potential impact on overall social policy and priorities in the United States. The evaluation of the direction, methods, and effects of these programs advocated by black moderates is reserved for a later chapter.

CHAPTER 6

Programs of White Majority Businesses

Since 1967, the black economic development problem has taken on a new dimension. The white businessman has become concerned with the economic advancement of the Negro. This statement may appear to be tautological, but it is highly significant in historical perspective. The urban decay syndrome presents a new set of problems for American business. As David Kennedy, Secretary of Treasury, said, "the men who run American industry today can no longer shrug their shoulders and say that the poor are always with us and there is little we can do about it."[1] In that significant speech Kennedy noted that "it may be fairly said that American industry has embraced the urban crisis as the most important challenge it has faced in a generation. . . ."[2]

For Notes to Chapter 6 see pages 344–345.

The American corporation is not without prior experience in dealing with these hard-core unemployed. But no concerted or significantly functional programs had dealt directly with the necessary conditions to alleviate ghetto problems. There was little evidence of an extensive private-sector commitment prior to 1967. The private-sector participation has evolved slowly, but gathered momentum in 1967.

The change from the passive to an active position by business in socioeconomic affairs can be rationalized in the following way.

Businessmen have been complaining for too many years now about government competition in the private sector. Although many, if not most, of these complaints have been amply justified, it would be refreshing and beneficial change to hear government bureaucrats complaining that business is competing in their activities. This would also be a healthy thing for our economy and a formidable hedge against a future in which we must grapple with the social and economic "fall out" of technological advances.

Business must move from the defensive to the offensive and begin pushing the boundary line between public and private sectors the other way.[3]

Private-Sector
Employment Programs

As early as 1962, the Yellow Cab Company in Chicago designed a training program to offset a shortage of cab drivers. Graduates of this program are now driving cabs. Shell Oil Company has a service station attendant program. Eighty-five per cent of the people placed in jobs as a result of these programs by Shell and the Yellow Cab Company were formerly on relief.

During the mid-sixties, Diamond Alkali Company in Houston needed more skilled employees, but was facing difficulty in finding "in-plant" employees because of reading, writing, and arithmetic limitations. An "in-plant" educational program was started. Some employees advanced the equivalent of four grades with less than $100 worth of instruction, and the cost was only about $140 per employee.

Immediately after the Watts riot, H. C. McClennan of Old Colony Paint Company sent a wire to a hundred company presidents in the Los Angeles area requesting their help. The program that came out of that conference resulted in 12,000 jobs for Los Angeles Negroes.

Other examples of involvement by businessmen in education and training to make effective employees are components in the National Association of Manufacturers STEP (Solutions to Employment Problems) coordination efforts (Table 1).

Table 1 **National Association of Manufacturers STEP Program**

Company Sponsoring	Name of Program	Number of Participants
Campbell Soup Company	In-Plant Educational Program 　　Basic grammar school education.	228
Carson Pirie Scott and Company	"Double E" Training Program 　　Training program for high-school drop-outs, work-school program.	
Chase Manhattan Bank	Business Experience Training (BET) 　　On-the-job training for high-school seniors, particularly those from minority groups.	19 (1967)
Pacific Telephone Company	"Bridging the Gap" 　　Practical program involving educators and students and the company organization.	
Diamond Alkali Company	In-Plant Basic Education Program 　　Program for employees working at low-skill levels to prepare them for entry-level job-training programs.	20 originally
Xerox Corporation	Project Step Up 　　Program designed to prepare disadvantaged Negroes and Puerto Ricans to meet the company's standard employment requirements and qualify for entry-level positions in the Machine Manufacturing Department.	16

Table 1   (continued)

Company Sponsoring	Name of Program	Number of Participants
Corn Products (Argo Plant)	MIND Company-sponsored basic education program for basic education utilizing an innovative pathway to learning.	33
Chemical New York Trust Company	MIND (Laboratory TEE-Lab 1) Company-sponsored training program to prepare individuals for jobs when and where available.	12
E. I. duPont de Nemours	Industrial Training Library Program to increase efficiency and productivity of the work force through the use of programmed instruction courses.	20,000
KLH Research and Development Corporation	A company policy established for the purpose of employing released prisoners, in addition to other "special" groups.	50
Federal Correctional Institution, Danbury, Conn.	Work Release Program, Federal Correctional Institution Joint venture involving a federal prison and industry in preparing prisoners to secure employment when released.	
Aerojet-General, Watts Manufacturing Company	Large corporation establishes a subsidiary in an urban slum and effectively employs local residents.	438
Bedford High School	Industrial Education-Vocational Program, Bedford, Ohio Designed to teach high-school students industrial skills that are in demand in the Bedford-Cleveland area.	
Jobs Clearing House, Boston	Results-oriented program designed to locate, train, upgrade, and encourage minority group individuals to find and hold jobs.	6000

Table 1 (continued)

Company Sponsoring	Name of Program	Number of Participants
Newark, New Jersey Board of Education, and Bambergers, New Jersey Bell, Public Service Gas and Electric, Humble, Esso, Westinghouse, Western Electric, Prudential	"Learn-and-Earn" Establishment of a special high school for high-school drop-outs.	14 graduates (1965)
Anti-Crime Crusade's Stay-in-School Committee, Indianapolis	Stay-in-School Program.	2000
Federal Bureau of Prisons, Petersburg, Virginia	Application of du Pont's programmed instruction techniques for pilot project in a federal prison.	
Western Electric Company, Phoenix	SLIP (Skill Level Improvement Project) Designed to upgrade existing work skills and improve the personal character traits of trainees (clerical skills).	32
Indianapolis Chamber of Commerce	Job Opportunities Fair Organization and conduct of an effective community effort to assist the usually unemployed person to secure a suitable entry-level job.	
Businessmen's Development Corporation, Philadelphia	Establishment of the BDC by the grass roots Negro community to provide guidance and assistance in obtaining funds for those persons who wish to enter business and for Negro businessmen to expand businesses or to start new enterprises	78
3M Company, St. Paul	Community Business Services Associates (CBSA) A company program established for the purpose of sponsoring self-employment for the handicapped.	150 CBSA centers in 20 states

From *Journal of Small Business Management*, National Council for Small Business Management Development, October 1967, p. 7.

A contemporary catalog of activities by businessmen must include the Control Data Corporation in Minneapolis where unemployables are now being taught to manufacture precision parts. McDonald-Douglas Corporation in St. Louis is hiring men and women who have had neither high-school education nor special skills for space-age production that demands accuracy and precise workmanship.

In other words, the doors are being opened in large American industries for the black man, either by now permitting him to work or training him to be an effective employee. Corporate giants such as General Motors, Chrysler, and Ford have also participated. GM has about 68,000 black employees. The firm added 6,000 black workers in 1968 after waiving educational requirements for job qualification. Ford provided 6,500 job openings, and these were made available without education or background constraints. Chrysler, where at least one third of its total employees in its Detroit plant are blacks, has been bringing men in who have police records or who could not have been hired before.

In the communications industry, AT&T has doubled the number of its black workers in the Bell System in the last three years. Lockheed Aircraft has recruited hard-core unemployed for its program with the help of the Urban League, the NAACP, and other agencies. Lockheed set up a program aimed at the hardest of the hard core. These particular unemployables were identified through negative rather than positive standards—that is, sustained unemployment, records of delinquency, low income, little working experience, and lack of education. The Lockheed trainee had to possess at least four of these qualities in order to participate in the program. Lockheed's experience was similar to that of other white corporations attempting to get into this kind of employment program. They reported very high cost and a variety of unanticipated problems before favorably assessing the results.

By 1968, corporations in many urban areas had joined into consortiums to bring the black jobless or hard-core unemployed into contact with job opportunities. For example, the consortium approach is typified in Cleveland, Ohio's AIM-JOBS Program, which has helped nearly a thousand applicants find work. The St. Louis Work Opportunities Unlimited has also provided work for about 7,000 people, while more than 6,000 more have been aided by either pre-job training or on-the-job counseling by the Boston Community Development Corporation. The new Detroit Committee and the Los Angeles Management Council have been successful in similar efforts.

Detroit's consortium approach is illustrative of this joint effort of many corporations acting to alleviate not only tensions in the city, but doing something practical about the income and employ-ability features of the hard-core unemployed. General Motors, Chrysler, and Ford reacted to the request of the consortium approach. They have recruited hard-core unemployed by lowering educational requirements and taking people with criminal records. The automobile manufacturers confirmed difficulty in recruiting the hard core and in keeping them for a reasonable retention rate. Counselors were hired for ghetto employment and at least 20,000 hard-core unemployed have been retained among these automobile industries. An outgrowth of the earlier experience of the automobile manufacturers helped to provide the motivational force to create what is now the consortium, the New Detroit Committee. The New Detroit Committee is composed of thirty-nine members, including the President of General Motors, Chairman of the Board of Chrysler, and Henry Ford II. The Committee is currently chaired by Joseph L. Hudson of the Hudson Department Store. The NDC is basically concerned with the variety of ghetto ills—how to upgrade the disadvantaged, how to get the hard-core unemployed off the streets and how to motivate them and get them to work, how to eliminate or disperse the ghettos and make living areas more humane, and how to break through the so-called cycle of welfarism to integrate the black into the mainstream of society. The New Detroit Committee has endured a variety of frustrations. The Hudson Company, early in its efforts, experienced a kind of backlash because of its activity. The Hudson Stores were picketed with signs indicating that the "NDC rewards the rioters." There were a variety of other problems introduced by the black militants. Several of the militants who had participated earlier left the group late in 1967 over a dispute about the allocation of funds. The Committee is still in operation and has tried to increase the understanding of the dimensions of the problems in Detroit. It is estimated that a $10-million budget is required to generate the necessary involvement. Detroit businessmen also have been active in other areas, such as the Inner-City Business Information Forum, which is primarily a Negro organization that promotes black capitalism. Michigan Bell Telephone and Chrysler have adopted a Detroit school as an innovation and project to upgrade education. The Chevrolet Division of General Motors and Detroit Edison and Fruehauf Trailer Corporation are active in a project, Handyman, which helps ghetto residents fix up their homes.

A variety of white corporations have helped to establish organizations to combine their business activities and relate these activities to the National Association of Businessmen. For example, the Urban Institute sponsors research. The Committee for Economic Development, U.S. Chamber of Commerce, National Association of Manufacturers are all involved in generalized support programs for the NAB. Most of these associations direct their attention to the ways in which businessmen can coordinate their experience, talents, and influence to give the NAB and other related programs a national impact.

Urban Coalition

In the summer of 1967, about 1,200 individuals gathered at a meeting in Washington, D.C. to attempt to form an organization that could deal effectively with the urban crisis. Out of that meeting came a private agency, the Urban Coalition. Whitney Young, in commenting on the organization meeting, said that an organization was needed which was strong enough to turn this country around. The Coalition draws its resources from five segments in the economy: business, labor, religious, minority groups, and local government leaders.

Urban coalitionists are attempting to deal creatively with the crisis in the cities by encouraging community participation. A. Philip Randolph, President of the International Brotherhood of Sleeping Car Porters, and Andrew I. Heiskell, Chairman of Time, Inc., were the co-chairmen at the organization meeting. John Gardner, former Secretary of Health, Education and Welfare, became chairman in 1968. A steering committee of thirty-eight members works with him. The Urban Coalition is a tax-exempt or nonprofit corporation funded by contributions from foundations, businesses, and other private institutions. All members or participants in the coalition are expected to contribute, in some way, either money or services or staff members to be loaned, or office space, or supplies. The major effort of the Urban Coalition is to encourage community participation. It recognizes the lack of community identity with projects as a principal handicap in pursuing any effective program. Fragmentation of the community leads to fragmented and thus ineffective community leadership. The Urban Coalition is attempting to unite leaders as the first step to meaningful approaches to attack its specific problems. Each city that participates in the Urban Coalition develops its own plans and uses resources from the national agency. The National Alliance of Businessmen and the Chamber of Commerce cooperate in individual cities. Minneapolis, New York City, Detroit, and other cities use the coalition approach. In New York, for example, the work-study program administered by the city's police department, financed by a grant from Standard Oil of New Jersey, is an example of the local-coalition approach. The Urban Coalition is attempting to expand to one hundred more cities. In its own activities, primarily at the national level, the Coalition functions as a kind of clearing house for information and policy ideas. The Coalition offices offer direction as well as information and has been quick to take stands to advocate specific programs for antipoverty measures.

The Kodak Experience

Businesses have been acting privately, that is, out from under the umbrella of the stimulus of the Urban Coalition and the National Association of Businessmen. Eastman Kodak is a good example. Kodak, a large employer in Rochester, New York, was one of the first companies to join President Kennedy's Plans for Progress program in 1962. Kodak has always been rather proud of its image as an "equal-opportunities employer." Kodak did incur difficulties with the FIGHT organization from charges that Kodak didn't have enough black employees. Since 1967 Kodak has hired one black out of every ten new employees. Kodak has also expanded its professional recruiting and contacts to at least three-score Negro colleges and is making an effort to hire more Negro professional and technical graduates. Kodak operates more than fifty different training programs and has enrolled more than 200 members of minority groups in these training programs. The firm has also influenced other industries in the Rochester area in dealing with the hard-core ghetto employment problems.

In the spring of 1969 Kodak announced that it had helped two new enterprises organize in the Rochester inner city. The two new companies are Camura Inc., a camera and small appliance-repair business sponsored by the Urban League of Rochester, and T. A. Plastics, Inc., a plastics-forming firm which was set up with the aid of the Rochester Business Opportunities Corporation. The two businesses were originally proposed by Kodak in 1968 as part of the plan to stimulate the development of an independent enterprise in Rochester's inner city. The large photographic producer provided training for managers on business and technical elements of operations, as well as employee training for both companies. Kodak was also Camura's first customer and has contracted with the firm for repair services on a large number of its cameras.[4]

The National Alliance of Businessmen

Since early 1968 when former President Johnson appealed to business leaders to participate in a national drive to hire the hard-core unemployed, many large corporations, including Ford, Chrysler, International Harvester, General Motors, IBM, and many others, have drastically altered hiring and training policies to reduce ghetto unemployment. The National Alliance of Businessmen, formed as a result of President Johnson's appeal, has been responsible for operating a program called Job Opportunities in the Business Sector (JOBS). NAB, originally formed by Henry Ford and now under the leadership of Lynn Townsend, President of Chrysler, obtained pledges for 165,000 new permanent jobs for the hard-core unemployed from these American corporations.

While the NAB's immediate goal is to find jobs and match them with people who need work, its long-run aim is to help a non-productive, unqualified individual—one who, in many instances, may have lost help—become a viable, productive member of an organization and society. This involves more than bringing together individual and job. It means coping with the complex array of problems in fitting human beings into organizational settings. In some cases it requires extensive human rehabilitation, tasks that will undoubtedly prove to be one of the most difficult undertakings ever attempted by the business community.[5]

The task that the NAB JOBS program has undertaken with the American business sector is extremely difficult. Personnel departments of participating corporations are drastically revising hiring processes or are doing almost the opposite of everything done during the past twenty years in hiring and job-placement procedures. Efforts under this ambitious program have drastically altered stereotyped training and hiring practices long held in the corporate community. In looking back at the record of the program, some 23,520 companies hired about 300,000 people through JOBS. In early 1970, 200,000 were still on the job for a retention rate of about 66 per cent. The long-run task of this organization is to put about 614,000 severely disadvantaged workers on the business payrolls by 1971. The 1970–1971 program will require expansion of existing operations in fifty cities, to encompass at least seventy-five cities. The 1969 goal was to add at least an additional 200,000 jobs.

During the short-term period of operation of NAB, additional fundamental information has been garnered to provide for future, more effective, operations.

The need for special training and new standards for dealing with the disadvantaged workers if anything has become more apparent. In Seattle, where industry has strongly backed the project, NAB official Robert McAvoy feels that NAB representatives initially did not "realistically portray the type of man or woman the employer would be receiving." The lesson that he and many others have learned is: "It takes time and training." Other cities found that the kind of job is important. Atlanta runs into resistance on taking low-status jobs. . . . In many cities keeping the disadvantaged on the job rates as a high priority. . . . trying to improve job retention, NAB will be wrestling with the more difficult prospective job seekers.[6]

The first year's experience with the JOB program has indicated that the nature of the local labor markets make a great deal of difference in the status of the job, and the vigor with which the corporations pursue their activity is significant. Whether or not the firm is a large-size or a small-size employer becomes significant, as well as whether or not the community or the chambers of commerce carry on vigorous efforts to expand the programs. The intensity of the problem faced by corporations participating in this job program can be understood from a question that might be asked by employers: "How do I go about hiring and training uneducated, unskilled, untrained, and unmotivated individuals?"[7]

Experience suggests that companies involved with the hard-core unemployed have incurred training costs of one man that range from between $3,000 and $5,000. The U.S. Department of Labor now offers up to $3,500 to employers to prepare a trainee who is classified as "hard-core unemployed." The Manpower Administration Program of the Department of Labor (MA-3) will provide the $3,500 if a trainee is given at least one year of training plus promotion opportunity in addition to counseling and other supportive services such as remedial education. The company must insure that the trainee will have the job-holding power to keep him in the labor force.

The JOBS program, although nominally dominated by the private corporations, is supported by federal-government subsidies. The JOBS program was the outgrowth of the government's TEST program and TEN Cities program as well as experience obtained with on-the-job training under earlier Manpower Development and Training Administration activities. The JOBS program really looks to industry as the best source of training for eventual employment. From the government point of view, it places the services and the facilities of the government at the disposal of industry. It is understood that this is essential if the hard-core unemployment problem is to be eradicated. Thus, the JOBS program is linked with the existing federal programs and is especially concentrated on employment. Under the JOBS activity, the companies bear the nominal normal training costs. But costs are higher because the persons hired are less qualified than those typically hired by the participating employers. Besides needing more training than the typical new employee, unemployables require basic education, transportation services, consideration of health problems, personal counseling, and other special help. The extra cost for these services is to be borne by the government.[8]

Although the goals of the JOBS program may be met, there is a basic question as to whether or not private-sector job experiments can provide long-term employment of the hard-core unemployed.

Furthermore, many businesses involved in the NAB effort characterize it as a nationwide "United Fund" campaign complete with the hoopla, rhetoric, and the trappings of pledge meetings and collection and reporting of pledges at the local, state, and national level. Furthermore, there are questions as to the meaning of the report figures. There is evidence that many of the jobs pledged are either menial, low-paying, dead-end jobs, or at levels too high as yet for the hard core to handle. Nevertheless, a number of employers are seriously engaged in this effort, and many others are casting about for practical ways and means to be involved.[9]

Ghetto Employment Opportunities

At the end of March in 1969, *Business Week* summarized the experience of a number of large corporations which were taking jobs to Negroes in the ghetto. These companies may or may not have been participating in the JOBS program, since there is no NAB emphasis that industries locate in the ghetto to provide employment for the Negro. Most of the participating JOBS firms have attempted to bring the hard-core unemployed into their existing plant sites rather than move the plant sites to the ghetto. The idea of bringing new plants into the black slums or black ghettos represents another approach to dealing with the hard-core unemployed. Most of the programs that the Negro moderates advocated (see Chapter 4) contained suggestions for locating new industries in the ghetto. The new firms were either financed and/ or operated by blacks or by the majority white community. Basically, this is not black capitalism, but an extension of productive facilities in inner-city neighborhoods. This is an attempt to move the jobs to the locale of the black unemployed.

Of the fifteen firms reported in this *Business Week* article, the programs were first initiated by Aerojet General in Los Angeles in 1966, and the most recent program was reported by Control Data Corporation in Washington, D.C., in 1969. The other firms were Avco; Economics Systems; Brown Shoe; one other control data plant in Minneapolis; Edgerton, Germeshausen and Grier;

Fairchild Hiller; IBM; General Dynamics; International Rectifier; Lockheed Aircraft, Ling-Temco-Vought Aerospace; McDonald-Douglas; Universal Plastics; and Thiokol Chemicals. These fifteen firms took only a total of about 3,000 jobs to seven different ghettos in the United States.

In addition to providing employment in these areas, several of these corporations, profit and nonprofit, have been building industrial parks in ghetto areas. A forty-five-acre industrial park is being developed in Watts in Los Angeles as well as in the flatland area of Brooklyn adjacent to some of that borough's poorest neighborhoods. The old Brooklyn Navy Yard which the city is buying will also provide jobs near the slums. Chicago, with its Economic and Cultural Development Committee, has two parks in the development stage in the inner city.[10]

The Bell System is one of the firms that has moved a plant into the Newark, New Jersey, riot area. This new plant offers employment for approximately 300 Negroes. The Aerojet-General subsidiary, Watts Manufacturing Company, which is Negro-managed employs about 500 blacks with 1,000 more on the waiting list. The Watts Manufacturing experiment seems to be a successful enterprise. It has a backlog of orders for $2.5 million and plans to expand employment. In another successful experiment, the Avco Corporation operates a new plant in Boston's Roxbury ghetto. Avco estimates the business volume in the plant at over $4 million a year. This Roxbury experiment is unique because Avco explicitly follows unique guidelines in selecting employees. At least 15 per cent of the employees must be ex-convicts; another 10 per cent will be mothers on welfare; at least 25 per cent are hard-core unemployed; the remainder will be people who have been working on part-time or "marginal" jobs.

Business has also made initial attempts at ghetto renewal. The effort is modest and is illustrated in the following brief commentary.

**Private-Sector
Urban Renewal**

The most significant effort among American corporations to do something about the physical environment of ghettos is the United States Gypsum Company's private urban-redevelopment program. U.S. Gypsum was the first major corporation to enter the slum-rehabilitation field. The corporation has already refurbished several of the half-dozen tenements it owns. The company installs new bathrooms and kitchens and redecorates the interior and the exterior after gutting the building to the exterior walls.

In Gypsum's East Harlem experience, about one third of the tenants in the rehabilitated buildings pay the entire rent themselves, another third receive federal rent-supplement programs, and the remainder are on welfare. The rents have been raised from a low of $50 a month to as much as $127 for a four-bedroom apartment after rehabilitation.[11]

In commenting on the business activity, a spokesman for Gypsum noted that in these endeavors "there must be a profit incentive—and there must be developed a good training program to teach slum people how to staff these projects .... every major corporation should get in on this. One big reason is that it can turn poor customers into good ones."[12]

In the area of urban renewal, in addition to Gypsum's more publicized effort, several other American corporations have been extremely active in private urban-renewal programs. As early as 1966, Hallmark Cards, Inc. announced that it would branch out from the greeting-card business and would support a $100-million urban-renewal project in Kansas City. In the twenty-five-block section adjacent to corporate headquarters, the company sought to improve its neighborhood, but also to make some profit in the deal. U.S. Gypsum will expand its operation with the expansion of its ghetto rehabilitation program to the Cleveland Hough area and plans to introduce shopping-center construction in Los

Angeles, Chicago, Philadelphia, and San Francisco. The American Plywood Association has invested approximately $150,000 in the Cleveland area as well. Armstrong Cork is still evaluating a rehabilitation plan in a North Philadelphia ghetto.

Another of the older and more publicized examples of private urban renewal took place in Pittsburgh. Business initiated and completely renovated the run-down portions of that city. There were eight private projects involved, and the investment totaled over a quarter of a billion dollars. Two million dollars came from local government, but no money came from Washington. The Pennsylvania Railroad contributed by clearing 148 acres of forty city blocks and erecting apartments and research and educational buildings. The land cost in that Pittsburgh development has been $125 million. No government funds will be used.

In a recent assessment of private-enterprise activity in the private urban renewal program, it was noted that rehabilitation of slum housing is a highly publicized solution, but it is hardly a cure-all. Rehabilitation has not added to the supply of new housing and may in fact reduce the number of units available. Such programs have not performed the social function of rehabilitating the community. In addition to the negligible effect upon the expansion of available housing supply, there is really still no evidence that urban renewal can be profitable for the firms' undertaking. "The best-known effort is U.S. Gypsum's rebuilding of several hundred units of New York City's Harlem and its plan for similar work in Chicago and Cleveland. But USG has yet to say how its venture is fairing financially."[13] Profitability of ghetto rehabilitation is a function of many factors. For example, whenever a businessman sets out to fix an old apartment or to build a new one he faces the reality of a money shortage to finance low-rent housing. Government-assistance programs in this area are extremely time consuming. The procedures or regulations frustrate the erection of every prospective building. "In New York City it takes at least two years to process the average FHA 221 d3 project, and by that time costs have risen 10%. Furthermore, builders often run into delays before their projects' proposals even reach FHA. A case in point: late last year a 1,450 unit project proposed by HRH Construction Company in 1961, was still awaiting approval by the New York City Board of Estimate."[14]

The future of private-sector urban renewal is uncertain. Whether or not the private sector will bear the cost in terms of leadership and finances will be a function of the nature of the factors that precipitate a business reaction.

Harvard Business Review calls Gypsum's first undertaking an experiment or an example of a sociocommercial enterprise. This term is a way of describing an entirely new view of the true "business" and its role in the so-called public sector of the economy.

In essence, socio-commercial enterprise is based on the theory that if we are going to be successful in solving such crucial problems as water and air pollution, race relations, unemployment, education, we must commit the vast resources of private business on a businesslike basis. Thus, such an approach is particularly social in motivation and goals; but is also partially commercial in that it is helping to shape an environment in which business can continue to operate profitably 5 or 10 years from now.

What is involved here is not masked "do-goodism" on the part of business at the expense of stockholders. Rather it is the application of the skills, knowledge, funds, and particular resources of a company in a social problem area on a scale comparable to that on which the company attacks day-to-day commercial tasks.[15]

Banker Involvement

The American Bankers Association has also become concerned with the plight of minority groups and their problems. This trade association through a committee of urban affairs has developed policies and a program for urban progress. The Urban Affairs Committee of the ABA has analyzed the banking industry's involvement in urban affairs in three areas: (1) housing, (2) jobs and training, and (3) business development in the inner city.

In the matter of employment of minority groups, several bank-operated programs designed to provide opportunities for the inner-city disadvantaged have been developed. Business experience education programs of the First Pennsylvania Bank in Philadelphia, the Store Front Academy Program in New York City (Chase Manhattan Bank and First National City Bank), and the Jobs Now program in Chicago are good examples of bank participation. There is a wide range of other similar programs in other areas involving bank participation to various degrees.

In the field of minority ownership, the ABA is working with the Small Business Administration in developing a major national program. The program recently announced by the SBA, Project OWN, is designed to increase minority group business ownership. A prominent feature of the program is bank financing. A great number of banks are already involved in similar efforts. For example, the banking communities in New York, Philadelphia, Boston, Cleveland, and Rochester, N.Y., are participating in comprehensive programs of inner-city business development.[16]

The ABA policy on business relates primarily to technical assistance to business, or assistance in the development of enterprise in critical urban areas. Banks should provide personnel for training and counseling in business finance and development. Banks in localities are asked to combine to provide a consortium of special skills. The consortium would include other community institutions, but provide a comprehensive business counseling service. Banks are also urged to contribute personnel to a counseling service consortium on a temporary-loan basis without fee, and all banks within the community are asked to share in providing the personnel. The ABA policy to promote economic development represents an even greater commitment to development of local enterprise. Their policy statement includes reference to encouraging entrepreneurship in economic development in critical urban areas with members of the banking industry adopting positive action programs to locate, recruit, develop such business prospects. Banks are advised to take affirmative action in reaching prospective minority businessmen to help them get established. Banks are thus urged to establish the practice of dealing with business prospects in the critical inner-city areas in exactly the same manner that they do with more established customers. This has required the opening of new lines of communication and thus more consideration given to working through a neighborhood group so that banks communicate more effectively with the disadvantaged poor. The bankers' committee on urban affairs has developed, after careful study, a policy on employment and career advancement for the disadvantaged poor. Managers are urged to establish policies and practices that would advance meaningful employment and career opportunities for the poor. Banks are also urged to implement new and more aggressive policies for recruiting the disadvantaged poor for jobs in the banking business. In order to hire the formerly unemployable, the banks are asked to develop new techniques for the selection of employees that are based on the abilities to perform rather than on the background and particular experience or training for the job. A related commitment under the Negro employment emphasis is that members of the banking industry should insure that their employment and advancements policy apply equally to all and that the criteria are in fact fairly developed to promote the maximum opportunity for the disadvantaged. For example, banks must participate in and develop kinds of programs that will be utilized by the entire labor market of disadvantaged people, including those physically and mentally disadvantaged. Employment of these people has to be in more than "token" or "dead-end" jobs when qualification or training potential could permit higher-level performance. Banks, then, are supposed to develop special counseling programs as well as training programs in order to insure that the job opportunities in the banking industry will be long term and meaningful.

Donald Graham of the Board of Directors of Continental Illinois National Bank and Trust Company of Chicago has provided a commentary on the ABA's efforts to deal with urban problems:

The bankers' committee on urban affairs has embarked on a new venture which is unique in the banking industry's history.

Historically the nation's bankers have played a leading and positive role in the development of American life. Many individual banks have been working toward alleviation of inner city problems for some time. Now, however, banking as an industry has made a commitment to help solve today's greatest challenge in America—to rebuild and revitalize the inner cities and help the residents gain personal dignity, a meaningful sense of community spirit and activity, and material benefits which elude them. The bankers have capacity for civic leadership, his knowledge of constructive financing, his experience in all financial and investment levels and his careful interpretation of the mood and conscience of his community must be utilized to help solve the urban crisis. And this effort fully embraces the cooperation of the National Bankers Association so that black and white bankers are truly working shoulder to shoulder. It also embraces the Investment Bankers Association of America as we seek to work out equity capital arrangements which will provide seed money for the inner city entrepreneurs.

Initially the industry's effort is being focused on the major problems of housing, jobs, and businesses in the inner city. While much remains to be done in the search for positive solution to the critical urban problems, I believe we have made a good start. . . . We recognize that the real test of the banking industry's commitment to the urban challenge will be the visible, actual results—good housing, trained and employed workers, and new businessmen.[17]

Graham in that speech commented on the underlying causes of the ghetto problem as it is related to the supply of credit and investment capital, and noted that banks have been making progress in making credit available for rehabilitation and for other programs in the city. "Yet to achieve the degree of private sector investment in the cities which is required, it will be necessary for government to provide special inducements which will assure a competitive yield and repayment of the extended credit. Without such incentives it would be extremely difficult for the inner city market to attract funds from more competitive and insured investments."[18]

For example, legislation affecting the Small Business Administration's lending and financial policies have been directed toward meeting some of the financial constraints facing minority businesses. The Small Business Administration's Project OWN is designed to establish 20,000 new minority businesses by the end of the fiscal year 1970. This expansion of minority ownership will require investment at the rate of $250 million by the first year of the program and $500 million through the fiscal year 1970.

Project OWN will continue to enlist banks, industries, and community organizations with the leadership and backing of the federal government. Project OWN is supposed to be "a giant step toward closing the gap between black and white in the owner-ship and management of American business."[19] Howard J. Samuels announced at the same time that OWN was "a program to answer the appeal from the ghettos for a stake in American capitalism. . . ."[20]

The 1968 SBA program asked the banking community to in-crease its commitment to minority borrowers and play an active role in selecting and supervising loans. SBA asked industry groups to volunteer management assistance and other support, including increased franchise opportunities. Community groups were asked to become involved in identifying potential owners and managers and organize local efforts to develop business sites to help process loans and to coordinate managerial assistance. Such groups as the National Business League, Urban Coalition, Urban League, and the Puerto Rican Forum were expected to participate in this activity. SBA itself was supposed to assume leadership on behalf of the federal government in guaranteeing loans and coordinating the work of the other agencies. The Labor Department, Commerce Department, and the Office of Economic Opportunity had pledged to make resources available and had assigned liaison officers to the SBA.

Section 502 of the Small Business Act is another recent example of the legislative sponsorship of development financing for indig-enous community groups. The U.S. Department of Commerce, through its Affirmative Action Programs, has developed and imple-mented a variety of specific projects designed to aid the disadvan-taged minority businesses. These elements of the Economic

Development Administration's activity include credit pools and loan guarantees, the development of additional leadership in the Negro business community (Youth Enterprises, Inc.), franchise opportunities, and aid to Negro construction companies in urban and housing development projects.[21]

Summary

Given the pace of current business sector aid to the ghetto resident, it appears that the corporations are now considering a more active, positive role in social progress. Since the summer of 1968, it has become virtually impossible to chronicle or catalog all the programs that have been initiated by the private sector. Trade association publications, house organs, business magazines, and financial chronicles almost daily report new programs initiated by another firm or corporation. Despite the large number of programs and the diversity of the features of the programs, the white-oriented solutions activities are directed principally at skills training, job placement, and the employment emphasis and/or various forms of private urban renewal within the ghetto regions. In terms of popular support, the skills training, job placement, and employment emphasis is becoming the chief contribution of the white business community.

The businessmen have learned that in jobs training there is no simple answer. Brief experience over the last two years has provided some experience that is important. No program to hire the hard core will succeed unless top management is totally committed. Recruiting requires special efforts. The under-educated black does not seek out employment opportunities. Communitywide groups are necessary to seek to reconcile moderate and militant. Most companies find that they have had to drastically alter their hiring bars, to take unqualified people. Businessmen have to restructure their concept of the role that can be functional in solving the problems of the unemployed. Business must play a role that will convince the black that the white majority corporations are not party to the continued suppression of his innate desire to become a productive participant in the economy.

It is difficult to evaluate private-sector job or employment and development programs in terms of probable success in eliminating the underprivileged status of the American Negro. With the exception of one or two programs, all are new and untested. There are, however, some general guidelines that can be used to provide a frame of reference for future critical studies.

Private industry assumes that it can attack the problem of underemployment and unemployment. There is also an assumption related to efficiency and the greatest possibility of success that underlies the vigor of the business-sector activity. One black militant leader described the importance of the private sector when he told a group of Detroit businessmen that "if you cats can't do it, it's never going to get done."[22]

The noted Negro educator and President of the Metropolitan Applied Research Center, Kenneth Clark, has argued that:

. . . business and industry are a last hope. They are the most realistic elements of our society. Other areas in our society—government, education, churches, labor—have defaulted in dealing with Negro problems.

It is now up to business. Other elements can lose in terms of guilt or conscience. But business has profits to lose also. It has efficiency to use, economy, and, of course, it has tremendous investment it can lose unless there is a lasting racial peace.[23]

Clark, however, is not uncritical of the role that business has undertaken. It is his belief that the private sector has exhibited insensitivity, indifference, apathy, and Pilate-like washing of the hands; unwilling to become involved and more willing to regard it as somebody else's responsibility—either the government's or the churches.[24] A variety of other issues must be confronted when evaluating the business sector's contribution to the solution of manpower unemployment problems:

☐ **1**   Can private industry provide a more efficient and thus a

low-cost approach to the problem of skills training and job placement than the public sector?

☐ **2**   If cost efficiency studies indicate that private industry is
best suited to provide a solution to this problem, would business be
willing to provide jobs if it meant a reduction in profitability?

☐ **3**   If this were the case, does the private sector have a social
responsibility to proceed in this effort?

☐ **4**   Could the magnitude of any programs provided by the
private sector ever be great enough to eliminate the mass unemployment in our nation's ghettos?

☐ **5**   Even if the private sector would provide sufficient jobs, can
business cope with the arguments of the militants and many
moderates that jobs are not wanted? (Blacks had full employment
under slavery.)

There are few adequate comparative estimates of the efficiency
of the private as opposed to the public sectors in providing skills,
training, and jobs. Even minimum information is necessary before
any relevant policy conclusions can be drawn. Experience is not
adequate to indicate which sector would prove superior. Perhaps
the strongest argument for industry's role is the "incentive effect,"
which is a result of private training.

. . . . In on-the-job training, jobs are directly, visibly, and risklessly
tied to completing training programs. A visible job can provide
the incentives necessary to persuade workers to complete the cour-
ses in instruction. Without a visible job, the risk of not finding a
job or refusing a job offer given during the training period may
be so large as to not make training worthwhile.[25]

Although private-versus-public-sector effectiveness remains at
issue, private industry cannot significantly reduce urban unemployment without a sharp increase in cost with a resultant reduction in profitability. In addition to the cost of training the hard-
core unemployed, industries may have to redesign basic production processes to reintroduce labor-intensive low-skill-rated jobs.
These types of jobs are being eliminated through technological

advance and automation. Reduced efficiency and other sources of higher costs will occur.

In assessing the alternative of "industry in the ghetto," the business sector recognizes the inner city as a high-cost, high-risk area. The disadvantages to this approach are obvious. The assumption of high-risk operations is not practicable when alternative options are evaluated on an opportunity cost basis. Thus, there is no substantive evidence that white businesses are prepared to take the high risks, other than on a very highly selective basis. The presence of large numbers of potentially employable low-wage cost workers is not a sufficient reason for firms to locate operations in the ghetto. The low-wage costs mask the total very high cost of such locations and of employing the black unemployed. There is little evidence to disprove the position that business is not now willing to embark upon the high-cost programs required to move industry to the unemployables.

The effort to create job mobility by locating enterprises within the ghetto also would result in higher industry costs because of the paucity of positive locational factors in these areas. Adverse locational factors within the ghetto or the positive factors outside the ghetto (cheaper land outside the central city, developments in transportation including growth of air and highway transportation) make it less unnecessary for plants to be located near the center of the city. Technological developments favor the use of single-storey continuous-process plants; less crowding away from the central city makes it easier for employees to find housing near their work and to commute more easily. The types of industries that have been growing most rapidly tend to hire highly skilled and technically trained workers who are both attracted to and can afford relatively improved and modern public facilities characteristic of the environment of the new suburb.[26]

With the increased costs of ghetto job training and ghetto sites and the concern of businesses with profit making, private industry can be induced to tackle the problem of inner-city employment only if it is guaranteed no net increase in cost. The public sector must actually provide incentives through subsidies or new tax concessions to encourage industry to undertake this task. "To make a substantial impact on poverty ... the government must provide financial incentives to train the poor. The real cost of training the hard core unemployed or sub-employed are high enough so that private firms simply will not (and should not be asked) to undertake any more in token training without financial incentives. ... .[27]

Private-sector jobs and employment programs are likely to have very little effect on the total number of jobs available. Private-sector programs represent devices to ration jobs or to reallocate jobs in the direction of the poor black.

The Administration's three-year target of 500,000 jobs is the official estimate of hard-core unemployment in the 50 cities, averaging out to a little over 3,000 in each city each year. But many experts believe that the real number is two to six times the 500,000 counting such groups as those who have simply given up the search for work. In the district of Columbia, for instance, where the first-year JOBS quota is 2,000, even the official estimate of hard-core joblessness is 8,000 to 12,000, and "for every hard core unemployed person we go out to recruit, we find several more," says Fred Hetzel, the local U.S. Employment Service Director. ...

As fast as some hard-core unemployed find jobs, the other low-skill workers are losing theirs to automation and other factors. The very success of the newly employed persons may draw into the labor force friends and relatives who haven't been looking for work, or attract to the big cities still more poor families from rural areas. Even if the 500,000 goal is fully achieved, says manpower specialist Garth Mangum of George Washington University, "we will never notice the difference."[28]

The question of whether industry has a social responsibility to attempt to deal directly with social problems is debatable. Private enterprise is acting in an area of uncertainty. Society has changed the traditional ground rules for turning to the private sector to find appropriate solutions to social problems. Business finds itself facing a philosophy gap as well as "a morass of fuzzy moral questions more befitting academicians than men of trade and commerce .... they are confused, frustrated, and largely immobilized."[29] The same author evokes a sobering warning on allocating social problems to the industrial sector:

It is when we get into the dangerously fuzzy area of begging and pleading with companies to act that trouble can arise. For if we, through our government, abdicate areas of public concern, then we abdicate all rights to criticize performance, and we may find it increasingly difficult to regain control of the situation. If companies are reacting to all this entreating really begin to tool up their productive capacity to handle central problems, and start pouring investment capital into setting up "operations divisions," we may find it very hard to stop such a juggernaut.[30]

If industry can attack the problem of urban unemployment more efficiently; if, with a sufficient tax incentive or subsidy program, industry could enter the activity with no net reduction in productivity; and if industry does visualize social problems as a legitimate concern, then the issue is whether the magnitude of any programs by private industry can be massive enough to eliminate or significantly reduce urban unemployment. Present efforts are inadequate and only a full-scale mobilization of the private sector would be solutions-oriented.

. . . . It is wishful to believe the JOBS program in itself can ever be a complete solution. The 40,000 jobs filled in the first 6 months of the effort—assuming that the placement turns out to be successful, and no statistics have been obtained on that—take the country less than one-tenth of the way toward the goals of 500,000 jobs the President set-up for the program, only one-twenty-fifth of the way toward the Kerner Commission's goal of a million private jobs, and only one-fiftieth of the way toward the commission's goal of two million to be equally divided between private and public employment.[31]

It matters very little to the black ghetto resident whether or not private industry can conduct efficient jobs programs.

. . . . The first thing we must do is to separate the question of providing an adequate level of income from the question of how best to accomplish production in the economy.

To a very substantial extent the current problems of chronic unemployment and underemployment arise from attempts to legislate the productive mechanism and factor prices to achieve income redistribution objectives. This just doesn't work. If an individual can't produce enough in the private economy to be paid the minimum wage, the private economy just won't hire him. It can't be stressed enough that there is a pressing need to begin restructuring the incentives in our economy and modifying our approach toward insuring an adequate income. The need is to separate income maintenance from the way in which we produce output in the economy.[32]

Kain continued his testimony before the Joint Economic Committee by stating emphatically that

. . . when we talk about the Negro worker, the problem is not principally his lack of skills, rather it is the fact that he is systematically discriminated against, because he is a Negro, from participation in the economy.[33]

A comprehensive and adequate manpower policy is the causal element in any substantial reduction in Negro underemployment, unemployment and poverty. The federal government must play a more active role in formulating a more adequate total manpower policy. The priority private sector role is that of eliminating discriminatory barriers to employment and promotion. Private industry must also make available more job opportunities for the lower skilled members of the labor force. But the private sector by simply hiring more Negroes cannot provide all of the needed elements to solve the economic plight of the Negro. In regard to the JOBS program, the private sector's principal efforts should be directed to removing traditional job promotion and job qualification policies. A necessary condition for expanding and upgrading Negro employment is a massive and immediate effort by employers, labor unions and the government to increase training and education opportunities and to abandon racial barriers in employment.

The point may also be made that federal government cooperation with the private sector is a *sine qua non* without which solutions-oriented programs can be undertaken in our system.

Federal Incentive
Programs

Any assessment of potential and costs of federal financial assistance and incentive proposals must recognize the need to separate the effects of incentives and concessions on newly established black businesses from those on white-established corporations. But a general evaluation of all incentives programs can be made in terms of the repercussions on resource allocation and programs' potential success.

At this juncture, it is important to assume that the tax concession and/or investment incentives are short-run alternatives. Longer-run restructuring of many basic institutions is part of the long-term solution.

Investment Credit—Is It Effective? The federal government implemented a 7 per cent investment tax credit in 1962. This tax credit is a form of business subsidy for firms with taxable profits. For the first two years after adoption of the tax-credit program, business investment spending in the United States did proceed at a high rate. This would seem to underscore the efficacy of tax policy in influencing investment behavior. It is not clear, however, whether or not the investment tax credit played the responsible role in the high rate of investment. Firms invested on the basis of traditional investment determinants, including need for additional capacity, or replacement or because of expected economic conditions. But the investment tax credit does increase the return from a given investment.

For the successfully operating firm, certain marginal capital expenditures become profitable. The increase profit margin may or may not be the determinant variable to induce additional investment. The increased profit margin may or may not be associated with the investment credit used by the business firm.[34]

From the point of view of permitting informed public discussion, a tax credit is inferior to a direct subsidy as a means of producing investment incentives. The tax credit conceals potential changes in the firm's income. In other words, an increase in earnings would be needed to make the firm as well off without the credit. This would not be the case if a similar incentive were provided by direct subsidy. In the case of any form of a subsidy, whether an investment credit or a tax incentive, it is important to be able to predict whether or not "a given subsidy device is consistent with the requirements for an optimal allocation of resources."[35]

A Critical Approach to Tax Credits Criticisms of the tax-credit approach outnumber the advantages. The tax-credit method is too limited in scope. It is of value only to firms that have tax liabilities. The credit encourages large firms but offers little help to newly formed businesses, including black ghetto businesses. An equal-percentage tax credit for all firms endows a larger income subsidy upon firms with higher marginal tax rates.

Tax-credit critics question the intentions of businessmen receiving the concessions. If the investment credit does provide a general stimulus to investment, the direction of that stimulus is determined by decisions of individual producers. Furthermore, regulations would be required so that income from tax benefits would be returned to ghetto development. The Advisory Committee on Intergovernment Relations in the *Report on Urban and Rural America* noted that critics of their tax-credit recommendation object to the fact that the incentive approach relies on the profit motive, which is in some way related to the corporation's focus on increasing the productivity of trained workers rather than on the need for new and unskilled or unemployed workers. Critics object to this likely result "because the governmental costs covered by tax incentives are less obvious to the public than direct expenditures."[36]

The Use of Tax Concessions Tax concessions are often justified as an investment in jobs and payrolls. But there is fundamental agreement among economists that taxes are not an important determinant of plant location. Financial inducements of the tax type are a secondary factor in choice of a region and are also a subsidiary factor in the choice of location within a given region. From a national point of view, selected financial inducements have support if they are used in labor surplus areas. But "With regard to national resource allocation effects, other methods of aiding people of labor surplus areas may be preferable to financial inducements."[37]

Resources Allocation Concerns   Tax concessions and investment credits distort resource allocation and lead to inefficiencies in the use of those resources in economic activity. However, this is a tautological concept because the intent of the incentives must be the distortion of the existing pattern of resource use into areas of underdevelopment. No program of fiscal aid, whether it is the tax-incentive type or the subsidy type for (regional development), "will be of much use unless there is also some plan for that development—some system of rational balancing of the cost and benefits of devoting so many resources to the achievement of such and such goals."[38]

Tax concessions of whatever type are subject to strong criticism and weak support based on resource distortion, accountability, and other administrative problems, as well as equity and discrimination. Yet, the federal government must use its financial or fiscal resources to aid the black community if the economy is to avoid future sacrifices from underutilized resources. At issue is the type and appropriate use of federal fiscal aids. Resource allocation must be redesigned to bring the black into the mainstream of economic life. Because the dilemma exists of needs for action versus the criticism of existing industrial schemes, there is no consensus as to which public financial support program is appropriate.

A survey of selected forms of the federal government's programs now in effect is introduced in the next chapter.

CHAPTER 7

Private- and Public-Sector Cooperation

James L. Sunquist, in discussing jobs training and welfare for the "underclass," raised questions as to the future of private-sector programs.[1] It is his contention that in the future corporations will need new tax and other incentives plus a subsidy to continue costly programs if they are to play the role of employer of the last resort. There are few notable exceptions in business-sponsored programs that can be undertaken without financial and other help from the public sector. The public sector is asked typically to co-operate with the private sector in programs nominally originated by banks, corporations, and other private-business entities. For example, the Chamber of Commerce for the United States in its statements on the disadvantaged poor reflects this need for private-public cooperation.

For Notes to Chapter 7 see pages 346–347.

173

Solutions to the problem of the chronically unemployed workers should give priority to programs that offer basic education and training in skills leading to jobs in the competitive labor market. . . .

. . . Emphasis should be placed upon upgrading the ability of these workers. Administrative improvement in government manpower programs should be undertaken particularly so as to coordinate and rationalize efforts at the local level. Government programs should be refocused increasingly in helping the hard-core unemployed. Massive federally financed employment programs in public and non-profit jobs should be avoided. Such programs could lead to the development of a locked-in class of workers unprepared for the transition of regular jobs.[2]

In the experimental demonstration projects involving the disadvantaged and hard-core unemployed during the last year and a half, several difficulties and costs have been encountered.

The time has come for a change in the continuing pattern of the employers engaging in experimental and demonstration projects, each learning *de novo* what others have learned about hiring, training, promoting, and providing compensatory and remedial services for the hard-core unemployed. To correct this situation, assistance and guidance must be provided to employers by government agencies whose staff have acquired knowledge and competence in the field of working with the hard-core unemployed. Beyond this, government agencies must begin to view themselves as major employers and to "practice what they preach" to non-government employers in terms of seeking out and providing meaningful job opportunities to the unemployed.[3]

There may be new recognition by the leaders of industry that their corporations must become involved in all types of public-service activity designed to improve the welfare of the community. These private manpower development activities are a new area of activity for most firms in the private sector, and to be effective they must be expanded on a massive scale. Yet, only very large employers are administratively responsible or capable of mounting the necessary effort. Furthermore, only a very few of the large corporations can afford to become involved in the effort in a meaningful way. It may be assumed that these aggressive, socially oriented enterprises have the responsibility to ask government to give aid to the private sector. Businesses also have the right to ask government to take the initiative in its own agencies to practice what it preaches in regard to employment problems. Almost no private-sector employer of the hard-core unemployed disavows the need to have the federal government become more active as a direct employer and as a subsidiary financial source in private-sector employment programs. Government agencies probably will need to provide employers with more help in overcoming the experimental nature of the employment problems of programs for the hard-core unemployed.[4]

Government has been active in manpower-training programs for a number of years. The current emphasis in federal manpower programs is to rely on the private sector to employ and train the disadvantaged. This is significant and of future importance. Federal government agencies are not being used to create extensive employment in the form of new starts or new jobs as a part of overall public manpower programs.

There are a variety of objectives of federal manpower programs, but a significant one is to increase employability through training or what is referred to as "sheltered work experience." The justification for this objective is an assumption that there is inadequate basic education, ineffective formal vocational training, and limitation of the ghetto workers' employability and productivity by the status of on-the-job training. It is assumed that federal welfare programs and various forms of discrimination also contribute to the unemployability characteristics of ghetto workers. The ghetto worker is not competitive in existing labor markets.

The federal government's overall poverty policy or impoverishment presents two alternative approaches. It has inaugurated programs that try to equip the poor to earn higher incomes through normal employment or other training programs that increase earning capacity. This policy is sometimes referred to as a "structurally oriented" approach. A second basic orientation is referred to as the "distributive alternative" and involves a wide range of programs designed to increase the income of the poor. The income may be in the form of direct cash grants from the government, or goods in kind as under the Food Stamp Program and through subsidized employment. Federal manpower policies currently include elements of both alternative approaches.

In the case of the structural approach, the federal government is attempting to change the nature of the labor market as well as improve the competitive capacity of individuals in that market. In regard to the labor market itself, the federal government is performing more aggressively to make sure that conditions exist that will make the market structure more competitive. In regard to the role of the individual in the structural policy, skill development and experience, plus on-the-job training programs will improve worker capacity so that he will be more effective in the labor market. Economists usually refer to the education, job-training, and retraining elements as social capital, or human capital investment. Investment in human capital is a long-run effort that is extremely slow and very costly.

Office of
Economic Opportunity

The most popularized efforts of the federal government in dealing with the poverty problem are the programs administered by the Office of Economic Opportunity. The programs inaugurated in 1964 set up the basis for indigenous or local participation in the design of activities. Comprehensive work and training programs administered by OEO and the Bureau of Work Training of the Department of Labor comprise the Neighborhood Youth Corps. The School Program provides part-time employment and training of high-school students of low-income families so that they can remain in school. The Neighborhood Youth Corps is designed to provide useful work and training for unemployed or local-income persons who are over sixteen. NYC assists these persons to obtain regular competitive employment. Operation Mainstream, which is a special work activity for the chronically unemployed poor, is specifically aimed at improving parks and recreational areas and protecting natural resources in areas where projects are located. The participants in this program are typically unable to secure appropriate work and training. A companion work-training program is designated New Careers. This is also a work and training activity for adults that leads to new career opportunities, particularly in service fields such as education, neighborhood redevelopment, health, and public safety. In the New Careers program the objective is to both provide training and establish, on a competitive basis, new career opportunities.

Under the OEO's Community Action Program, such programs as Upward-Bound; provision of legal services; care for older people; the Headstart Program, now under the Department of Health, Education and Welfare; the Neighborhood Health Centers; and Family Planning are generalized activities designed to alleviate some of the social conditions or social problems of the poor. These activities are consistent with the efforts of OEO's Community Action Programs (CAP) to have local participants attack the local poverty problems.

Another element of the "in-service" programs administered by OEO is the Volunteers in Service to America. This program gives adults of eighteen years of age or over an opportunity to join the efforts of OEO against poverty. The volunteers typically work with migrant workers, or on Indian reservations, in rural and urban CAP programs, in Job Corps centers, and anywhere else they are needed. The volunteers organize and help others to organize remedial action or work in adult education or health and recreation or other community activity. The volunteers offer service-training information and other help to the poor.

There is no evident coordination in the federal government among its agencies or departments responsible for programs that directly or indirectly affect the hard-core unemployed or the urban-racial problems. The Nixon administration in the spring of 1969 did make a first effort to introduce an element of coordination of selected agencies when the President established the Office of Minority Business Enterprise in the Department of Commerce. The explicit purpose of this new office was to coordinate all federal programs in this one area. The federal government had at least 116 different programs operated by about 21 different departments and agencies of government.

The Office will also seek to develop new business opportunities for minorities as well as coordinate the efforts of other government agencies in encouraging minority enterprises. It has the capacity to mobilize financial and other resources, both public and private, and to provide for centralized leadership that has not been available in the past. The Office will seek to provide a better focus of government programs at the local level. The Office reviews existing and potentially new programs for the encouragement of the minority enterprise and recommends further action to the executive and legislative branches of the government. The executive order that created this new office of Minority Business Enterprise also provided for the creation of an Advisory Council and an information center for compiling and disseminating information on successful business enterprise activities. The establishment of the office gave evidence of the recognition that, in addition to alleviating the basic problem of poverty itself, there is a need to stimulate those enterprises that will give members of minority groups the confidence that opportunity is open and unlimited. The Office is supposed to help demonstrate that all Americans can participate in a growing economy on the basis of equal opportunity. The Office is charged with the responsibility of encouraging the efforts of the private sector as well as state and local government activities. There was a requirement for close liaison with business and trade associations, universities, foundations, professional organizations, and other groups working in the area. A small professional staff of experts was thus drawn from those representative groups. "It is also an act of faith in individual initiative in the competitive free enterprise system. And most important of all it is an expression of faith in the abilities of potential enterprises in minority groups and a recognition of their eagerness to become profit-making participants in our competitive system."[5]

The Secretary of Commerce is responsible for developing plans for federal action and for proposing changes in federal programs as required. The Secretary is also required to submit information, from such departments and agencies, necessary to carry out the purpose of the President's order and/or to convene meetings of heads of departments whose programs and activities may contribute to growth of minority businesses.

The Advisory Council is composed of members appointed by the President. The membership includes representatives of minority groups and minority enterprises and those people knowledgeable about minority business activity. The Council is advisory to the Secretary of Commerce and serves as a source of information on developments in the field. The Council also keeps the Secretary abreast of plans, programs, and activities in the public and private sector which relate to minority business enterprises, and evaluates any problems referred to the Council.

All other agencies of government are required to furnish information and assistance to the Secretary of Commerce for his minority business activity. There were no new funds appropriated or requested to carry out this activity. The responsibilities of the Secretary or the Department of Commerce and other departments are limited by funds available under existing laws. In commenting on the Executive Order, Maurice Stans, Secretary of Commerce, noted that

This new office of Minority Business Enterprise, by providing better coordination of both public and private efforts, will help give our minority members an equal chance at the starting line as entrepreneurs, as managers and owners of their own business.

I would like to point out that this effort will produce a highly important by-product for all members of minority groups.

There are many responsible leaders among our minorities. But there are many other members who have never had a chance to develop their leadership qualities.

... business is one of the great training grounds for leaders because to organize and operate a business successfully requires responsible leadership.

Those trained in this program can help their people along constructive paths to many areas, social and economic.[6]

This new program is essentially a coordinating activity and in no way makes the government responsible for undertaking specific efforts to help black businessmen who embark upon business ventures.

Other programs or other federal legislation that establish programs of the distributive and structural types that deal directly with poverty problems include manpower programs, the reform of vocational education in 1963, increased support for higher education in 1964, the Civil Rights Act of 1964, the Elementary and Secondary Education Act of 1965, the Higher Education Act of 1965, the Appalachian Region Development Act of 1965, and Public Works and Economic Development Acts of 1965, as well as the Housing and Urban Development Act of 1965. A chronicle of all the poverty-oriented programs administered by the U.S. government requires a book-length compilation. It is informative, however, to make reference to programs administered by various government agencies and to dwell only on programs or legislation that are particularly important in attacking the black or the ghetto problem. (The list of agencies described in the following text is not intended to be comprehensive. For more complete information, the reader should use other sources such as Clair Wilcox's *Toward Social Welfare* published by the Irwin Company in 1969. Department of Commerce listing of programs related to minority business enterprise published in the spring of 1969 is appended to this chapter.)

The Array of
Federal Programs

The Department of Agriculture administers the special school lunch program as well as the special milk program which provides commodities for schools as well as whole milk for children in schools and day camps. The Department of Agriculture also administers the Food Stamp Plan and donates commodities to needy persons other than those in the Food Plan or school lunch milk program. Its rural community developments service, although not administered under a large budget outlay, is also active in the area of what is nominally referred to as rural development.

The Department of Health, Education and Welfare (HEW) has a large number of programs that would be oriented principally to the social capital or human capital investment activity of the poor. The Vocational Education Act, which includes the Student Loan Program, improved counseling and guidance in schools, cooperative research and demonstration grants, and education for handicapped children, needs to be included in the HEW list. HEW's Vocational Rehabilitation Programs, which provide for grants to states as well as for rehabilitation research and training, may become more significant within the next few years. The Public Health Service of HEW, with its chronic diseases and health programs for the aged as well as a communicable disease program and its emphasis on community health practices, has played a significant role in explaining the nature of the health problem of the ghetto and other minority poor. The Hill-Burton Act, has provided funds for hospital construction. The HEW administers social security programs that include old-age and survivors insurance and unemployment compensation and employment services. The HEW's welfare administration provides public assistance grants to the states for administration of Bureau of

Family Services and Maternal and Child Welfare, as well as all the activities under the omnibus Office for the Aging. The Housing and Home Finance Agency is responsible for the low-income housing demonstration programs as well as the urban renewal grants, the low-rent public housing grants, low-rent public housing development loans, and the Model Cities Program, in addition to administration of certain sections of the massive housing program passed by Congress in 1968.

The Department of Labor, through its unemployment insurance service and U.S. employment service, sponsors significant activity in the federal manpower programs. It is through the State Employment Services that most of the federal manpower programs, other than those administered by OEO, are implemented. The Manpower Development and Training Act elements are also administered by the Department of Labor. The Labor Department has cumulated an extensive experience rating in regard to federal manpower policy. It is the programs of the Labor Department, particularly MDTA, that deserve special emphasis in regard to the federal actions that are directly oriented toward the structural and distributive objectives of federal government's overall poverty policies. The following sections summarize activities carried out, as manpower policy, by the OEO, EDA, and Department of Labor.

The Manpower Development and Training Act of 1962 was the first major manpower program ever to be enacted in the United States. It established job-development activities to improve labor mobility, funded demonstration programs, installed on-the-job training and placement assistance projects, and generally has provided funds for occupational training and redevelopment.

The MDTA programs, which are administered jointly by the U.S. Department of Labor and Department of Health, Education and Welfare, is generally thought to be the most significant manpower legislation of the 1960's. The Act symbolizes an evolution of congressional attitude. Manpower shortages existed alongside the manpower surpluses and indicated wasteful human resources and a different challenge to reconcile economic growth with employment opportunities. Congress has recognized that the

Negro poor have been and are outside the economic mainstream, and that manpower legislation must incorporate selected programs to deal with the hard-core unemployed. Congress has set up the Job Corps under OEO, the Neighborhood Youth Corps (under the Department of Labor), "work study" programs (under HEW), the Appalachian Regional Development Act, and the Public Works and Economic Development Act (EDA). There are several premises for these acts. Labor markets will function more smoothly if adequate opportunities for education training or retraining plus competition for job openings are established. Imbalances in labor markets may be removed, as between the poor and the productively employed, between developed and distressed areas, and between businesses seeking workers and workers seeking jobs. Titles 2, 3, and 4 of OEO set up programs designed to extend loans to cooperatives for jobs creating investment, and to supply financial assistance to selected small businesses.

The Economic Development Corporation (EDA) stresses regional development and economic efficiency as opposed to social or welfare programs. EDA programs generally try to foster a process of development within which business capital and careful planning result in a sustained growth process. EDA considers its primary function to be one of matching jobs with people.[7]

Federal Manpower Programs

The underlying justification of the training provisions in the Manpower Development and Training Act was the assumption that government-supported training programs would equip unemployed workers to fill existing job vacancies. Using the indicator of placement rates, the training programs are apparently reasonably successful.

When Congress enacted the MDTA, it was anticipated that substantial funds would be used for on-the-job training. This concept was based on the fact that businesses had traditionally assumed responsibility for the training of their employees. It was also expected that federal support under MDTA would stimulate employers to expand their own on-the-job-training programs. It was before 1966 that the MDTA modified and expanded federal programs to focus on the disadvantaged poor. Two years after that new emphasis, the 1968 Manpower Report of the President noted that "our past efforts, vital as they are, have not yet effectively reached the hard-core unemployed." . . .

"These hard core are America's forgotten men and women, many of them have not worked for a long time and some of them have never worked at all. Some have had only odd jobs. Many of them have been so discouraged by life that they have lost their sense of purpose."[8]

The concentrated employment program was established to unify all the various manpower and related programs which could help these people in the worst areas and some of our major cities. The first task was to find the hard-core unemployed to determine who they are and where and how they live. Most of the work in identifying the unemployed has occurred and the concentrated employment program was inaugurated in 22 rural and urban areas and will expand to 76 and then to 146 areas for providing a variety of services to the hard-core unemployed. In addition to the CEP Program, expansion, the Cooperative Area Manpower Planning Service, CAMPS, integrated all of the programs within the manpower system providing the training and work experience for 1.3 million and related programs in fiscal 1969. It should be noted that the Manpower Development and Training Administration feels that the JOBS Program is an integral part of their efforts to provide job opportunities for the disadvantaged poor.

If federal manpower programs are to be effective, blacks must be participants in the programs. The 1968 Manpower Report of the President (see Table 1) listed programs and actions, by industry and government, that give evidence of new types of programs designed to increase aid to the hard-core unemployed. The CEP

Table 1 **Estimated Number of First-Time Enrollments in Federally Assisted Manpower Programs, Fiscal Years 1962-1968**

| | | | | FISCAL YEAR | | | |
Program	1962	1963	1964	1965	1966	1967	1968
Total[a]	11,900	66,600	108,500	481,400	1,079,000	1,434,900	1,287,000
Structured training:							
Redevelopment area (Area Redevelopment Act)	8,600	12,600	11,300	10,400	(b)		
Manpower Development and Training Act		34,100	77,600	156,900	235,800	265,000	265,000
On-the-job training		2,100	9,000	11,600	58,300	115,000	125,000
Institutional		32,000	68,600	145,300	177,500	150,000	140,000
Job Corps				12,400	47,100	70,700	64,600
New Careers						1,000	4,300
Manpower activities of Bureau of Indian Affairs	3,300	3,500	3,900	5,000	6,700	7,700	7,900
Work experience:							
Neighborhood Youth Corps				137,900	422,900	556,300	467,400
Operation Mainstream						11,000	12,600
Work-Study (college)				48,000[c]	262,000	431,000	405,000
Work Experience (Title V, Economic Opportunity Act)				88,700	84,800	77,200	27,600[d]
Community Work and Training (Title IV, Social Security Act)		16,400	15,700	22,100	19,700	15,000	14,000
Program support:							
Concentrated Employment Program (special funds)[e]						(f)	16,000
Special Impact							2,600

a Excludes regular placements by the public Employment Service; also the registration of apprenticeship programs by the U.S. Department of Labor's Bureau of Apprenticeship and Training. The JOBS and WIN programs do not appear because the first enrollees were not recorded until fiscal 1969. It should be noted that the figures may include some double counting of persons enrolled in more than one program.
b Merged with MDTA program.
c Program in operation only five months in fiscal 1965.
d Program phased out in fiscal 1968 and 1969. Clients to be served by the new WIN Program.
e Other participants in CEP are included in training or work-experience programs to which they were referred. These persons received some service but were not enrolled in any of the above programs.
f Not available.

Note: Detail may not add to totals due to rounding.   *Source:* Manpower Report of the President, January, 1969, p. 140.

(Concentrated Employment Program) and CAMPS programs, begun in 1967 but scheduled for expansion thereafter, were established to concentrate on poverty problems. CEP programs provide a system for "delivering manpower services to the disadvantaged." CEP has four principal features: (1) it enlists the support and cooperation of business and labor organizations in local types; (2) it provides a range of counseling, health, education, and training services to individuals; (3) it develops employment opportunities for individuals; and (4) it provides follow-up assistance to assure that new jobs once obtained will not be lost. Local employment contracts are entered into by the Labor Department with a single sponsor who arranges to supply any services disadvantaged workers need, such as job placement, and assistance on the job. The CEP program had involved more than 51,000 individuals (1967). Of these 51,000, 34,000 received such services as education, skills training in MDTA, and work experience in the Neighborhood Youth Program and in New Careers in special impact projects. About 22 per cent had found employment, and 11 per cent had been offered other training programs.

The Comparative Area Manpower Planning project is locally oriented and set to operate in sixty-eight labor areas to coordinate manpower plans. Area committees share information that identifies manpower needs and problems so they can assess the needs for manpower resources that may be available or develop a manpower plan that avoids duplication with other programs. Information, advice, and assistance is sought from local educators, community leaders, trade union representatives, and others. A representative area committee might include participants from twenty or so different manpower-related programs. CAMPS is producing an inventory of manpower programs as well as an assessment of unmet needs so that any current projects can be better evaluated. It is really a way of linking many programs designed to serve persons in need. A particular function of the CAMPS program is to coordinate manpower services, which are part of the Model Cities program.

Other new manpower development and training programs

undertaken since 1967 include institutional training, that is, employment orientation training, or pre-job education for many who have skills but poor work levels. Training is given in grooming, personal hygiene, behavior, and communication, in addition to techniques of job hunting and the use of local transportation.

Although altogether 132,000 training opportunities were approved in MDTA institutional programs during 1967, only 65 per cent were disadvantaged enrollees. The follow-up on these people during the next year found 72 per cent were employed when contacted. Total number of full-time trainees in institutional programs during 1968 was about 129,000. Efforts to attack the skills shortage problems through part-time, upgrading training, however, were less successful.

Another expanded MDTA program was the on-the-job type training. The OJT training opportunities target was substantially met in 1967 and 1968. To make on-the-job training possible for most of the severely disadvantaged, nearly 60 per cent of OJT funds (in 1967) were used to couple skills training with supplementary basic education training. Problems have been encountered in retaining disadvantaged trainees during the first stages of classroom training programs. Many trainees are school dropouts. They have already rejected the school setting and are reluctant to return to it. It has been found that a change of the training setting—for example, using vestibule training on the employer's premises for classes—is somewhat more effective. A larger federal investment will be necessary to get employers to attract the disadvantaged into the programs and/or keep them in training and employment. This finding is the rationale for increasing government payments to employers to compensate for the added indirect cost attributable to losses in productivity involved in training the hard-core employees. More initial counseling help and other supportive services must be provided. In developing new OJT contracts more attention is now given to better-paying jobs that offer promotional opportunities. More cooperation in creating new opportunities will be sought from large corporations.[9]

Although there are a large number of different federal manpower programs, there are only two basic types. The first type provides a basic education and skills training to prepare the unemployed. Given training, the unemployed worker is able to compete effectively for existing jobs. The second basic type of program is on-the-job training, sometimes referred to as work experience. Several commentators on the work experience programs refer to the second category as "work relief." Many of these manpower programs seek to improve the employability and employment of racial minorities. Implicit in the programs are efforts to indoctrinate the younger slum residents with a sense of values regarding work.

An example of work relief is the Neighborhood Youth Corps, where the government actually serves as an "employer of the last resort." There is little information about the productivity or the potential productivity of the workers involved. Basically the Youth Corps programs provide income maintenance and some type of activity for those participating. There is no stress that people in this program be productively occupied. There is little productive work experience available to participants in this program. The Kerner Commission Report indicated that the typical rioter was between 15 and 24 years old, a high-school drop-out, a resident of the area, and probably had been employed in a menial job frequently on a part-time basis, sometimes unemployed, and was aware of discrimination. The fact that the participants in the Youth Corps are drawn from the same group may mean that they are being kept off the streets in order to keep them from additional destructive activity.

It may be an error, however, to characterize "public-service" jobs such as in the NYC only as employment opportunities for the low skilled and poorly trained. The concept of public service jobs is broader than "employer of the last resort." If the federal government were to act as the principle employer of non-white minorities and provide occupations at all skill levels with on-the-job training and a kind of career development of new workers, some of the stereotypes about the concept of "employer of the last resort" would be alleviated.

The government can actually create new employment. The new employment could result in an expansion of output of goods and/or public services in a variety of areas such as police and fire protection, mail delivery, urban reconditioning, education, health, and other categories that affect the public interest. The government-sponsored employment could provide on-the-job training opportunities, which are now emphasized as part of the MDTA program, and also provide what is called "career ladders" for new potential professional and managerial employees. The federal government's existing New Careers program is already part of current work programs. It is, however, new and impossible to evaluate at this time. The purpose of New Careers was to move the unemployed and underemployed up through subprofessional jobs into the useful public service jobs. This program is, however, unlikely to provide any large-scale job creation activities. Another experimental program in providing public employment for the disadvantaged is Operation Mainstream. Both of these programs are on an experimental basis, but are designed to provide at least limited expansion of public employment opportunities.

There are many difficulties in applying the concept of public employment or the government as an employer of the first resort. Existing job openings for public employment are at rates of pay that are near the minimum wage. These low-paid jobs are turned down by the young unemployed ghetto worker unless there are built-in features that assure him of further and better opportunities. However, the older employed workers who have welfare and poverty incomes may be attracted by these government job opportunities. But again, unless better opportunities are available in the long run, these programs may not really solve any of their employment problems. It is apparent that very little is known about the nonincentives that influence economic attitudes in the ghetto area. Job opportunities alone, unless they are coordinated with other elements of economic forces that pattern activity in the poverty neighborhoods, cannot possibly be effective. Job programs that are designed to deal with employment must be in harmony with the conditions that influence attitudes about work in ghetto areas. Most of the federal government manpower programs depend fundamentally on the structure of incentives established by the white community.

In addition, present government employment programs are a patchwork and in many respects facilitate income transfers as opposed to providing basic skills training and higher-paying potential necessary for effective attacks on the personal problems of the unemployed. However, in contrast with the private-sector jobs program, the government or public-sector approach can actually create new jobs as opposed to merely rationing new jobs. Public employment is not incumbered, as is the private sector, by the market test of profitability. In the short run there is no requirement in new employment opportunities or new employees of the federal government to contribute productively in the physical output sense, as required by the private corporation. Social capital programs, such as health care, air and water pollution, have extensive spill-over benefits that accrue to the total society and are difficult to measure in individual terms.

There is no indication that the concept of government as an employer of the first or the last resort is a panacea for the total manpower problem. Government employment is one tool that is necessary in a comprehensive program. Government responsibility for maximum employment is clearly stated in the Employment Act of 1946. In addition to the fact that monetary and fiscal policies must be designed to expand aggregate demand, there is also a related requirement that government provide both the necessary procedural elements and training to make the minorities or underprivileged qualifiable in the job market. It is implicit in the modern interpretations of the Employment Act that the government has a responsibility to the unemployed who are "left over" after the aggregative demand policy efforts have failed to make more competitive jobs available.

Neither the federal government nor any level of government has made a full commitment as an "employer of the last resort."

Yet jobs for the poor and the otherwise impoverished is a current emphasis of federal manpower policy. It should be understood that current manpower policy focuses on the private sector to provide these jobs. Subsidized employment or minimal interference with profitability in the private sector is the incentive for firms to create employment for the hard-core unemployed. Some type of subsidy or reimbursement of costs makes the hard-core unemployed from minority groups at least competitive on an alternative costing basis with other available employees. This incentive system has produced a great deal of progress in the six or so years since MDTA inaugurated its programs. However, it may be said that all existing federal programs which try to bring employment to the minority groups either in the ghetto or by transporting them outside of the ghetto can be looked upon as short-run insurance against frustration and rioting.

The economic concept of alternative costing becomes significant in any evaluation of employment opportunities. Federal government money spent on job creation, training programs, or job-placement services is lost to other programs such as education and other broad-gauged capital programs for transportation improvement, housing, and programs for air or water pollution or related social capital undertakings. The alternative costing element again is significant because any government program, whatever its type, that is aimed at employment as opposed to broad-gauged social capital improvements, may be evaluated in the short-term sense by comparing the cost of such a program, whether or not it is effective or productive in the long run, to the cost of rebuilding cities destroyed by black rioters. With the climate in the nation "to do something" about the black problem, there may not be the time to evaluate whether or not expenditure on each program accomplishes more per dollar than other alternatives. In terms of employment programs, a short-run program of subsidized private employment could be either a very attractive or very unattractive element in the total remedial program designed to deal directly with manpower problems. The ultimate result depends in part upon cooperation, effectiveness, and implementation inherent in the programs now available. One essential point to make in any discussion of an evaluation of manpower programs or career development programs is the magnitude of the problems to be attacked. The Kerner Commission's Report made a number of proposals for providing job opportunities for the ghetto resident, including the creation of a million new jobs in the public sector in three years. But the government record to date does not lead one to be optimistic about the possibility of the government accomplishing this goal. The federal government must give additional support to existing programs such as JOBS, CEP, CAMPS, Model Cities, Neighborhood Youth Corps, New Careers, MDTA training, and Operation Mainstream. In addition, the government must be prepared to be the employer of the first resort. This may require a movement toward a new concept of full employment, which would mean that government must guarantee everyone a right to work or the right to earn a living. However, the current emphasis of federal programs is placed not on the employer as the last resort, but on improvement of the effective functioning of the nominally private labor markets and those who are participants in the markets.

***Summary of Public-Private
Sector Cooperation in
Employment Programs***

The dramatic change that occurred in the administration of manpower services originally begun with the Office of Economic Opportunity and its local Community Action Agencies has continued since 1965. In fact, the most significant effort in manpower policy recently undertaken by the federal government has been the improvement in its administration of manpower agencies. In effect, the Concentrated Employment Program (CEP) is a current effort to administer all the manpower programs as a single system. As noted before, under CEP the Labor Department does have access to funds for various federal training and employment programs in selected areas of concentrated hard-core unemployment. But the CEP organization, although nominally created to administer manpower service, is usually subservient to a Community Action organization in the locality. Simply because the federal government is the dominant administering agency for its manpower policy, it has used powers to force more full cooperation or to get more action from state employment services. It is the state employment services that are responsible for interviewing, counseling, and establishing training programs as well as job placement and follow-up. The CEP program is designed to achieve more effective cooperation between the variety of federal, state, and local agencies that are involved in manpower policy. CEP is providing a mechanism on the supply side for jobs or employment programs. The Labor Department's JOBS program may be conceived of as developing opportunities for the hard-core unemployed. The CEP feeds individuals into the JOBS program. The role of the CEP currently reflects some maturation on the part of the federal government's attitudes in its role in manpower programs. Despite the long period of activity in manpower development and training programs, the federal government's role has principally been that of a supra-agency which approves or screens, and reviews, programs implemented at the community and/or state level. The CEP innovation implies that the federal government will play a more responsible role as consultant or adviser in the local experiments. Federal government attention now is directed toward the planning process rather than the production of job openings.

Jobs, more and better jobs, are certainly the most appealing solution to these poor families—let them earn their way out of poverty. This is undoubtedly the path that they would prefer. It is also, the public opinion polls tell us, the path that the general American public prefers. It accords with the work ethic of the society, strongly ingrained in both the poor minority and the affluent majority. Moreover, so long as there are socially useful tasks to be done, it is a national economic waste to leave willing and able hands unemployed or underemployed.[10]

Americans are reluctant to support federal government policies that conflict with the Protestant or Puritan ethic which suggests that individuals ought to work hard to push up through the system, to be aggressively competitive in order to earn more. The American typically assumes that equality of opportunity in regard to jobs or career development and the money rewards for productive activity are administered effectively in our system. In American folklore we accept the fact that our system of income distribution based on productivity and aggressive competition is fair, and just.

But this proud history does not mean that America has equality of opportunity and a fair race today. First of all, the concept has never fitted the Negro, the victim of America's own brand of feudalism and prescribed inferiority. Second, the inequalities of achievement and reward in one generation are inequalities of opportunity for the next. The United States allows vast differences in inherited material wealth and, what is probably even more important, vast differences in the health, informal education, and formal schooling which children bring to adulthood.[11]

Thus, the federal government's responsibility in the area of manpower problems still continues to be significant since there are too few good jobs for Negroes. Education is inadequate—whether it is formal, informal, on-the-job training, or otherwise—to put the black into a competitive position with his contemporary white. There are inadequacies in job information, job placement, and hiring procedures that reflect poorly structured programs in addition to elements of anachronistic racial discrimination. There is little prospect that the federal government will find it possible to develop a job-creation program that does provide an extremely large number of good jobs for the Negro. Without being unduly pessimistic, there is little reason to attach too much significance to the fact that federal manpower programs can really remedy the difficulties in employment conditions that affect so many Negroes. It may also require extraordinary optimism to believe that the federal government will undertake the necessary financing to make a significant impact upon the quality of education and employment of the disadvantaged Negro. Large-scale programs may, in fact, fail. More importantly, large-scale programs of massive federal government outlays on extension of federal government services will encounter the same kind of negative impact associated with the financing of any major effort, such as a war. Such programs, relying upon federal government purchasing and federal government employment or conscription of manpower, tends to raise taxes and increase government expenditure and, more importantly, contribute to inflationary pressures.

The pattern of changes that has taken place in the last few years typifies the action that is feasible at the federal level.

The obstacle to employment, whether in the private sector or the public sector, is the cost of adapting the worker to the performance requirements of the work place. The degree of disadvantage is defined by the magnitude of this cost. Providing a permanent wage subsidy for public employment of the disadvantaged may well entail an acceptance of extremely low levels of work performance. Few employers in the private sector will hire even small numbers of "free workers" if a guarantee of employment were required; and it is a misunderstanding of work and work management to believe that public managers could provide productive employment experience on a large scale under these terms.

Moreover, estimates of the potential clientele for such a program of public employment ranged between 3,000,000 and 8,000,000 persons, depending upon assumptions about the attractiveness of stable public employment to the working poor. Its direct cost as well as the profound effect it would have on wage and price levels suggest that only a program for limited eligibility is politically viable.[12]

It may be emphasized, then, that any greater reliance, in the short run, on the federal government other than in its present capacity requires additional research as well as substantial additional funding. Programs of the federal government aimed at labor-market deficiencies should be expanded and amplified. Thus, an expansion of the existing kinds of programs, plus careful evaluation of the supportive programs to be offered by the private sector, is probably the significant short-run contribution of the federal government to manpower policies.

There are a variety of other federal government-administered programs that are directly oriented toward the so-called environmental conditions of the ghetto as well as the social capital requirement for improving productivity. These activities include programs designed to improve the physical environment of the ghetto.

Environmental
Improvement Programs

The concentration of nonwhite poverty in metropolitan areas is well documented. Although the proportion of nonwhite poor in the central cities is somewhat less than the proportion of nonwhites in other areas, the concentration in the city of nonwhite poor is in limited residential areas that have a distinctly larger proportion of young children in poor families and unemployed youth. The poverty problem in urban areas has not grown because there is a greater proportion of poverty in the urban cores, but because social problems are more visible when brought together in one place. Men can do less for themselves individually in the city, but they act in groups politically and otherwise only when they have good leadership and strong associations. The cities are characterized with distinctly higher welfare allowances; higher school costs; higher outlays for police and traffic control; more expensive housing, health, and hospital services, as well as sanitation. Immigration to the city is not significantly new, neither are the socioeconomic problems of deficient education and lack of marketable skills and language handicaps. These problems are not the fault of those people who migrate. Our current system in the metropolitan areas has failed to provide methods of assimilation of minority groups. The system has introduced rigidities in education and employment, separation of work and home, rigidities in unions and working-wage standards, and criteria of health and housing that have eroded the first steps in the traditional ladder of success. There are thousands of potentially productive people existing in the frustrating trap of poverty. The most easily identified needs today in urban areas are for better schools, more hospitals, more adequate highways, more extensive systems of parks, better water and drainage facilities, better methods of hand-ling waste and pollution, more libraries, more museums, improved mass transportation, including the integration of local transportation with the outside; and a restructuring of welfare programs, expanded adult education, effective slum-clearance programs, and significant reconstruction of urban areas.[13]

Model Cities Act of 1966   The federal government does have enabling legislation to permit it to bring together programs to focus on all these areas. The focus and concentration emphasis was a prime objective in the ideas underlying the Model Cities Act of 1966. The Model Cities Program recognized that cities do not have the resources to meet critical problems. The Model Cities Act provided additional funds for cities that specifically recognize their needs for programs, calculate costs, and embark upon innova-tive programs. If these local programs produced desirable or positive results in selected demonstration areas, cities could apply the momentum to successive programs elsewhere. Under the Model Cities program, funds go to cities of all sizes; it was there-fore not a big-city program but supposedly an all-city program. The Act's purpose was to enable cities to plan, develop, and carry out locally prepared, comprehensive, city demonstration proposals. It was the Act's stated proposals to (1) rebuild or revitalize large slum and blighted areas; (2) expand housing, job, and income opportunities, (3) reduce dependence upon welfare payments; (4) improve educational programs and facilities; (5) combat disease and ill health; (6) reduce the incidence of crime and delinquency; (7) enhance recreational and cultural opportunities; (8) establish better access between homes and jobs; (9) improve living condi-tions for the people who live in slum areas. The Model Cities Program hoped to accomplish these objectives through the most effective and economical concentration of coordination and federal, state, and local and private efforts. In asking the cities to provide a five-year estimate of their needs and costs to be developed on a year-to-year basis, it was hoped that funds would not be spent on a series of individual or scattered projects, but that a system of expenditures would evolve designed to achieve the comprehensive goals. Under the old program by program approach, a variety of local agencies had administered their own narrow programs with little or no coordination with the needs of other programs in the cities as a whole. Federal government obviously had inaugurated the variety and dispersal of these programs, although independently of each other. Now, under the Model Cities Program, a comprehensive program designed at local levels permits funds and activities to be concentrated on the total needs of the community. For the first time, many of our cities will be dealing simultaneously with the totality of problems of the slum areas and concentrating their resources on solving the problem under the Model Cities Program.

The federal government is primarily responsible for the financing of the Model Cities Program. Department of Housing and Urban Development (HUD), through sixty-three planning grants in the fiscal year 1968, scheduled seventy more for fiscal year 1969. HUD requested a billion dollars for fiscal year 1969, but was granted $625 million, which was divided between grants for the cities and an urban renewal bonus for urban-renewal activities specifically identified and scheduled to be carried out under the Model Cities Program. In December, 1968, seventy-five cities had already received Model Cities Planning Grants and planned to start action on the program in 1969. Planning grants are also to be made for an additional seventy to eighty cities. The total population of cities then included in the Model Cities program was nearly 34,000,000, and a total population in model neighborhoods within selected cities was approximately 4,000,000. The total number of substandard dwellings registered in the Model Cities neighborhoods was approximately 365,000, while the total number of families earning less than $3,000 in these neighborhoods was about 285,000.

Because the program is still in its relatively early stages, it is difficult to assess it. One of the problems encountered early in the program is the coordination of the many agencies and groups that are involved in the so-called planning process. There have been fears that the planning process will bog down the program. Most of the discussion or evaluations of the programs are in terms of organization, or the administrative structure, rather than how many houses are going to be built or how garbage is going to be collected or how job training classes are going to be planned and opened. Part of the problem of getting the program underway is a matter of funding. Unless there is enough money to carry out the programs, Model Cities will become nothing more than a planning or "talking" type of program. Obviously, the program cannot be implemented if funds are not available, and as of the end of 1968 Congress, with the pressures of alternative financing, did not seem to be enthusiastically supporting the Model Cities Program when in fact it cut requests about 40 per cent.[14]

Housing Act of 1968 Another significant legislative step in creating the permissive environment for attacking the physical problems of the ghetto was the Housing Act of 1968. It was viewed as a landmark of housing legislation and excelled in significance only by the original 1949 Housing Act. The Housing Act of 1968 reaffirms the goals stated in the 1949 Act: "to provide a decent home and suitable living environment for every American family." In addition to calling for massive programs to build both sale and rental housing for low-income families, the 1968 Act has the following objectives: improvement of public housing by additional assistance to larger families; greater ease in the purchase of units by occupants and improvement of tenant services; upgrading of management personnel; restriction of high-rise project construction and allowance of greater freedom of design.

The 1968 Act shifted the emphasis in renewal projects from high-income luxury housing to low- and moderate-income housing. It also provided for improved programs for rehabilitation, loans and grants, and for interim assistance grants to blighted areas for relocation payments and for housing-code administration and enforcements. The Act also made funds available to nonprofit, limited-dividend, and cooperative housing groups for seed money and for housing services. The lack of money had been a major limiting factor in moderate-income programs. The 1968 Act did phase out existing moderate income programs while providing mortgage insurance in high-risk areas as well as guarantees for financing new town developments. A billion-dollar increase in Model City authority was provided and included the housing elements in 701 urban-planning programs. There was a major provision for experimental housing programs that will attempt to reduce costs, and establishment of a kind of national housing partnership between the federal government and local contractors to attract more private financial resources into the low- and moderate-income housing fields.

Potentially, about 500,000 low-income families could buy new housing, and another 700,000 units might be provided for low- and moderate-income renters in a period of three years. Subsidized interest rates for families meeting the income qualifications to a level of about 1 per cent and other similar subsidies are available for rental units for low-income families. In the past, Congress has been reluctant to provide funds for low-income housing programs and has in effect restricted the use of such funds in ways that have diminished the housing program. FHA and HUD have been often criticized for administrative difficulty and related delays in implementing publicly assisted programs. The private sector has also given no significant sponsorship to such programs. Adequate funds have not been attracted from private sources into this kind of market. Contractors and builders have also been reluctant to take part, and state and local governments have obviously been slow and sometimes openly hostile to housing programs for the poor. Because of these rather well-entrenched institutional attitudes, it is difficult and certainly premature to predict the future of the Housing Act of 1968.

This Act does have far greater possibilities than any other programs previously introduced and reflects awareness of the problems and of the difficulties in previous legislation. Housing experts have learned many lessons from past programs and hopefully have profited from that experience. It is actual implementation or experience only that can be used to measure the program's performance against its potential.

An example of the difficulty in implementing prior federal programs that were designed to enhance the physical characteristics was the experience with the urban-renewal programs. A study by the National Commission on Urban Problems indicated that only one third of urban renewal projects were completed in six years or less, and over a third took nine years to complete. Many functions that should have been funded or completed early in the process must wait until the project is completed before they can move forward. The 1968 Housing Act did make three major changes in urban renewal programs. The recent legislation specifically attempts to meet the problems of delay in earlier urban renewal projects by providing for planning and execution on an annual-increments basis. In addition to funding on an annual basis, the 1968 Act authorizes a Neighborhood Development Program to cover activities of several contiguous or noncontiguous urban-renewal areas. Loans and grants may be based on funds needed to carry out planned activities during a twelve-month period. Since the Act of 1968, urban renewal programs must emphasize housing for low- and moderate-income families. In urban-renewal projects for predominately residential areas at least 20 per cent of the housing must be for low-income families. New provisions were made for improved programs for rehabilitation grants and loans, including interim assistance for blighted areas, relocation payments, and additional payments to owner occupants to purchase replacement dwellings. This effort is designed to remove the "Negro removal" syndrome that identified most urban-renewal projects. The effect of these new provisions is a step toward transferring urban renewal into a program of help to the people who live in the blighted or slum areas, thus restoring the objectives or the original sponsorship of urban-renewal programs.

The 1968 Act was designed explicitly to stop "red-lining,"

the practical device by which banking mortgage and insurance mortgage insuring institutions outlined areas that would not be eligible for loans.

Another new feature of the Housing Act is a new-towns concept. The Housing Act authorizes the Secretary of HUD to guarantee bonds, debentures, and other obligations issued by new community developers up to a total of $250 million and up to $50 million for any one new town or new community.

The significance of the 1968 Act, which encompasses the earlier Model Cities Program, is that it represents recognition of the fact that urban problems do exist. Also, the Acts fully recognize that the problem will not go away by itself and that the free-enterprise mechanism will not act effectively in solving the dilemmas of the metropolitan areas. The specific examples of housing programs and urban redevelopment actions also recognize the need for approaching government action on a nonconflicting or an integrated comprehensive basis.[15]

In regard to the capacity to implement the Housing Act of 1968, it is instructive to look at the legislative requests as opposed to the funds appropriated for the various sections under that program. The Congress was requested to provide $15 million for tenant services under public housing programs. None was appropriated. $75 million was requested for the 1 per cent interest rate housing programs (sales housing), and only $25 million was appropriated. Exactly the same request and exactly the same appropriation occurred for the rental-housing segment under that subsidized interest-rate provision. The Model Cities request was $500,000,000 for supplemental grants while $312,500,000 was appropriated. Additional urban-renewal features called for $500,000,000 appropriation, but only $312,500,000 were made available. Urban renewal programs for fiscal year 1970, which includes Model Cities programs requests, were at the $1-billion, $450 million level, and Congress saw fit to appropriate $750 million.

In a MIT-Harvard Joint Center for Urban Studies Report on "The Ghetto, the Metropolis, and the Nation," Professors Kain and Persky noted that the

. . . . residential pattern imposed on the Negro has led to an unduly large proportion of poverty-linked services being demanded of central cities. At the same time the expansion of the ghetto has encouraged the exodus of middle-income whites, both directly through its effects on housing market and indirectly through its effects on industrial locations. . . . the problem can be handled in the short run by various schemes for redistributing governmental revenues; a preferable long-run solution would involve a major dispersal of the low-income population in particular the Negro. Central cities will continue to have a high proportion of the poor as long as they contain a large proportion of metropolitan jobs. . . .

. . . Housing segregation has also frustrated efforts to renew the city. At first sight the logic of renewal is strong. By offering federal subsidies to higher-income whites locating within their boundaries, central cities have hoped to improve their tax base. The same logic underlies community efforts to woo industry. However, to the extent that these groups consider the city an inferior location, because of the ghetto, such subsidies will continue to fail. As long as the ghetto exists much of white America will write off the central city. Spot renewal, even on the scale envisioned in the Model Cities Program, cannot alter this basic fact. . . .

The continued rapid growth of central cities ghettos has seriously expanded the realm of *de facto* segregation and limited the range of possible corrective actions . . . . in addition to sharply curtailing Negro economic and educational opportunities, the ghetto is an important disorganizing force. It represents the power of the outside community and the frustration of the Negro.[16]

The Harvard urban specialists indicate that "nothing less than a complete change in the structure of the metropolis will solve the problem of the ghetto." These professors point out that it is ironic and almost cynical the extent to which current programs that are ostensibly concerned with the welfare of the urban Negro accept the permanence of the central ghettos. Programs such as those of the Housing Act and the Model Cities Act will only serve to strengthen the ghetto and all the problems that it generates. "In particular, these programs concentrate on beautifying the fundamentally ugly structure of the current metropolis and not on providing individuals with the tools necessary to break out of that structure."[17]

Appendix:
Federal Assistance Programs
Related to Minority
Business Enterprise

The following list indicates federal assistance programs by agency, prepared by the Economic Development Administration, that might in one way or another help in the development of minority business enterprise. The list was compiled from the Catalog of Federal Assistance Programs issued by the Office of Economic Opportunity on June 1, 1967.

The listed programs include not only those involving loans, guarantees, and direct financial assistance, but many which provide other forms of assistance, such as relevant statistical information.

In addition to the attached list, it should be noted that many federal regulations relating to the conduct of business also have an important bearing on the climate within which minority business enterprises are launched or conducted. Such things as bonding requirements, various procurement policies, and Internal Revenue Service rules, and even the manner and timing of rulings by many federal regulatory agencies, can all have significance.

The Office of Minority Business Enterprise is now soliciting the assistance of other departments and agencies of the federal government in reviewing the funding of federal assistance programs relating to minority business enterprise and in reappraising established rules and regulations regarding the conduct of business which may indirectly or inadvertently create barriers to the establishment and growth of minority business enterprise.

U.S. Department of Labor

1 Apprenticeship and Training
2 Community Employment Program
3 Employment Service—Industrial Services
4 Farm Labor Contractor Registration
5 Farm Labor Services
6 Federal Minimum Wage and Hour Standards
7 Job Market Information
8 Labor Mobility—Relocation Assistance Allowances

9   Labor Standards
10 Manpower Development and Training
11 New Careers Program
12 Unemployment Insurance
13 U.S. Employment Services
14 Occupational Training in Redevelopment Areas
15 Trade Readjustment Allowances for Workers
16 Operation Mainstream
17 Youth Opportunity Centers
18 Special Impact Program
19 Concentrated Employment Program

Veterans Administration

1   Veterans' Business Loans

Office of Economic Opportunity

1   Job Corps
2   Assistance for Migrant and Seasonal Farm Workers
3   Volunteers in Service to America (VISTA)

Federal Power Commission

1   Beautification of Hydroelectric Projects
2   Forestry Tree Planting
3   Water Resources Development
4   Wholesale Electric Power Service
5   Wholesale Natural Gas Service

U.S. Department of Agriculture

1   Agricultural Conservation Program
2   Agricultural Research Service
3   Agricultural Stabilization Programs
4   Cooperative Agriculture and Forestry Research Program
5   Cooperative Extension Service
6   Cropland Adjustment Program
7   Economic Research Service
8   Emergency Loans
9   Export Market Development
10 Farm Ownership Loans
11 Forest Service Cooperative State and Private Programs
12 Land Stabilization, Conservation, and Erosion Control
        in Appalachia
13 Loans and Grants for Farm Labor Housing
14 Loans for Forestry Purposes
15 Loans for Recreation Purposes

16   Loans to Rural Families with Small Incomes
17   Multiple-Purpose Watershed Projects
18   Operating Loans
19   Price-Support Programs of the Agricultural Stabilization and
         Conservation Service
20   Rental Housing
21   Rural Electrification Program
22   Rural Housing Loans
23   Loans to Cooperatives

U.S. Department of Health, Education, and Welfare

1   Air Pollution Control
2   Arts and Humanities Research
3   Drug Abuse Control Program
4   Occupational Health Program
5   Vocational Rehabilitation Services to Blind Persons
6   Work Experience Program
7   Training for Cuban Refugee Professional Personnel
8   Adult Basic Education
9   Cuban Refugee Program
10   Vocational Education Grants
11   Vocational Education—Residential Schools and Work-Study
         Programs

General Services Administration

1   Nonmilitary Procurement from Labor Surplus and
         Redevelopment Areas
2   Payments to Small Lead and Zinc Mines
3   Sale of Federal Surplus Personal Property

Small Business Administration

1   Disaster Loans
2   Economic Opportunity Loans to Small Business
3   Loans to State and Local Development Companies
4   Procurement and Management Assistance to Small Business
5   Small Business Financial Assistance Program
6   Small Business Investment Company Program

U.S. Department of the Interior

1   American Indian Credit and Financing Program
2   American Indian Industrial Development Program
3   Appalachian Region Mining Area Restoration
4   Farm Fish Pond Management
5   Fisheries Assistance

6 Outdoor Recreation Technical Assistance
7 Construction of Reservation Roads and Bridges (American Indians)
8 Direct Employment Assistance (American Indians)
9 On-Reservation Adult Education Program (American Indians)
10 Outdoor Recreation Assistance

Farm Credit Administration

1 Federal Land Banks—Farm Real Estate Loans
2 Production Credit Associations—Agricultural Loans

Equal Employment Opportunity Commission

1 Affirmative Action Program—Equal Employment Opportunity
2 Equal Employment Opportunity Grants

Tennessee Valley Authority

1 Agricultural and Chemical Development Program
2 Electricity Supply and Utilization
3 Forestry, Fish and Wildlife
4 Industrial Development
5 Mineral Resources Development
6 Navigation Development and Waterway Transportation
7 Recreation Development
8 Topographic and Navigation Maps
9 Tributary Area Development
10 Unified Resource Development
11 Water Quality Control

U.S. Department of Commerce

1 Aids to Shipping and Shipbuilding
2 Census Data
3 Clearinghouse for Scientific and Technical Information
4 Commercial Intelligence Service
5 Gross National Product Estimates
6 Foreign Investment in the U.S.
7 Information and Services to Industrial Community
8 International Trade Promotion
9 Loans to Business or Development Companies
10 Nautical Charts and Related Data
11 River and Flood Forecasting
12 Ship Exchange Program
13 State Invention Programs
14 State Technical Services Program
15 Trade Adjustment Assistance
16 Weather and Climate Guidance

17 Weights, Measures, and Other Standards
18 Public Works and Economic Development
19 Grants and Loans for Public Works and Development Facilities
20 Technical Assistance, Research, and Information for Economic Development
21 Supplemental Grants-in-Aid for Appalachia

Federal Trade Commission

1 Consumer and Small Business Protection

U.S. Department of Housing and Urban Development

1 Low-Income Housing Demonstration Grants
2 Mortgage and Credit Insurance for Residential Rehabilitation and Home Purchase and Improvement
3 Mortgage Insurance for Housing for Families of Low and Moderate Income
4 Mortgage Insurance for Land Development and New Communities
5 Mortgage Insurance for Multifamily Rental Housing
6 Mortgage Insurance for Nursing Homes
7 Mortgage Insurance for Rental Housing for the Elderly
8 Mortgage Insurance for Urban Renewal
9 Rent Supplements for Disadvantaged Persons
10 Urban Renewal Projects
11 Community Renewal Program

U.S. Atomic Energy Commission

1 Construction of Nuclear Power Stations
2 Licensing of Nuclear Power Reactors
3 Nuclear Science Information
4 Radiological Safety Assistance
5 Research Support in the Physical Sciences
6 Transfer to Industry of AEC-Generated Technology

U.S. Department of Transportation

1 High-Speed Ground Transportation

National Aeronautics and Space Administration

1 Technology Utilization

U.S. Department of Defense

1 Community Economic Adjustment Program
2 Machine-Tool Loans to Vocational Schools

3 Military Procurement from Labor-Surplus Areas
4 Hydroelectric Power Development
5 Limited Water Resources Development Projects
6 Recreation Facilities at Federal Water Resource Projects

National Science Foundation

1 Graduate Education in Science

Post Office Department

1 Lease Construction Program

CHAPTER 8

The Financial Dimension of Development Programs

Role of Capital

One characteristic of all the black programs noted in this book is "newness." With the exception of selected "jobs-oriented" programs of the Urban League and selected National Business League activities, the programs are in the planning or formulation phases. A secondary characteristic of all the programs is the need for financing. The money capital necessary for successful implementation of programs becomes the principal impediment to getting the programs underway. The need for money or the need for the control of purchasing power over resources is a fundamental prerequisite in all capital development programs, whether in the American ghetto or in other areas of the world.

Capital accumulation is inexorably entwined in the folklore

For Notes to Chapter 8 see pages 347–348.

and formal analysis of economic development. The process of raising income and speeding wealth accumulation is a function of the capacity of the individual and the system, to exert economic power to substitute machinery for human motive power or to increase ownership and control of resources. The capital-scarcity syndrome, with its inherent restriction on economic accretion and expansion, has been applied to Negro economic problems in the United States.

The vicious cycle of poverty income is a generalized explanation of the fate of many individual blacks. If incomes are low, all of the income is committed to subsistence purchases or for debt retirement. No economic accretion occurs. In the entrepreneurship cases, the black businessman is typically in the service area, and his sales volume is relatively low. The business organization is invariably a proprietorship or partnership. The small volume, labor-intensive, limited-market, and high-risk elements have created credit limitations to supplement others already at work in the money market. Theodore L. Cross in his book *Black Capitalism*[1] and Eugene Foley is his, *The Achieving Ghetto*,[2] stress the primary importance of increasing the flow of investment capital into the central city as the most important factor in the economic development of the ghettos.

Isolating capital formation or financing as the fundamental causal factor in the failure of the black community to develop is simplistic. Capital sources are, however, a salient factor in a pattern of permissive factors which would aid in current and future economic development. Problems such as lack of skills training, discrimination, limited markets acquisitive motivation, management acuity, geographic mobility, and entry barriers other than capital interact with capital problems in black development. The capital problem is selective and its solution should not be viewed as a panacea even if the concept of black development has been defended satisfactorily. It is interesting to note the amount and sources of funds currently available or being sought for programs formally structured by blacks with an economic focus.

All programs call for direct financing, or a system of financial incentives to stimulate and advance effective implementation. The financing issue is twofold: (1) whether the private sector or the public sector should be responsible for funding productive programs, and (2) what are the alternative tactics available to implement successful financing. Designers of all programs have called for unique federal government encouragement or fiscal responsibility to aid whites and blacks in participating in these programs. The principal forms of public-sector support advocated are federal grants, tax incentives, and/or some form of investment credits for firms willing to undertake programs designed to bring the underprivileged Negro into the mainstream of economic life.

Moderate organizations have sought funds from both the private and public sectors and continue to do so. Funds for the National Business League's Project MAINSTREAM illustrate the public-private cooperative emphasis. In the twelve regions where NBL's Small Investment Companies are being organized, funds are sought from the white "majority business community." The NBL has solicited outright grants from large corporations and has offered a variety of equity and debt instruments for sale to any interested party. The Local and State Development Companies of the Project were created to utilize Section 502 of the Small Business Act, which provides financial support for plant and equipment for shopping centers and small industrial parks that employ the urban hard-core unemployed. Private funds are being sought to finance the data-processing centers.

The pilot project for management training, Outreach, activated by the NBL, is financed by the Department of Commerce, Economic Development Administration, and the Office of Economic Opportunity. The franchise and other similar projects are funded by private and public sources with emphasis placed on local sources of funds.

The massive "modular core" program of NBL, which is really a broad-gauged urban development program, must look to the majority white business community and the federal government for funds for various components.

The individual- and group-counseling activities of the Small Business Development and Guidance Center have been provided by the EDA. Modest funding, about $150,000 per year, has been used for actual operations. The constraints on the expansion of the SBDGC activities are currently physical facilities and staff. The SBDGC needs more space and more facilities than currently available in the temporary buildings at Howard University.

The Urban League has been tapping both private sector funds —personal and corporate—as well as government resources. Its highly successful job-placement and training programs have been funded by the Department of Labor. The Urban League's larger community development interest in housing, education, and health care requires extremely large amounts of capital. As noted earlier, Whitney Young has argued for "A Freedom Budget" before the Senate Sub-Committee on Executive Reorganization (Committee on Government Operations).

The CORE development program, which provides for community corporations, community development banks, and other programs to mobilize the resources of the black, would require $1 billion in federal-government funding in fiscal year 1970. Additional federal funds would be required each year the program is being implemented. Private and public subscriptions would have to generate hundreds of millions of dollars to effectively finance the program that CORE advocates.

A Freedom Budget

The Freedom Budget was developed under the auspices of the A. Philip Randolph Institute with professional advice by Leon Keyserling and others. This program is of particular interest because, like most of those noted, it is of black origin and advocated by blacks as consistent with their views on economic development. It is important because of the black estimates of the magnitude of funds needed for an omnibus approach to the overall development. The Freedom Budget provides for seven basic objectives: full employment, decent and adequate wages, a decent standard of living to those who cannot or should not work; decent homes for all Americans; decent medical care and adequate educational opportunities; improvement of transportation and natural resources development; and sustained full employment, sustained full production, and high economic growth.

These goals must be implemented through national programs with federal government leadership. The Freedom Budget assumes that if the federal authorities exercise prudent monetary and fiscal policies that the national output should rise to $1,085 then to $1,120 billion by 1975. For the ten years used in the Freedom Budget, a level of "total national production *averaging per year . . .* 231.5–244.2 billion dollars higher, and *aggregating* during the ten-year period . . . 2,315–2,442 billion dollars higher, if total production remained at the 1965 rate."[3] This aggregate ten-year figure of $2.3 to $2.4 billion in the "economic growth dividend" upon which the Freedom Budget draws to fulfill its purposes.

The allocation of the economic growth dividend would be for expanded and new programs. For example, the funds for the Economic Opportunity Program should have increased from $1.4 billion in 1967 to $3.0 billion in 1970 and then increase to $4.0 billion in 1975. Housing and community development programs should have risen from $0.1 to $3.3 billion and then on up to $3.8 billion; for agriculture and natural resources combined outlays should have jumped from $5.9 to $10.5 billion and then to $12.0 billion; for education the increase should have been from $2.6 to $7.0 to $9.5 billion; health services must rise to $7.0 billion in 1975; public assistance, labor and manpower, and other welfare services total budget expenditures should be at the $7.5-billion mark in 1975.

Total federal budget outlays with the Freedom Budget allocation would not increase as a percentage of GNP over the ten-year period. Stated in different terms, at the time the Freedom Budget was developed average GNP per capita was $3,500. "We grant to the Federal Government a slice equal to roughly $500 in the form of taxes, leaving us an average of about $3,000 to spend on our other needs."[4]

If our nation's productivity continues growing at the same rate as in recent years—and it will if the Freedom Budget is adopted—each share will grow at about $5,000. Thus the Federal government's slice will grow to $700, . . . and we will still have $4,300 left for our other needs.

What the Freedom Budget proposes is this: Budget a fraction of this $200 increase in Federal tax revenues to provide jobs for all who can work and adequate income of other types for those who cannot.[5]

In commenting on the Freedom Budget, A. Philip Randolph points to necessity for government-channeled resources to eradicate poverty.

But the very nature of a total war against unemployment and poverty and all their manifestations calls for greatly increased emphasis upon adequate Federal programs and huge increase in Federal expenditures. Increases in private incomes alone, while necessary, cannot themselves at appreciable speed channel a large enough part of our resource into clearance of slums, the rebuilding of our cities, the construction of schools and hospitals, the recruitment and adequate pay of teachers and nurses.[6]

Randolph expects the federal government to serve as the catalyst in developing full employment and estimates that a financial commitment of at least $185 billion is necessary. It is interesting to note that Randolph's budget would also directly alter the economic well-being of white Americans in similar poverty conditions.

The GHEDIplan

Sources of government funds are the principal concern of another capital funding program suggested by Dr. Dunbar S. McLaurin. McLaurin's program, called the "Ghetto Economic Development and Industrialization Plan," was prepared for the

Human Resources Administration of the city of New York. The GHEDIplan has two basic components: (1) a source of funds for business in the ghettos and (2) a guaranteed market for the ghetto businesses once established (see Chapter 5).

Of the $200 million potentially available under this plan, half would represent guaranteed financing for businesses and half would be in guaranteed markets for products and services of the businesses. The plan has elements of an approach to the restructuring of New York slums similar to those found for developing nations on an international basis. In the particular plan proposed, the city of New York would provide the financing by depositing a portion of city funds in slum-area banks on the condition that the banks make development loans to ten newly formed corporations created to funnel the monies into local businesses. Five of these corporations would be nonprofit Local Development Corporations to attract new industry and to otherwise stimulate the ghetto community. The remaining corporations would be Small Business Investment Companies which would help convert the local-government deposits into venture capital and loans.[7]

The Ghetto Economic Development and Industrialization Plan would increase the productivity of the ghetto's private sector and employ the city's underutilized fiscal and purchasing resources.[8]

The magnitude of the estimates of the capital resources necessary to revitalize the ghettos and to eradicate poverty throughout the nation should be noted. The Freedom Budget makes reference to $185 billion over a ten-year period, the local GHEDIplan project estimates the use of $200 million for New York City alone, while the National Business League's initial and single modular core costs are set at $75 million.

A nonblack estimate of the capital cost of urban development was made for Goodbody and Company, an investment banker and financial services organization, by economist Lawrence Ritter of New York University. Ritter estimates that the cost of a "domestic Marshall Plan" is likely to range between $150 billion and $250 billion over a ten-year period, or about $15 billion to $25 billion annually at current prices."[9]

Each of the programs noted are directed at total or fractional economic development of the black community and require the large outlays of money and resources. One issue in the potential success of this myriad system of programs is adequate financing.

**The Report of the National
Advisory Commission on
Civil Disorders—
The Kerner Report**

The Kerner Report stated that only a "greatly enlarged commitment to national action . . . can shape a future that is compatible with the historic ideas of American society." The Commission reported that it had taken into account the magnitude of the commitment necessary by the American system to alleviate the conditions associated with urban disorders. The financing of the cost of a variety of programs was also studied by the Commission. The Kerner Commission's policy recommendations include adopting a national system of income supplements; providing on-the-job training with federal support; stepped-up programs of urban renewal and housing for low- and moderate-income families; creating employment opportunities in both the private and public sectors, and improving the standards of social assistance programs as well as additional support for education of the disadvantaged.

The Report noted that "the nation has substantial financial resources—not enough to do everything some might wish, but enough to make an important start in reducing our critical 'social deficit' in spite of a war and in spite of current requirements."[10]

The Report referred, in a rather cursory way, to a fiscal dividend or positive increase that accrues to the Federal Revenue System at the rate of about $11 to $14 billion a year because of steady economic growth as a source of funds for the programs. In later sections the specific financial mechanisms were recommended as sources of funds to meet costs of particular programs.

It should be stated at the outset that federal-government expenditures for public programs have been large during the last decade. If consideration includes social programs as well as all programs that include health, education, low-income housing, social insurance, and welfare, expenditures have nearly doubled in the seven-year period between 1960 and 1967. Using the National Planning Association's estimate for total social expenditures, the 1966–1967 level of such expenditures was slightly over $100 billion. Social expenditures at all levels represent about 44 per cent of total public expenditures and about 13 per cent of GNP.

According to the National Planning Association in a report prepared by Mrs. Joyce Powell under the direction of Dr. Leonard Lecht, the total additional outlays for Kerner Report programs would amount to about $40 billion per year if the programs were accomplished within a relatively short period of time. Using the NPA information, if the full Kerner Commission program were implemented at a rapid pace, housing would cost $18.8 billion, employment programs $8.5 billion, welfare (public assistance only) would cost $7.8 billion, and educational programs $5.4 billion. Of the $40-billion total, the public sector would bear about $22 billion of that total cost, and the private sector would be responsible for the remainder. If a slower pace were adopted to implement the Kerner Commission's proposals, the annual average cost for the slower pace would be $14 to $15 billion with the public sector's cost in the $7-billion range and the private sector's in the $8-billion range. The NPA also made estimates of the employment opportunities that would be created through the completion of these programs. If all the Kerner Commission programs were recommended there would be an increase in employment in the range of 3.5 million. Most of these programs would involve work in the urban core areas and are designed to absorb existing unemployment and underemployment of Negroes and whites in the city. The NPA estimates that if the national economy expands over the years by an annual average rate of a conservative 4 per cent, the increase in GNP at constant prices and the increase in labor force —for example, for the next three years—could be estimated as follows: In 1970 the GNP increase would be $35 billion and the employment increase would be 1.51 million. In 1971, the GNP accretion would be $36 billion while the increase in the total labor force over the preceding year would be 1.53 million.[11] Whether or not the economy can actually accomplish these required financial responsibilities is debatable.

Productivity-Cost Offsets as a Source of Funds

Proposals in the Kerner Commission Report included need for the creation of a million new jobs in the public sector in a three-year period of time and a million new jobs in the private sector during the same period. The related programs in manpower and economic development, including education and housing, were never detailed as to cost or source of funding. The Commission estimated hard-core training costs at about $3,000 to $5,000. The assumption of training costs and related services and the impact on productivity during the training period would be the basis for financial incentives and the proposed tax-credit arrangement.

It should be noted that the concern for the cost of the employment program is largely offset by benefits that accrue to the system as a whole through the increase in jobs and productivity and the elimination of high social costs, such as welfare payments. In estimating the costs and benefits of manpower development or employment programs, other federal government programs provide basic information. In the case of Job Corps trainees under the OEO Program, the average cost per trainee was over $6,000. As of mid-1968 there are over 75,000 youths who had Job Corps experience. Out of that 75,000 almost 53,000 had found jobs or had returned to school. Those people who sought jobs generally were able to obtain better-paying jobs. The average hourly rate was $1.71 compared to $1.19 paid prior to their Job Corps training. On the basis of that $1.71 an hour for the rest of the working life, these Job Corps employees will be paying back to the government an aggregate of over $11 million in future income taxes. Similar estimates and experience are also available for MDTA Programs.

The MDTA has helped approximately 200,000 low-income people over a period of the last five years. More than three fourths of the institutional trainees and about half of the on-the-job trainees in training in 1966 had previously earned under $3,000 a year or had received no income for the year before employment began. The Labor Department, in producing estimates for a five-year period ending January, 1968, indicated that about 75 per cent of those people receiving institutional training were employed at the time they were contacted, and slightly more than 75 per cent of these were in training-related jobs. Before training, in early 1967 the median pretraining earnings of persons enrolled in MDTA was $1.44 an hour. After training, this hourly rate increased to $1.74. The government now estimates that the average trainee costs are repaid in taxes in about two years. If the trainee continues to work during his lifetime he more than repays the public investment.

These cost-and-repayment estimates are significant as they relate to other social costs involved when individuals do not have productive employment. For example, a man confined in prison for ten years with his wife and children on welfare, produces a much greater cost than does a man in the MDTA or the Job Corps training program. In the mid-1960's, the average cost per offender per year in a penal institution was about $2,000. In estimating future revenue returns from increased productivity, on a GNP basis, the training of the hard-core unemployed may produce an average potential revenue of about $11,000 per job. With a need for approximately 4,000,000 jobs in the system to deal with the hard-core unemployed, the gross national product should increase in the range of $10 to $30 billion annually. The Kerner Commission's estimates of the fiscal dividend is probably based on this type of rise in GNP or national income attributable to increased productivity. The amount of that dividend largely depends on the assumptions regarding changing price levels and inflation. It might be noted that no economist would argue that if employment is increased without inflation, and if a larger number of individuals are earning higher levels of income, the increased earnings must be reflected in GNP increases. Correspondingly, unemployment can be measured on the same basis to indicate the total negative cost to the system, in terms of an equivalent amount of resources underemployed or underutilized. In order to achieve full employment to get the hard-core unemployed into the manpower stream and improve social and economic mobility, the outlays to implement the Kerner Report must be large and continued over a period of at least a decade as a "crash" program.

Tax Incentives

In dealing with the hard-core unemployed, the Kerner Report recommended that a tax incentive be allowed for private-sector employers who provided training environment and/or retain the hard-core unemployed. The tax incentive would be in the form of a credit against tax in the amount of 50 per cent of the wages and fringe benefits paid to the employer during six months of employment, and 25 per cent of the wages and fringe benefits paid during the second year of employment. In an example of the way in which the tax incentive might operate, the Report noted that "an employer paying the minimum wage of $1.60 per hour, or over $3,300 per year, with no fringe benefit, would receive a $1,248 credit against his net corporation income tax. And if the employee were retained for the next half year a $832 additional benefit would be received for a total of slightly over $2,000 in the form of a tax credit for the first year and this would continue over a two-year period of time." The Report also recommended a 7 per cent tax investment credit for new equipment if the necessity arose out of the corporate's attempt to hire the hard-core unemployed. The employer of the hard core would be limited to $25,000 plus 50 per cent of the amount of the company's tax exceeding $25,000 so that no employer would receive a particular competitive advantage. The idea of the tax incentive for investment in poverty areas was also suggested for rural poverty programs, as well as for a variety of special development programs.

Other Use of Tax Incentives   An early advocate of the tax incentive and investment credit approach was the late Senator Robert F. Kennedy, Democrat of New York. Legislation introduced in the first session of the Ninetieth Congress (S2088, July 12, 1967) called for tax reductions for industries willing to establish operations in slum areas, or industries that foster programs which would provide employment for indigenous residents.[12] The fiscal and financial incentives called for were a 10 per cent credit on machinery and equipment and a 7 per cent credit on costs of construction or leasing facilities. A credit carryback of three taxable years and a ten-year carryover were included. A net operating loss of ten taxable years instead of the present five-year limit was recommended as well as a special deduction of an additional 25 per cent of salaries paid to ghetto employees. The Kennedy program also liberalized depreciation. In the second session of the Ninetieth Congress, a bill (H.R. 17567) introduced by twenty House members called for revision of the Internal Revenue Code of 1954 to provide a tax credit for employers who employ the hard-core unemployed.

The Advisory Commission on Inter-Governmental Relations in its 1968 Commission Report on Urban and Rural America also called for government incentive techniques to influence industrial locations. Tax-incentive options were suggested:

"A federal income tax credit might be a percentage of various bases: (1) investment plant equipment; (2) amount of payroll; (3) value added to produce. . . . the first would tend to encourage investment in the non-labor factors of production, thus emphasizing automation and technological improvements. The second would emphasize the use of labor and thus would more immediately further the objectives of an urbanization policy seeking to attract people by jobs. But it might tend to discourage technological improvements. The value added base—relating the amount of tax credit to the amount of value added by business or industries own achievement—would steer a course between the other two.

Under any of these three approaches, the Secretary of the Treasury would be required to grant a tax cut upon certification of eligibility by the Secretary of Commerce.[18]

Representative Evins of Tennessee introduced H.R. 14600 (Ninetieth Congress, Second Session) to encourage rural development by providing incentives for new or expanded job-producing industries or commercial facilities in rural areas with high proportions of low-income populations. This bill also calls for an investment tax credit of 7 per cent and other additional tax credits. Amendments of the Internal Revenue Code would have the effect of reducing the corporation income tax on those firms that were certified for purposes of the bill.

Another form of the tax-incentive approach produced in the Ninety-First Congress, First Session, is included in S 3376. This bill, which is the formal statement of the CORE development program, is designed to facilitate self-determination for people of urban and rural communities by setting up employment opportunities through the ownership and control of resources in the black community.

Under Title IV of this bill, the Community Development Corporations receive multiple surtax exemptions and are subject to a corporation income tax less than that levied on other corporations. The tax on the community development corporation would be computed with reference to a so-called "development index." The "development index" for any community within which the community development corporation is operating is computed according to: (1) the ratio of (a) the percentage of the labor force unemployed on a national basis, or within the relevant standard metropolitan statistical area, whichever is lower, to (b) the percentage of the labor force unemployed in the appropriate community area; (2) the ratio of (a) the median family income in the appropriate community area to (b) the median family income on a national basis or within the relevant standard metropolitan area, whichever is greater. The development index of the area shall be the lesser of the two ratios computed.

For tax purposes, the normal tax is equal to 22 per cent if the development index is 100 or over. With a development index of 90 or over but less than 100, the rate is 12 per cent of the first $50,000 and 22 per cent of the amounts in excess of $50,000. If the development index is below 80, tax rate is 0 per cent on the first $50,000, 6 per cent on the next $50,000, 12 per cent on the next $50,000 and 22 per cent on amounts in excess of $150,000.

A surtax would also be levied equal to 26 per cent of the amount by which the taxable income exceeds the surtax exemptions of the taxable year. For purposes of the self-determination program, the surtax exemption for any taxable year is related to the level of the development index. The unique bill also provides (Section 403, page 148) for "dividends received" deductions. There would be a 100 per cent deduction in the case of dividends received by a Community Corporation.

Other sections provide for more rapid write-off or more rapid amortization as well as an investment credit for turn-key facilities. The investment credit could be equal to 10 per cent of the wages of qualified employers. The credit allowed for the taxable year should not exceed so much of the liability for the taxable year as does not exceed $25,000 plus 50 per cent, or so much of the liability for the taxable year as exceeds $25,000. Special tax relief is also provided in the form of tax liability limitations. The taxable income from turn-key facilities is computed by deducting from the gross-income expenses of losses and deductions of any expense losses or other deductions that cannot be allocated to some other item or class of gross income of Community Development subsidiary. A net operating loss arising from the operation of a turn-key facility is treated as a net operating loss carryback or net operating loss carryover in computing taxable income.

T. L. Cross in his *Black Capitalism,* advocates an omnibus array of tax-credit programs to encourage private sector sources to speed the flow of investment capital and credit money into the ghetto. Income tax credits are recommended by Cross to apply to:

(a) owners of demand and time deposits and certificates of deposits deposited in ghetto banks;

(b) franchise income derived by the franchiser from poverty-area franchised businesses;

(c) the lender who provides the capital for new ghetto franchised businesses;

(d) corporations which provide licenses and working advice for franchising in the ghetto;

(e) any bank or finance company which provides credit to set up a franchised ghetto business;

(f) any manufacturer, wholesaler or retailer who sets up a new plant facility in a poverty area;

(g) corporations establishing entrepreneurial development centers in the ghetto;

(h) and to any tax payer who maintains and operates poverty area facilities used for vocational and job training.[14]

Other Tax-Incentive Legislation   H.R. 17567 provided a tax credit for employers who employ the hard-core unemployed. H.R. 244 provided tax deductions to individuals in businesses who create new jobs. The Kerner Commission Report and the Advisory Commission on Intergovernmental Relations recommendations call for tax incentives for established business to create new employment opportunities. Senate 3376 is designed to provide for self-determination and black development in ghetto areas. The tax incentives would provide financial advantages for the Negro community development corporations and turn-key facilities by establishing employment opportunities and black ownership of businesses and apartment buildings. Thus, for job and entrepreneurship options, tax incentives are an integral element in encouraging the white-establishment corporations to participate in hard-core employment. Tax incentives are to be used to provide a better environment, more conducive to the development of embryonic black establishments in the ghetto area.

These are extraordinary recommendations for the use of federal tax concessions and the investment credit incentives to encourage the private sector to participate more actively in the financing of aid to the Negro. Such tax concessions and similar provisions raise old issues about the use of taxation and government subsidy for particular groups or sectors of the economy.

Financial incentives for the embryonic black businesses can be justified more easily and completely than similar financial support for successfully functioning, established corporations, and direct government financing of it is the most propitious approach.

White-Versus-Black
Ghetto Development

Large, established corporations will not react to the exigencies of social problems without adequate economic incentives. This troublesome attitude compounds the equity issue in credits or concessions to white business. Huge, undistributed, corporate profits of major United States corporations may appear as a ready source of funds to be tapped to absorb the costs of reducing the hard-core unemployed. But pressures such as profit level and stability eliminate this cost-absorption premise. In order to get white business participation, some form of financial outlay must be made. Whether or not priority should be placed on business participation as an employer of the last resort is an idea that is clouded with ideological preconception. Private-sector businesses cannot produce or create enough new jobs to hire all the hard-core unemployed. Whether or not such businesses should be financed by tax or other incentives for even a proportional share of job creation can be answered only by the relative effectiveness of this financing in actually making a breakthrough to the causes of the Negroes' economic malaise.

The Subsidy Alternative

Direct government payments for ghetto development is the most straightforward method. Direct subsidy payments should be paid to black, not white, entrepreneurs who locate in the selected areas. Payments would offset either capital outlays or operating costs. A direct subsidy based upon cost differentials would equalize direct business costs between areas of desired economic growth and other areas. The federal government could apply the eminent-domain theory to acquire land and lease it to private black enterprise.

This subsidy approach is recommended because the precise costs to the public can be determined readily. Detailed planning by the business applicant is required, however. This prerequisite increases the prospect that the subsidy will fulfill its purpose. For the black businessman the subsidy approach represents a "no-strings" financial contribution to the firm, to be used as management best sees fit.

Given the venture opportunities plus lower initial costs of establishing a business, such businesses can contribute to a reduction of the unemployment and an improved emotional milieu in the affected areas. The use of favorable depreciation schedules and advantageous loss-carryover features are also consistent with the most advantageous devices to foster successful business undertakings.

Additional Support for Black Businesses

Even with government-financed new business ventures (sources of government support could be general revenues, or a new federal type of the industrial development revenue bonds), only the most optimistic black nationalist would argue that the enterprises could generate significant increases in labor demand or significantly redistribute personal income. The task is too formidable and the number of potential black businesses too few. But of more significance is the viability of the black enterprises. Given the subsidy advantage, can these firms meet the competitive and market tests? Without additional forms of continuing government assistance, the answers must be couched in great uncertainty.

A Guaranteed Market

A final recommendation for public financing involves control of the market. The government should set aside a percentage of its procurement for ghetto businesses in depressed areas. The government market assures the ghetto company a return comparable to the non-ghetto company. Price supports may also be needed by the ghetto company. A related problem would be a type of market disruption. Many ghetto manufacturing firms would be needed. Government would have to spend enough to offer an adequate preferential market. By identifying the type of goods and services ghetto firms should provide, and the potential markets for these goods, a successful program could be set up. Unless adequate markets are found, this urban employment solution will result only in manpower redistribution.

The federal responsibility is much more extensive than previously noted. The federal government must act to make other governments as well as the private sector more active in problem-solving programs.

Federal Revenue-Sharing

The principal responsibilities assigned to governments through the various programs noted earlier are either a reallocation of existing expenditure priorities, or increase in federal government outlays, or tax concessions that would have the effect of reducing total revenues of the federal government and providing additional funds for private-sector corporations and employers in order to create employment options for the hard-core unemployed. Another dimension of the government responsibility is the manner in which the funds should be allocated among various programs, the timing of the funds, and the agency responsible for the administration of such programs. It is assumed that because of the "crisis in local government finance and administration" state and local governments have abdicated their responsibility in the solutions-oriented approach to the urban crisis. This point is highly significant because, despite any changes that might occur in the physical environment of the ghetto, or an increase in job opportunities, and/or improvement in employment opportunties, and/or increase in the capacity to share in the wealth, the fundamental problems facing the Negro in regard to his pattern of living will not be changed unless there are improvements in the services provided by state and local government.

The Report of the National Commission on Urban Problems summarized the factors contributing to the current pressure and the additional requirements of the central city. The Report, of course, recognizes the serious and growing disparity and the relative fiscal capacity between the central cities and the suburbs. Higher public-expenditure needs in the cities, rather than the deficiency in its tax base, are the significant factors in the cities' or states' capacity to deal with local problems. At least three factors contribute to the fiscal stress of the metropolitan area: (1) The central city is where the poor and disadvantaged tend to be concentrated. They are high-cost citizens, inasmuch as they require poverty-linked services such as public assistance, public health and hospital care, housing, and other social services, plus education for disadvantaged children. (2) Population concentration increases the scope of costly functions such as police and fire protection, parks, recreation, and sanitation. In most urban cores, these services, as well as the highway and traffic system, have to meet the need of a large daytime population plus a net inflow of suburban commuters. (3) The central cities developed after suburbia, and therefore their schools, hospitals, and water-supply and sewage-supply systems typically include a higher proportion of deteriorated structures and equipment that need replacement or renovation. As a result of these factors, most urban-core areas have higher taxes than the average for the suburban fringe.

A fragmented local government structure has resulted in metropolitan cores having tax rates far above those in the suburban areas. Because of these factors, local financing conditions add to other factors that encourage fringe area growth and discourage growth in central cities. These functions are not self-correcting and in fact tend to be self-reinforcing. There is no market mechanism available to reallocate the resources between ghetto and the suburban areas. If programs to improve the service capacity of local governments are to be implemented, there is a requirement for improvement in present intergovernmental fiscal relationships. Only the federal government can make a significant contribution to increasing the fiscal capacities of state and local governments.

Intergovernmental revenue from state and local sources is a significant component in urban finance. In the mid-1960's, intergovernmental revenue provided about a fourth of all the revenue local governments received. Only a minor part of these payments came directly from the federal government. A larger part of state and local payments was financed by federal government grants. It should be noted that state and federal payments to local governments have in fact been increasing rapidly. For example, in the period between 1962 and 1967, state aid to local governments rose from $10.9 billion to $19 billion. The federal payments also increased to $15.2 billion from $7.7 billion. The absolute increases are not as significant as they first appear, since there has been rapidly rising costs of state and local government services as well as significant increases in the state and local government revenues from their own sources. The general revenue of state and local governments provided by federal aid changed only from 13.5 per cent to 16.5 per cent in the five-year period before 1967. The proportion of all local governments' income from other governmental sources rose only 4.5 per cent in that period. In summary, intergovernmental receipts have accounted for less than one fourth of the total increase in state and local government general revenue, and for only 44 per cent of the increase in general revenue to local governments from 1962 to 1967. The rest of the increase was met from taxes or from other local revenue sources of the aid of government.[15]

The National Commission on Urban Problems recommended

an improved method of federal revenue-sharing with state and local governments. The federal government, of course, has been active in its form of revenue-sharing called "categorical grants." The grants are payments to help finance particular programs or types of projects tied to conditions and actions by the local government. Numerous measures have been introduced in Congress over the years which contemplate a different approach to the distribution of funds on a less narrowly oriented basis. The basic idea for increased federal financial assistance was given impetus by the Council of Economic Advisers' Chairman, Walter Heller, in 1964. The federal government should share some of its growing income-tax collections with the states. Heller had argued for the tax on the basis of increasing needs, as well as improvement in the fairness of the overall tax system.[16] In the Eighty-ninth Congress, at least fifty-seven congressmen sponsored or co-sponsored fifty-one different tax-sharing bills. In the first session of the Ninetieth Congress, there were almost double that number. At least 110 members sponsored or co-sponsored ninety separate bills with thirty-five variations in the tax-sharing theme.[17] However, the most popularized form is the Heller-Pechman Plan. When first proposed, Heller advocated revenue-sharing only to state government. The originators conceded that the problems of public services and financing are the most critical at the local level, particularly in urban areas. State governments, however, had been responsive to rising public service needs as evidenced by tax-sharing efforts and improved local grant-in-aid programs. Local government representatives argued that major urban areas needed more funds than those provided by the state government. Pechman and Heller, as well as the National Commission on Urban Problems, recommended a "pass-through" allocation which recognizes the legitimate claims of local governments for additional funds. The Commission pointed out the urgent need for early action to establish an improved revenue-sharing system. The Commission proposal was that Congress adopt a system for regular revenue-sharing with state governments and major cities and urban counties. The formula's recommendations are as follows:

(1) earnings reserves should be made in a federal trust fund sum for annual allocation consisting of a legally authorized percentage of the total new taxable income reported under the Federal Individual Income Tax form; (2) an allocation should be provided each state area, based primarily upon population, but with an adjustment for relative total state-local tax effort and additional crediting for state revenue for taxation of individual income; and (3) provision should be made for a portion of the allocation of individual state areas to be paid directly to major municipalities and urban county governments on a basis determined by their respective shares of all state and local tax revenue in that particular state. This system should encourage recipient governments to exercise a high degree of discretion regarding the application of the distributed funds.[18]

As noted, the Commission proposal put added emphasis on revenue from state individual income taxes to encourage further use of this kind of tax. It was implied that states have not yet used this tax as extensively as possible or as necessary. The apportionment processes emphasize the local government responsibility.

The direct-formula allocation payments to major cities for urban problems are focused on municipalities of 50,000 or more and county governments about that same size in which half of the population is urban. This selective approach would probably avoid the undesirable features of the system that used direct federal and local sharing to local governments in general. The arguments against making direct payments to local governments include the fact that there are tremendous administrative complexities because of the 80,000 or so local governments involved, and that the prospect of federal aid with "no strings attached" tends to entrench many local governments that are too small to really be operational units. Under the suggested two-stage distribution formula the total allocation would be determined on a uniform basis, but the intrastate shares to be paid directly to major local governments and to state governments would take account of the particular state's prevailing pattern of functional responsibility and financing as reflected by state revenue proportions.[19]

The Nixon Administration apparently accepted the basic thesis of the Commission's Report when it inaugurated a system of federal revenue-sharing. Although there is nothing new in the Nixon proposal, it differs in at least one fundamental and significant feature from the Commission recommendations. The size of the total fund to be shared is smaller at five-twelfths of one per cent of personal taxable income in fiscal 1971. The percentage will increase and reach one per cent in fiscal 1976. Only an estimated $500 million will be distributed when the program is implemented and only about $5 billion will be available under the one per cent rate at the end of five years.

The administration approach provides for a "pass-through" feature to allow local governments to use money as determined by local conditions. The state governments play a role in determining the potential amount of money to be returned to state and local governments by the level of taxes exacted from the available tax base. Thus high "taxing effort" states will receive a larger allocation. The distribution of shared moneys from the state to local governments is determined by a formula based on local government shares of total local government revenue raised in the state. It is possible for state governments to qualify for alternative distribution systems if the state legislature approve an alternative plan, and if two-thirds of local governments consent to the alternative plan, and when localities which raise two-thirds of the total revenue in the state agree. This process safeguards large cities such as New York City against less than a fair share of revenues under alternate state plans.

Although the revenue-sharing concept is a practicality, the existing plan is a financial palliative and provides less financial support than deemed desirable by the Commission on Urban Problems.

The Commission report was oriented toward approval of the original Heller recommendation. In that proposal 2 per cent of the federal income tax base is earmarked for the trust fund for the new form of federal revenue sharing. If that 2 per cent had been implemented in the period of 1966, it would have supplied about

$5.8 billion to state and local governments. This would have been a 44 per cent addition to the amount received from the traditional federal conditional grants-in-aid. But that $5.8 billion would still have been less than 6 per cent of state and local revenue and less than 7 per cent of the state and local revenue from their own sources. The 1966 amount of $5.8 billion was about 10 per cent of the total state and local state revenue, or about as much as the year-to-year increase in state-local tax revenue. These figures, in the Commission's view, indicated that even a full 2 per cent of base would have only superficially dampened the fiscal pressures falling on state and local governments. By 1972, assuming a moderate rate of economic growth in the system, $5.8 billion could be available from the 2 per cent of individual income tax base. Coupled with the projected rises in their own revenue sources, this would still mean very little change in the resulting proportion of the total being supplied by the federal government in 1972.

The Commission on Urban Problems recommended to Congress that the federal government maintain and provide adequate financing for federal programs that have specific uses in improving the disadvantaged position of people in urban areas. Their recommendation included not only federal aids for housing and city rebuilding, but also appropriations to poverty programs, grants for education of children in low-income families, and additional aid for urban mass transit programs as well as programs for training the unemployed. This recommendation makes it quite clear that the revenue-sharing system should be adopted in addition to, rather than a substitute for, conditional federal grants for particular programs.

The Commission also noted the need for the President and the Bureau of the Budget to review existing procedures and requirements of programs sponsored by the federal government and usually funded through state governments. There is a need for statutory changes that eliminate discrimination between state and local governments in regard to existing federal government grants-in-aid programs. This pattern of federal discrimination in grants may be regarded as interferences with local governments trying to include existing districts and other local governments into larger, more viable, governmental units.

The Commission's Report also pointed out the need for local government tax administration changes, particularly in the property tax. The property tax was and is a burden on home ownership and on low-income individuals. In addition to the emphasis on the property tax, the excise tax base of state and local government finances are nominally regressive in regard to income and place a heavier burden on low-income taxpayers.

Thus, if the total financial dimensions of the urban crisis are to be recognized, there must be concurrent revenue and structural changes in local government funding and responsibilities to accomplish any of the necessary goals recognized in the improvement of the urban living environment. The financial dimension requires a more massive commitment than that made to date by the Nixon administration.

Feasibility of
Government Support

The National Advisory Commission on Civil Disorders chose a critical time to announce the need for money to implement recommendations in the area of education, housing, welfare, and employment. At the same time the Commission made its recommendation (without a price tag), a meeting was held in Washington and later in Stockholm with managing boards of central banks from throughout the free world. The heads of these central banks were trying to implement short-term action to save the American dollar and other Western currencies from devaluation. This period of time was described by William McChesney Martin, Jr., Chairman of the Federal Reserve Board of Governors, as a period of "the worst financial crisis we have had since 1931." The interest rate charged on loans to member commercial banks had been raised by the Federal Reserve Bank to the highest levels since the stock market crash in 1929. European banks were watching U.S.

fiscal policies to determine if American policy-makers were going to fulfill a pledge to adopt a more responsible fiscal policy. This pledge had been made on a *quid pro quo* basis for their support of our dollar. Federal spending was cut and a corresponding surtax was added to give symbolic evidence of fiscal responsibility and restraint by the U.S. government.

Despite the dire economic conditions at the time, the recommendations of the Kerner Report were to be financed through the "great productivity of the American economy and a Federal Reserve System which is highly responsive to economic growth. In combination these produce truly astonishing automatic increase in federal budget receipts, providing only that the national economy is kept functioning at capacity so that the actual income expanse is in line with the potential." Years after the Report and its recommendations, the economic and financial stringency in the United States has not significantly eased, although it can be argued that no war in the history of the United States has been financed in a noninflationary manner. But the federal government's previous commitment to a domestic war, the "war on poverty," was started when outlays did not contribute to inflationary pressures. It can be argued that the nation should accept inflation as a necessary cost of necessary domestic wars—on poverty, poor education, inadequate housing, and other social ills. It is important to understand that price rises or inflationary pressures should be glossed over as only a token cost. Inflationary pressures have very real repercussions on both the international and domestic state of economic well-being.

In evaluating the economic implications of the Report of the National Advisory Commission on Civil Disorders, Gerhard Colm, commented on two economic concerns of the Commission's recommendations. The first was the determination of the cost of the stated recommendations in terms of resource, particularly manpower requirements, and money cost. The other was the resulting fiscal repercussions or implications on the total system in terms of growth, inflation, and other elements if the recommendations were adopted.

Estimated cost of implementing the Kerner Report recommendations is about $40 billion above the level of the 1968 budget. Such an outlay would entail adding this amount to our gross national product, or channeling it away from other programs. The $40 billion estimates include both public and private outlays since some of the programs, such as housing, could be financed by the private sector.

The Commission's housing recommendations were to be completed in five years, and the employment goal of an additional two million jobs was to be accomplished in three years after the publication of the Report. The total increase in U.S. gross national product, which currently grows at about $35 to $40 billion a year, would be required to meet these housing and employment goals. In other words, most increases in production and income would necessarily have to be directed toward implementing Kerner Commission Reports. According to Colm, such an enormous redistribution of our national wealth is unrealistic. Thus a slower goal, or five years to achieve the employment goals and ten years to reach the housing goals, is much more realistic.

In assessing the financial implications, there are several important issues. Government expenditures of about $23 billion would be necessary to carry out all the recommendations of the Report in the suggested time period. In attempting to finance such an expenditure, singular emphasis is placed on the so-called "fiscal dividend." This fiscal dividend represents the increase in tax receipts resulting from existing tax rates, and an increasing tax base. The fiscal dividend was estimated at between $11 and $14 billion. Thus, two years of the fiscal dividend, or a total of $28 billion, plus two years of receipts from the surcharge put into effect in 1968 ($16 billion), would produce $44 billion, or an amount necessary to produce or finance the Kerner Report recommendations. The fiscal dividend of $14 billion is based on price increases as well as increased productivity in the system.

Twenty-eight billion dollars of the financing is based on two years' receipts from the surcharge continued at 10 per cent. The continuation of the life of the surcharge is in question. In early

1969 it was recommended by President Nixon that the surtax rate be reduced to 5 per cent in January, 1970, and be completely removed after June 30, 1970. Extensive commitments for the use of the fiscal dividend have already been determined by previous legislation. Thus, if a surtax is removed the recommendations would face the dilemma of achieving redistribution of the fiscal dividend from prior established programs, or a new commitment to the importance of the war on urban ills as opposed to other alternative needs.

What would happen to the economy if peace were to break out? Could additional monies be made available without the fiscal dividend in order to finance needed domestic programs? The $28 billion now spent for the war effort could potentially be channeled into domestic programs. The Cabinet Coordinating Committee on Economic Planning for the End of Vietnam Hostilities has made some assessment of the impact of de-escalation of that war. "The cost of the war has been a load for the economy to carry—not a supporting 'prop.' Prosperity has not depended on the defense build-up and will not need our military spending to support it in peace time. On the contrary, peace will provide the nation with welcome opportunities to channel into civilian use manpower and material resources now being devoted to war."[20]

With de-escalation, policies would necessarily be adjusted to avoid an excessively restrictive effect of the decline in defense expenditures. It would be necessary to weigh priorities in advance among a variety of fiscal adjustment alternatives, that is, reducing taxes, strengthening existing programs, and launching new programs. About one half of the expanding peace-time revenues have already been committed to existing expenditures, assuming peace is accomplished by 1972 and that the surtax has expired. Estimates made by the Cabinet Coordinating Committee on Economic Planning indicate that a "peace-and-growth dividend" would be reached amounting to $22 billion by the fiscal year 1972. This dividend would increase by about $7 to $8 billion in the short run thereafter, amounts that are over and above the committed outlays. If social insurance and other cash benefits are adjusted for the cost of living, the estimated dividend would be reduced. In addition, a selection of major existing programs and new programs already designed are resting in abeyance until the peace-and-growth dividend becomes available. It is apparent that the $40 billion needed to implement all the recommendations of the Kerner Report will not be available in the immediate future. A difficult determination of priorities will become necessary. Areas that will be affected by demobilization along with other high-priority recommendations, such as housing, education, welfare, and manpower, could receive the greatest proportion of the peace-and-growth dividend. In the case of a very rapid demobilization, flexibility in U.S. fiscal and monetary policy decisions will be a vital element in the success of the readjustment. If the surcharge is still in effect when hostilities cease, its expiration could provide a major component in the necessary fiscal offsets. Contrary to the Committee's suggestion, the continuation of the surtax for two years following the end of the war would provide additional and perhaps necessary funds for setting up a totally effective social program. Any reduction in the excise tax on automobiles and telephones would also tend to complicate the fiscal readjustment at the expense of domestic programs.

It is necessary to consider the effect of additional outlays on the total demand pattern in the U.S. economy, as well as to determine the impact of alternative programs on the expected pattern of needed policies, both now and in the future. It is also noted that "now" is the "future" that the Kerner Report recommendations alluded to. There has already been a time lag in the implementation of Kerner Report recommendations in the economic area, and lags continue to occur at the rate the Nixon administration has chosen to deal with domestic issues. The pace of current funding is inadequate.

It seems apparent that a "peace-and growth-dividend" could be used to permit tax reductions to stimulate consumer demands, as well as alleviate the existing pressures from military activity on other federal programs and ease the pressures requiring stringent monetary policies. Past experience indicates that effective stimuli in the economy stem from a decrease in federal taxation. Tax reductions in 1964 and 1965 illustrate that the dividend could be used to some extent to finance the compelling needs of public expenditures from income generated by appropriate levels of economic growth.

Thus, at some time in the future the federal government could conceivably make adequate funding available for necessary domestic programs by either reducing taxes, which would stimulate private-sector growth, which in turn would generate additional government revenues to be authorized for necessary programs to meet the urban ills. The federal government could continue its high rates of taxation at the end of the hostilities and use the money formerly available for military purposes in Vietnam for needed domestic programs.

What is most important about these alternatives is that the references are to future funding. The need for the program implementation is now. Given the existing economic conditions, there is no fiscal dividend of the type described in the Kerner Report available for funding domestic programs on a scale necessary to show significant, short-term results.

CHAPTER 9

Progress and Poverty

Since the summer of 1967, when riots changed the American outlook on potential integration of the black and white races, a variety of new programs have been advanced to attack the basic economic problems of the black race. Whites and the blacks have participated in formulating these programs. Implicit in all white and several black economic plans is the movement toward integration through activity that will bring the blacks into the established institutional structure of white America. A polar-case thrust is identified with particular black-militant groups which advocate some form of economic separatism. Aside from the ideological elements of polar-case positions, the flow of new ideas from these black and white groups for economic improvement of the black

For Notes to Chapter 9 see page 349.

does not illustrate great or unique innovation. All the programs recognize the need to raise the income of the black so that he may increase his participation in education, have access to better-paying jobs and better communities, and may be permitted to obtain entrepreneural control over economic resources. A presumption is that race alone should not be the barrier to better living arrangements, better working conditions, high-quality education, or other economy-related opportunities. It is possible to generalize on the purpose of most of these programs, noted in the earlier sections of this book, to the extent that all recommend some sort of ghetto economic development or economic development within which ghetto residents can participate.

Ghetto problems thus must be attacked. The typical list of these includes high unemployment, low income, poor schools, and poor housing. It would seem important, then, that any ghetto-development program must deal directly with these basic and obvious problems. However, it is more important to recognize that there are complementary problems in the ghetto. The problems of the very slow rate of improvement in residential housing integration, a slow movement in school desegregation, and residual elements of unfair employment practices point out procedural, as well as institutional, barriers that mollify the appropriate recognition of the problems of ghetto development and the pace at which development can be implemented. The white obviously has experienced some of the spin-off problems of metropolitan financing, transportation, housing, and urban renewal. But the processes of overall metropolitan development are continuing to move in the same unilateral pattern as the past, and thus continue to amplify the economic problems identified for the Negro.

A cursory review of the program alternatives advocated by both black and white for ghetto economic development indicates that most programs are designated to attack unemployment through skills training, easier job access, or locating industrial sites in the ghetto area, and by ghetto beautification or improved housing and physical facilities and structures within the area where the black resides.

Housing and Ghetto
Beautification

In ghetto beautification, or betterment of housing standards, the federal government's record has been one of uneven and slow movement, which raises questions about the capacity of the federal government to guide the private sector into a program that would provide the necessary quality and quantity of housing. The Joint Economic Committee's Report on the 1969 Economic Report of the President noted that

. . . the area of housing is the most outstanding example of the federal government's failure to fulfill its own commitment. It is now two decades since the passage of the Housing Act of 1949. We have not yet constructed the number of housing units contemplated for the first 6 years of that act. According to the Report of the National Commission on Urban Problems, we have demolished more housing by public action—under such programs as highways and urban renewal—than has been built under all federally aided programs. There are approximately 11 million substandard and overcrowded housing units. Yet, new housing starts total less than 1.5 million units per year, far below the number required to effect a rapid replacement of substandard units and to provide for an expanding population.[1]

The National Commission on Urban Problems reviewed the reasons why government public-housing efforts have failed. Local administrative officials have sometimes argued that Congress, in fixing low ceilings on the number of units authorized, is really responsible for the slow pace of public housing. Congress has in fact fixed limits below those originally expected to have been set in the 1949 Act. The ceilings have changed from year to year, but they generally numbered about 35,000 units. As late as 1965 the yearly ceiling for the next four years was set at 60,000 units to provide a total of 240,000 units since 1965. The cities as a whole have never built public housing at the rate or the level authorized by Congress. New York City as an exception has moved ahead and has approximately 150,000 units in operation. For the country as a whole, in the middle 1950's housing starts fell even below the very low ceilings of 15,000 to 25,000 units. There was some progress in 1966 and 1967, but then only about half of these larger quotas was filled. In the Commission's interviews in various cities, it was revealed that the construction units per family had slowed or stopped, and few or no public housing units were being constructed.

The New York City
Housing Case

Although the city of New York has an unusual record in terms of the number of new housing starts, there are still paradoxes in the New York case which exemplify the problems shared in varying degrees in most central cities—that is, providing housing in the quality and quantity needed to serve the needs of a great variety of people living there. In a study of New York housing, The Chase Manhattan Bank noted several of these paradoxes in New York City.

More than 750,000 units have been built in New York City since 1946. Although this number of starts would be enough to house an entire city such as Philadelphia, New York's population has changed little in the period 1965–1968. But the city is hard pressed to maintain the housing *status quo*. New construction dropped off drastically during the period 1966 to 1968. An average of one-fifth more units were built per year in the 1960's than in the 1950's. Despite this rate of change in new construction, vacancy rates in 1968 were 1.2 per cent, as compared with 1.8 per cent in 1960. Over a decade when vacancy rates were falling, abandonment of living units increased. If the estimated 50,000 abandoned units were included in the housing stocks, vacancy rates would be about three times the level of 1968. Abandonment of housing units has not eased the housing market. In many older cities such as New York the abandonments reflect malfunctioning of the private-sector market. Specifically, landlords are not able to operate units at a profitable level when rents are set at the level low-income tenants can afford. Nevertheless, New York's total housing inventory has increased, but at a lower rate than the new construction would indicate, because old housing is being dropped from the counting. Since 1945, a quarter of a million units have been destroyed or demolished. Abandoned units, or condemned units, have neither been destroyed nor rehabilitated.

Locally collected statistics indicate that the housing stock has risen about 8 per cent since 1960. U.S. Census data shows a rise in the national housing stock under 2 per cent. In New York City housing density has declined. Households tend to be two tenths of a per cent smaller in 1968 than in 1960. There is evidence, then, that overcrowding has been reduced, and fewer than a tenth of all rental units have one or more persons per room.

Deterioration is a rapidly growing problem despite the fact that the worst units have apparently been removed from the housing stock. In a count in 1968, about five eighths of the city's units were sound and had all necessary plumbing facilities. This represented a very small increase over 1960. In 1968, dilapidated units and units lacking facilities declined 30 per cent. However, the number of deteriorating units increased in the period from 1960 (100,000) to 1968 (360,000). One of the reasons deterioration continues to be a problem in New York is the features of real-estate taxing. Improvements are assessed and are reflected in higher property-tax payments. The landlord must recover the added cost of the improvements in higher rents. Because landlords often cannot do this basically, their incentive to upgrade property is diminished. It is significant that in the ghetto neighborhoods tenants carry a relatively heavy rent burden. About 80 per cent of tenants with incomes under $3,000 pay 35 per cent or more of their income in rent. The system of rent controls in effect in New York City for 375,000 apartments seem to aggravate the property-tax dilemma even farther. Rent-controlled apartments do not turn out to be particularly profitable investments. Maintenance costs and services tend to be reduced to maintain net income. On the other hand, higher-income tenants tend to convert buildings to tenant ownership, which is to the advantage of both the owner and the resident. In the last several years, condominiums and cooperatives increased dramatically to a new high level. Cooperatives are not typically available in low-income units. Thus, buildings of absentee landlords are particularly subject to deterioration. The owner will simply abandon the building when he does not have necessary capital or cash flow to manage repairs. It would seem that developers might rush in to the abandoned and deteriorated housings because of the typically low prices. But private contractors or developers find it is impossible to build low- and middle-income tenant housing without subsidies. Private developers will not build profitable luxury apartments in ghetto areas or areas with dilapidated houses.

Despite New York City's rate of progress, it still has need for additional units. It has been estimated that the overcrowding could be reduced with the addition of 135,000 units. There are over 500,000 units deemed inadequate by the U.S. Bureau of Census, and these units need to be either rehabilitated or replaced. About 800,000 units are required on the basis of local New York estimates of the potential renewal market. With the magnitude of the needs noted, the outlook is not bright in terms of adding the necessary units simply because of a steady decline in construction in the last three years. The rate of deterioration is too rapid, and deteriorating units will offset any new constructions at the current rate.

New York has done extremely well in the area of subsidized housing. A large part of the city's housing supply comes about through subsidized rent controls. Tenants paying less than normal rent-income ratios receive subsidies. Most of the people enjoying these subsidies are middle-income families. In apartments under rent control, 68 per cent of the residents earned between $8,000 and $15,000 and paid less than 15 per cent of their income in rent. In buildings constructed since 1946, only 16 per cent of those residents pay this low rent-income ratio. For practical purposes,

New York City is a middle-income city. More than 50 per cent of its households earn between $5,000 and $15,000 a year. The rent subsidies as distributed are inequitable in their impact between middle- and low-income families.

Subsidized housing from direct subsidies accounting for over 200,000 units since the end of World War II has declined when private housing was also cut back. The federally and other publicly aided programs are encumbered by cost limitations. There need to be special efforts in the New York area to speed up the momentum in public- and other-assisted programs. If New York is to make any headway at all in regard to its existing housing problems, change is needed in regard to priorities, in addition to laying out plans for a given number of public housing units per year. Any expectations of increased activity by the private sector must be associated with housing produced on a volume scale with an attractive profit potential.

For the national scene, the New York City case is an instructive microcosm of the problems that militate against long-term success in meeting housing needs. There are, however, a variety of other problem factors that plague the potential effectiveness of federal housing programs. For example, agency personnel and staffing problems are persistent.

Barriers to Progress

Personnel morale of the local housing authorities may be a factor. Programs that run over a long number of years provide for uncertain futures for dedicated people. The dedicated personnel are bid away to other activities rather than wait around for the potential implementation of the responsibilities which they have been assigned. When Congress acts there is no reason to believe that local housing authorities react in the same way for expansion or contraction.

For all the years of public housing since 1949, the real-estate interests, including house builders, realtors, mortgage lenders, and manufacturers, have been outspoken opponents and put forth extensive propaganda against public housing. In the last few years the antipublic housing efforts and propaganda have abated from the earlier extremists' claims, for example, that public housing was communistic, or anti-American, etc. There are very deep roots of opposition to public housing. Despite the fact that many whites still like to exercise their preferences of not wanting to live near the poor or the blacks, a substantial component of the opposition to public housing is economically based. Reasoning is based upon the following rationale. If low-income individuals, especially Negroes, come into a neighborhood, the crime rate climbs and housing is not cared for. This tends to lower real-estate value and to shatter the asset position of individuals who have invested in their own houses. The opposition people may be very normal, tolerant, church-loving, God-fearing people on the one hand, but on the other hand, they worry about their savings, their neighborhoods, their children, and their homes. They may or may not be disturbed to find their prejudices rise to the surface in the area of housing. The trade association and individual criticisms of public-housing programs have been reflected in the attitude of congressmen in dealing with public-housing programs. Congress has reacted to this so-called long, bitter battle and have been less than aggressive (in 1949 and 1968) in pushing for a more vigorous housing program.

The public housing program has been slowed to a faltering walk largely by economic class and racial antagonisms. Other conditions and influences have played considerable parts, but they have been and are relatively secondary. Only more confusion and frustration can come from evading this fact. It would be equally futile either to pretend that some new twist or gimmick in the subsidy formula would make much difference or to condemn out-of-hand all changes in law or administrative procedure, including some combined operation now being tried out in the Model Cities Program.[2]

Model Cities Potential

When the Model Cities program was advocated in 1965, individuals disenchanted with the chaos and the slow pace of federal aid to American cities looked to this program as a radical improvement. The Model Cities program is basically a coordination effort for other urban programs. In addition to providing funds, the federal government acts to develop a partnership relationship between local governments and the people in the neighborhoods who can be benefited, and to draw in private-sector resources from the community to aid. Housing and other characteristics of the urban environment are supposed to be attacked by the Model Cities programs. Education, health, and employment are other critical areas requiring community participation for the solutions-oriented approach. Since becoming law in 1966, more than 150 cities have at least begun the planning process to implement certain kinds of programs. Grants have been made available at the $512.5-million level with another $142 million designated for urban renewal within Model Cities neighborhoods.

There is evidence that the Model Cities program, although it continues to be funded as part of HUD's programs, is bogging down in the traditional problems illustrated in other housing programs since the late 1940's. For example, in Baltimore lack of cooperation and animosity have developed between the private sector and local participating citizens in the Model Cities governing board. Business participation is having difficulties with the Model Cities staff in Washington, D.C. The assessment of local-citizen participation is also negative insofar as selected representatives in the Detroit example would confirm. One of the directors of Detroit's Model Cities program noted that suspicion is strong in the community, because Model Cities proposals entail Negro removal from local neighborhoods. This action plays into the hands of militants who argue that their response would be a repeat of the 1967 riots. It may be necessary for the courts to force the city to listen to neighborhood residents for any effective cooperation in the future in Detroit. Moreover, specific business involvement in activities other than planning is slow in coming in Model Cities neighborhood projects. The attitude in Detroit and Baltimore seems to be that business should become involved, but only when the action starts.[3] It is not unexpected that the black-white confrontation appears with local participation in the Model Cities program. Sar Levitan and Robert H. Davidson have indicated in a study for the OEO that "programs aimed at alleviating poverty are likely to produce increased political participation by the poor. Such participation creates pressures upon established political leaders and may even generate hostility toward poverty programs. Articulate and activist representatives of the poor are bound to clash with the merchants, landlords, welfare officials, and politicians."[4]

It is essential that the white community recognize the response of the blacks in regard to Model Cities participation. It should be informative for white businessmen and other community leaders to recognize the extent to which the blacks are alienated by housing practices of the government and the white community. The thrust for black control may not be negative, except in an organizational sense, if the solutions-oriented approach involves black participation. These local participation groups cannot function effectively if alienation is widespread and if there is a polarization of views, or if the white establishment tends to mistrust or to back out of the black-dominated advisory groups. It is the blacks who should be heard in regard to the manner in which appropriate operational approaches can be developed. After all, local participation in programs means just that. Recognition of particular black needs is necessary, it is superfluous to invite black participation on a purely functional basis. Perhaps of more concern than the administrative dilemmas associated with implementing the Model Cities program is the absence of a willingness of federal authorities to make a full commitment through necessary funding to the organizational processes and other requirements. The estimated financial cost of Model Cities over the next five years is about

$27 billion. There is no assurance that the present Republican administration holds the Model Cities program in such high esteem as did the former Democratic administration. At this time it is estimated that there will be no expansion in the existing level of Model Cities programs from the 150 cities involved. Planning processes need to be coordinated within these cities. Time is needed for an integration of the federal, state, and local programs to improve the planning process. The planning, coordination, and simplification in the 150 cities projects will probably result in no increase in the $100-billion level of outlay until after the fiscal year 1971. The existing cost projections are based on a five-year plan submitted by a sample of the seventy-five "first-round" cities. The program has been even more fragmented since mid-1969, when a smaller budget request was to be spent within entire urban areas instead of on small selected local projects.

The Record—A Challenge

There has been some distinct improvement over the last year or two within public housing as starts rose from the general level of about 30,000 a year to 45,000, or a 50 per cent increase. This is still well below the 60,000 authorization. Rent supplements, leased public housing, and other programs raised the number of units "available for occupancy," as opposed to new starts to a respectable level.[5] In the Housing Act of 1968, Congress seemed to move forward despite the traditional emotional and economic objections to the public-housing program. It may be concluded—but without much optimism—that the potential for improved public housing is enhanced. But the Housing Act of 1968 should be evaluated only as enabling legislation. The Act reflects more the attitude of the administration and the Congress than the general public. Actual increases in the rate of starts stemming from the new private-public coordination necessary for a truly effective public-housing program must await some future evaluation.

Although there are a few new features of the 1968 Act, only

four programs can be termed innovative: (1) the New Communities Act, (2) change in the renewal process to allow a segment-by-segment execution, (3) insurance programs for slums and riot areas, and (4) federal flood insurance for lower-priced homes.[6]

The 1968 Housing Act cannot be a total solution to the housing problem nor, of course, other urban problems. The urban development portions of the program do not recognize the need for dramatically new innovations and ideas. The potential dimension of the scope of the programs is inadequate. It is apparent that most of the positive financial impact will be on middle- and not low-income families. The large quotas of housing starts cannot be met. This Act is the most far-reaching housing legislation ever enacted, but it is still not large enough to deal with the magnitude of the problems. The housing problem is not simply one of building new homes, since related problems associated with a myriad of environmental ills need directed action.

Researchers at the MIT-Harvard Joint Center on Urban Studies have advanced the thesis that

there is nothing less than a complete change in the structure of the metropolis that will solve the problems of the ghetto. Indeed it is ironical, almost cynical, the extent to which current problems that ostensibly are concerned with the welfare of urban Negroes are willing to accept and are even based upon the permanence of the central ghettos. Thus, under every heading, the social welfare legislation, education, income transfer, employment, housing, we find programs that can only serve to strengthen the ghetto and the serious problem that it generates. In particular, these programs concentrate on beautifying the fundamentally ugly structure of the current metropolis and not on providing individuals with tools necessary to break out of that structure.[7]

Earlier chapters of this book reviewed the government's thrust in housing and physical development areas. The assessment of federal activity over the past two decades indicates that problems remain. These problems will persist because housing development is directed toward ghetto beautification rather than a process of changing living and work environments.

Growth in Federal
Manpower Programs

In evaluating what has been accomplished by federal manpower programs, the assessment should be very favorable in
terms of rates of change. The years 1967 to 1970 were eventful
and recorded significant positive changes.

The Rate of Increase in Programs   In 1964, when the Job
Corps first got underway, there were openings for approximately
27,000 men in all government manpower programs. On the basis
of information included in the fiscal year 1970 budget, all manpower programs of the federal government could provide training
for some sort of employment opportunities for approximately 1.4
million men. In 1964 there were only $735 million spent on all
programs. A five-fold dollar increase in programs to increase the
employability of the disadvantaged was made in that six-year
period of time. There are six government agencies or departments
that administer the manpower programs. Labor, Defense, HEW,
and OEO, account for about 95 per cent of the manpower funds.
The U.S. Department of Labor now has the basic (50 per cent)
responsibility for administering the programs, even though only
29 per cent of the funds available for manpower programs were
appropriated directly to the Labor Department in 1970.

From the 1969 to the 1970 budget, manpower program funds
increased $458 million. About 25 per cent of this was for the JOBS
program and another 50-plus per cent was for the Concentrated
Employment Program, the Work Incentive Program, and vocational rehabilitation programs. The federal government, working
through the National Alliance of Businessmen, spent $200 million
to help provide jobs in public-private sector cooperation. Since
1968, approximately 100,000 trainees were semi-permanently
employed through JOBS. The outlook for this program is fairly
good in terms of the extension to a larger number of cities (125),

Table 1 Enrollment Opportunities and Federal Obligations for Training Programs, by Type of Program, Fiscal Years 1963-1968 (in thousands)

Item	Total	FY 1968	FY 1967	FY 1966	FY 1965	FY 1964	FY 1963
Total							
Enrollment opportunities	3,274.5	870.4	866.7	842.2	510.2	125.8	59.2
Federal obligations	$2,823,019	$785,007	$797,143	$628,441	$414,247	$142,111	$56,070
MDTA Institutional Training							
Enrollment opportunities	739.5	114.0	126.0	163.0	167.1	112.5	56.9
Federal obligations	$1,153,880	$216,586	$215,492	$281,710	$249,348	$135,525	$55,219
MDTA On-the-Job Training							
Enrollment opportunities	455.9	104.6	152.9	118.1	64.7	13.3	2.3
Federal obligations	$299,287	$89,837	$106,917	$57,939	$37,157	$6,586	$851
MDTA Part-time and other training							
Enrollment opportunities	8.7	8.3	.4				
Federal obligations	$5,597	$5,501	$96				
Neighborhood Youth Corps							
Enrollment opportunities	1,856.5	537.7	512.7	527.7	278.4		
In school	565.0	135.0	139.0	188.8	102.2		
Out of school	302.3	62.7	79.3	98.6	61.7		
Summer	988.2	339.1	294.3	240.3	114.5		
Work Training in Industry	1.1	.9	.2				

Federal obligations	$1,021,775	$281,863	$348,833	$263,337	$127,742
In school	(a)	58,908	67,448	(a)	(a)
Out of school	(a)	95,889	147,826	(a)	(a)
Summer	(a)	126,677	133,306	(a)	(a)
Work Training in Industry	(a)	390	253	(a)	(a)
Concentrated Employment Program					
Enrollment opportunities	159.6	67.9	58.3	33.4	
Federal obligations	$194,802	$89,743	$79,604	$25,455	
Operation Mainstream					
Enrollment opportunities	18.9	10.9	8.0		
Federal obligations	$45,947	$22,319	$23,628		
New Careers					
Enrollment opportunities	7.1	2.7	4.4		
Federal obligations	$23,130	$7,557	$15,573		
Special Impact					
Enrollment opportunities	8.3	4.3	4.0		
Federal obligations	$18,500	$11,500	$7,000		
JOBS—EOA Funds[b]					
Enrollment opportunities	20.0	20.0			
Federal obligations	$60,101	$60,101			

a Not available.

b The total JOBS Program through June 30, 1968, amounted to 41,880 enrollment opportunities and $114,178,000, including activities reported in other totals shown above: Special Impact—fiscal 1968, 3,050 enrollment opportunities, $9,462,000; MDTA–OJT—fiscal 1968, 9,533 enrollment opportunities, $20,357,000; and fiscal 1967, 9,311 enrollment opportunities, $24,258,000.

Source: Manpower Report of the President, January, 1969, p. 238.

the increase by mid-1971 to 614,000 people affected, and the lower-per-year per-trainee cost.

On-the-Job Training and Incentive Programs On-the-job training (Job Opportunities in Business Sector), initiated in 50 cities, will bring about 252,000 jobs under contract in the two-and-a-half years during which the program has been in effect. The estimated number of people who will be served in 1970 is ten times the number served in 1968.

Additional selected "on-the-job training" administered by the Manpower and Development Training Administration, increased the number of trainees by 48,000 in 1968. The government then paid over $43 million for training materials for supplementary classroom instruction. This type of on-the-job training programs has risen from $44 million in 1966 to $450-plus million in 1970, or from about 2 per cent to about 13 per cent of total manpower outlays. The Neighborhood Youth Corps in-school and summer programs were planned to have about 375,000 enrollees (at a cost of $185 million) during the fiscal year 1970. The Neighborhood Youth Corps out-of-school program, with its work experience and related services for unemployed youth, was expected to enroll about 115,000 youths and young adults in 1970 at an outlay estimated at $136 million. The OEO Department of Labor operation Mainstream, a program for older workers in rural areas, was also to expand. By 1970, approximately 15,000 enrollees were to have participated in Mainstream activities through an outlay of approximately $38 million. The combined work incentives programs and CEP programs will have increased from $25 million in 1968 to $118 million in 1970. WIN and CEP were to have served about 170,000 people during 1970. This is a sharp increase from the 22,000 involved in the program in 1968. All work-support programs involved approximately 780,000 people during the fiscal year 1970.

Careers and Incentives Modest increases in the number of individuals affected were to have occurred in the New Careers program. New Careers, which provides training opportunities for the poor in subprofessional public service jobs with a long-term career emphasis. The number of participants increased from only 12,000 to 20,000 between 1968 and 1970. The outlay for those career-ladder jobs was expected to increase from $24 million in 1968 to $38 million in 1970.

The industry incentive, or the special-impact program of the Department of Labor, which provides financial incentives for the location of plants in ghettos and reimburses employers to train the disadvantaged in these plants, was set to affect only about 10,000 people in 1970. This was a significant relative gain from 3,000 in 1968. Funds for that incentive program have about doubled in the three-year period of time.

Improved Coordination Perhaps the most significant new emphasis in government manpower activity is the coordination of the programs. In 1967, the CAMP Program was initiated to coordinate and plan manpower programs among federal, state, and local governments. In 1970, CEP, the manpower arm of Model Cities, was to provide manpower services in eighty-two urban and rural areas and will affect about 115,000 people. Approximately 50,000 of those will be referred to JOBS and other programs. Federal government has improved labor-market information, including national occupational trends, local labor-market studies, and specific data; and local job opportunities, primarily through MDTA budget authority. Outlays rose from about $2 million in 1969 to $14 million in 1970. The coordination and operation of local programs improved by providing training and technical assistance to staff, primarily under the MDT Act for which the budget authority of $14 million was sought.

Beginning in 1969, most of the Department of Labor's manpower services were funded through single sponsors as required by the comprehensive work and training program provision of the Economic Opportunity Act. In most cases, the Community Action programs coordinated the delivery of all of these services. The Work Incentive programs, started in 1968, were another of the federal government's coordination efforts. By 1970, the WIN program, which also provided child care and related services to public assistance recipients and welfare recipients, was to serve approximately 175,000 people. These welfare recipients were referred directly to jobs, and those who are not job-ready get basic education, training, and work experience to ready them for employment. This, and other manpower programs, are estimated to aid approximately an additional 400,000 welfare recipients.

In 1970, the Model Cities program expanded to about 150 cities. This program was expected to make a major contribution to manpower objectives by contributing to the capacity of the federal government to deliver total social services in the demonstration areas.

The Nixon Administration continued the pattern of consolidation of manpower programs in 1970, but added a new dimension—decentralization. The move for more consolidation and local manpower delivery systems eliminated the Office of Economic Opportunity from operational responsibility. All manpower programs were pulled together in the Department of Labor by a comprehensive manpower training act funded at the $2.3 billion level. Eighty per cent of the funds were for programs implemented by state and local governments and the remaining 20 per cent was used for national programs.

Decentralization of the administration of manpower programs requires state governors to determine the use of manpower program resources, to develop state comprehensive plans in the manpower area, to monitor performance after programs are implemented and to assure distribution of manpower services in rural as well as urban areas. Governors may appoint local administrators as sponsors unless a locality elects otherwise. Mayors in participating urban areas have similar responsibilities for manpower programs in urban areas. Funding for state and local programs is on an incremental basis with a state receiving initial funds when it designates a sponsoring agency and has developed comprehensive plans. Additional funding occurs when a state sets up an agency to operate "unified" programs plus a council to coordinate related programs and arranges to name mayors as sponsors. The remainder of the financing is received when a state meets "objective standards of exemplary performance in planning and carrying out its manpower service system."

Although the manpower program consolidation effort of the Nixon Administration included several needed features such as a computerized national job bank to match job vacancies and job seekers, and automatic increases in expenditures for manpower training as unemployment rises to critical levels, the comprehensive manpower concept may be neutralized by administrative problems. Decentralization actually increased rather than decreased the number of administrative agencies implementing manpower training programs. Decentralization places unique responsibility for innovation, imagination, and good management in the hands of local officials. Although the Secretary of Labor has extensive financial power to enforce local government efficacy, the effectiveness of the total manpower delivery system depends upon local government formulation and administration of specific manpower training programs. It is debatable whether or not the need for increased coordination of manpower training programs will be facilitated or impaired by decentralizing the delivery system. The Nixon Administration efforts were clearly designed to reduce the bureaucratic complexity of extensive and fragmented manpower training programs. But a new more complex and unwieldy state and local bureaucracy may undermine the newly designed delivery system.

The Program Emphases— The Poor

In 1968 there were approximately 11 million individuals who could benefit from manpower programs as the vehicle to escape poverty circumstances. About 3 million lived in urban areas and two fifths, or 4.5 million, of the potential enrollees were non-white, Mexican-Americans, or Puerto Ricans. Among the actual participants, 86 per cent were poor as compared to 11 per cent of the total labor force. In the total labor force, approximately 39 per cent did not have high-school diplomas. In manpower programs, 80 per cent of the participants had not graduated from high school. Only about 1 per cent of the total general labor force were welfare recipients, while 23 per cent of the manpower program trainees and enrollees were on welfare programs. The manpower programs have moved to increase their concentration on nonwhites who have special employment problems. Of the participants in manpower programs 44 per cent are now nonwhite.

In 1966, in the MDTA on-the-job program, only 15.4 per cent, or about 39,151, of the people involved were nonwhite. In the work experience and training programs, only 37.5 per cent, or about 67,000, were nonwhite. In the MDTA institutional programs, only 38.2 per cent were nonwhite. The Neighborhood Youth Corps, regular and summer, had slightly higher percentages of nonwhites. Regular Youth Corps had 46 per cent, the summer youth program, 52 per cent. The Job Corps had the largest number of nonwhite participants, approximately 41,500 involved; 69 per cent of these were nonwhite. The manpower training programs of the federal government do seem to be involving the hard-core unemployed. At least the programs are now so designed to potentially affect the youths, the welfare recipient, and the educationally disadvantaged. The record, as far as commitment of the federal government in the area of manpower training, is impressive. It should be noted, however, that the magnitude of the task involved requires an even greater effort.

The Magnitude
of the Task

Since 1968 the economy has typically created new jobs at the rate of about a million and a half a year. The Kerner Report recommended that in the next three years from the date of its publication the private sector and the public sector should produce an additional 2 million jobs.

The private sector has not been able to produce that number

of new jobs, nor has it been able to accommodate the hard-core unemployed. The rate of creation of private-sector jobs under the JOBS program will not meet the Kerner Report's required objective, nor will it deal effectively with all the people who need manpower programs.

Perhaps of greater significance in the development of employment opportunities is that the federal government continues to rely more and more on private-sector cooperation to create job opportunities. The government is funding programs such as on-the-job training under both the JOBS approach and purely public training programs in such a way that the private sector is required to accommodate an increasingly larger number of the hard-core unemployed. The New Careers program of the federal government and the Neighborhood Youth Corps, as examples of the "employer-of-the-last-resort" efforts, have not expanded at the same rate as private sector-subsidized job openings.

Another concern is whether or not men are being trained in such a way that they can stay in the labor force. The JOBS retention experience to date is not encouraging. Approximately 135,000 of the hard core have actually been involved in JOBS programs, and there are approximately 100,000 of these remaining on the job.

Of greater concern is the nature of the employment opportunities made available in JOBS and other NAB programs. A report by the Council of Economic Advisors noted that manpower programs over the last five years have been involved with skills that may or may not be of critical concern for our system. Only 18 per cent of participants were trained in skills deemed critical to the economy.

Vocational education programs have been training about 5 per cent of their enrollees for health and technical occupations. Yet, enrollment in vocational agriculture has remained constant over the past several years in spite of the fact that there has been a very persistent drop in the number of agricultural employment opportunities.

James Boggs commented on the types of jobs made available

in the core area of Detroit. Boggs implied that many jobs created in Detroit by programs to aid the hard-core unemployed can be eliminated through increased automation. These firms were creating employment in a noneconomic way; people were not actually needed for their productive activity. Boggs calls these industries— which should be automating rapidly, but are slowing the pace to handle token employment activity—dying industries. Programs such as JOBS should be oriented toward occupations that will be in existence as the technological base of the system changes. At best, most of these current jobs are in the "last-hired, first-fired" category.

Crucial to all the manpower-employment programs is the issue of whether or not skill-level improvement, easier job access, and higher-paying jobs are really what the black wants as the method of sharing in the wealth and economic accretion of the system. There is a dichotomy between the white majority and the black participants in manpower programs *vis à vis* the objectives of economic programs.

Ghetto Industrialization

In the programs with new plant locations in the ghetto for white or black firms, there are relatively few firms—perhaps twenty—which have initiated programs. The number of employees hired in white-based ghetto industries is extremely small. This number is extremely significant because it raises a question about the commitment to this method of attack on ghetto ills. Whether or not jobs can really be created more effectively by locating industries near the homes of the unemployed, or whether people ought to be moved to where existing jobs will develop within established enterprises, is a basic dilemma. The alternative costing question of establishing jobs within the ghetto or having the ghetto move out to employment options has never been answered satisfactorily. Locating plants in ghetto areas does not actually increase net new jobs, in the economy. These plants typically reallocate existing job openings. Ghetto economic development that simply shifts resources to provide economic development in a ghetto is inefficient and thus high cost. It is highly questionable whether or not the output of these firms is needed in terms of increased demand or whether normal market demand generated the need for the facility. A fundamental point should be underscored in regard to both the employment training of the private sector and the public sector and the thrust for economic development: If the private sector of the economy does not have demand generated for the purchase of its products, the creation of jobs and the training for jobs cannot be long lived. The economic functions really determine whether or not job creation should occur according to the needs of the system to purchase the products that are being produced. Earlier sections of this survey have indicated the high-cost characteristic of establishing plants in a ghetto area. Therefore, the arguments are weak for ghetto industrialization with an artificial base either by the federal government or the white business community. If the question is, "What is gained economically for the system, or for the Negro himself?" the answer is that job-location within the ghetto does not significantly produce positive results. A more important issue is the fact that the Negro may not identify with this general approach, which is controlled by the white community and establishes white-dominated employment options within the black community.

The Slow Pace of White Corporation Programs

The majority of white corporations' efforts in ghetto economic improvement or development are characterized by unique examples, as opposed to broad-gauged construction, in changing and rehabilitating the urban areas. Despite the fact that the U.S. Gypsum's much-publicized example illustrates a business commitment to changing the physical environment of the ghetto (see Chapter 6, p. 156), there are few other examples where the private sector has successfully embarked upon a ghetto development project.

The number of white firms participating in employment, training, and work-related education programs has increased significantly in the past two years. There is evidence of at least a numerical commitment to improving the economic condition of the urban ills by that white-majority community. Despite the rapid increase in the number of firms announcing participation in these employment and training programs, the number of Negroes affected by private-sector programs not subsidized by the federal government is extremely small. The white business-supported employment and training programs are not increasing at a pace rapidly enough to significantly affect the large number of blacks who need employment opportunities.

The total number of corporations participating is extremely small if compared to the total number of white corporations. The number of hard-core individuals hired, trained, and promoted in any corporation is small compared to the total employees of any represented company. Although many employers are still hiring disadvantaged individuals who are black and in other minority groups, there are probably other employers involved because of government and civil rights pressure. Except for a few unique programs, workers who are included in company programs usually have been selected and are from the best of the large pool of unemployed and underemployed.[8]

For the black, economic development from whatever source is not an end in or of itself. The black wants economic development as a technique to achieve social and political as well as economic ends. The white majority must recognize also that there is no homogeneity of purpose among the activists who design economic development programs. The black cannot be characterized as having unilateral ends in his focus on economics. In terms of the overall direction and impact of these ghetto development programs, no single program can alleviate the distortion and resource malallocation that has adversely affected urban growth during the last decade.

In terms of the pace of implementation of these industrialization programs, particularly those initiated by black groups, there is little evidence that the programs can have any significant immediate or short-run effect upon the economic plight of the Negro, simply because of inadequate funding. The progress in implementing most black-initiated economic programs has been painfully slow and discouraging.

Slow Progress of Black Programs

The National Business League's programs in creating entre-preneurship opportunities are moving at about the same pace enjoyed historically. Their efforts to create the basic training needed to enter into small enterprises is an example of an unful-filled need because it affects only a very small number of blacks. The Urban League's employment-related or job-placement apprenticeship programs continue to function at about the same level as in the past three years.

The Sullivan OIC effort, which has received support from the Urban Coalition, is not hampered by the lack of funds and is receiving increased funding from the federal government for more programs in other cities. The OIC is, however, encountering com-petition from expansion of federal manpower programs, but is receiving limited moral and financial support from the Nixon administration. The OIC's have been criticized for "creaming," that is, taking the most employable and the best educated. OIC has moved only moderately to increase the number of hard core in its training programs. The OIC approach is a unique "bright symbol" in black efforts to improve employment and business opportunities.

The National Business League's modular core or revitalization for urban blighted areas has not been funded and is not underway on a significant scale in any metropolitan area. This program is in the planning stages. President Burrell is still attempting to interest local groups in this type of development and improvement scheme.

The National Urban League's broad-gauged proposals on rural economic development, inner-city economic development, welfare, housing, and income maintenance rely almost exclusively on future federal government funding.

The A. Philip Randolph Institute proposal for a Freedom Budget has not been implemented and requires a change in attitude as well as a change in funding by the federal government. The Vietnamese War has virtually eliminated any possibility of government funding.

The actions of the federal government do not foster optimism about federal ability, capacity, or intent to implement broad-gauged, massive programs to affect the subsidiary as well as the primary economic problems of the Negro.

The NAACP has not yet developed an economic program. Its chief interest is in the important area of employment discrimination as it relates to the 1964 civil-rights legislation. The NAACP is organizing existing Negro businessmen to cooperate or to participate in federal housing programs that may be funded in the next few years.

The community corporations' approach, which is a broad-gauged, and the omnibus neighborhood development opportunity are not moving significantly into new and broader areas. It is true that in the spring of 1969 the East Central Citizens Organization, that very successful illustration of a neighborhood corporation in Columbus, Ohio, has rehabilitated several houses and made plans for a neighborhood retail store. But these products are modest and reflect a slow evolutionary pace of attack on the obvious ghetto ills.

Diversity of Groups
to be Served

The economic programs advocated by nonmilitant blacks to "make it in the system" have many of the same basic characteristics as programs advocated by the militant blacks. The processes and sources of capital are the same and function may be similar, but differences occur in whether or not there is a design for a separate black entity or for economic integration. All these black proposals are aimed at raising incomes by expanding business opportunities, sharing in business ownership, or improving skill levels to obtain higher-income jobs. Any evaluation of manpower and economic development programs should include social, financial, and conceptual issues as well as assessment of the format of the specific programs.

Although these programs are designed for the benefit of blacks, there are at least three distinct and diverse social classes represented in the black group; loosely categorized as the black middle class, the black student youths in universities, and black city youths, typically unemployed or on the streets. Members of the black middle class are almost part of the system and include businessmen, politicians, professionals, and ministers. Most black university youths are probably preparing to move into the system after their struggles for black power at the university.

The other youth segment may still be in school or may be working in unskilled jobs. Large numbers are in the armed forces and about a third are unemployed. Unlike the black middle-class student or businessman working to build black economic and political power through cooperation and financial association with the white power structure, these youth groups are engaged in preparing for confrontation and/or struggle against the white establishment. The struggle is for control of schools, industry and employment, housing, health, police, and most institutions inside the black community. The black youths' activities seem to be centered on real grievances, that is, typical everyday hardships suffered not only on the job but in the streets, in schools, at the welfare office, and in hospitals. The black youths recognize that the struggle is not with one or another individual, but against the whole power structure comprising politicians, school administrators, landlords, businessmen, realtors, contractors, union leaders, local bureaucrats, and so forth. The majority of those involved in these occupations are white, absentee, and looked upon by black youth as exploiters of the ghetto in much the same way as the colonial powers are regarded as exploiters of colonies. These youth take a position that is consciously anticapitalist; that is, they have no use for any person, black or white, who attempts to make a profit from the black community. The elimination of the profit system is probably considered as a component of black liberation. For black youth, this means a repudiation of the racist American capitalist system. Because this group is committed to the repudiation of the economic system, it is considered as revolutionary. It is difficult to determine the nature of the political system or the economic system which would be substituted or the method by which any new system would be implemented. There are no other patterns of revolution from which they can borrow or that can apply to an advanced economy like the United States. For this black group this country is economically and technically advanced but underdeveloped in regard to tolerance of racism. In general, any fundamental change in the American system must begin with the concept of the individual as being responsible for creating the social environment. However, personal political values cannot be developed in private or in secret, but in a relationship with others with whom he shares a sense of community. The course of actual and continuing struggle will conflict with people in power.[9] The perspective operative is the taking of power, which brings them the authority and the responsibility to create new types of social institutions. From the black-power advocates and the activities of these new youth on the streets, a new perspective of society appears. All the institutions of twentieth-century America would be completely transformed if this perspective were implemented.

Some black economic development programs, such as the CORE program, are subject to all the same economic constraints of the white ghetto industries, but have the advantage of being originated by militants. The CORE program is in jeopardy in Congress. There is only a doubtful chance that this program will be funded by the federal government, or that the white business community is willing to participate in the rather circuitous route of establishing black businesses under the CORE Development Corporation format.

The element of black power or the concept of black control in CORE's program should be considered by the white policy-makers as essential for an effective undertaking that has long-term support by the blacks. The idea of black power or black pride may be an essential element in any long-term, successful, development program. Black control, or at least black participation, is probably a necessity if these programs are to affect the young hard-core unemployed. There is a generic element in theories of development, which is the need for cohesiveness of participants in that program. If, in the short run, this cohesiveness helps programs that have elements of potential progress for the black, then black-power control or black control is necessary.

The Question of Black Power

Studies in the sociology and economics of development indicate that cultural and institutional changes are prerequisites for the development process in both the social and economic dimensions. One precondition for development is a sense of cultural pride or identity, such as nationalism, which can overcome traditional cultural constraints to attain high achievement and motivation in the populace. Viewed in this perspective, emphasis on "black power" and "black pride" is a coherent step in establishing pre-conditions for social and economic development of the Negro.

In the current focus on black separatism, a direct relationship is assumed between the acquisition of control over economic means and the acquisition of social and political leverage. This is an unsubstantiated assumption. Economic development alone has not been the panacea by which other minority groups have achieved social and political power or gained admittance to the institutional structure of American society. Even if economic integration into the American society is not the goal, the assumption that self-determination for the black populace can be achieved through economic power is critical. There are international examples of countries whose influential weight in world politics is disproportionate to their economic base. If this assumption of the relationship between economic wealth and political power is valid, the economic emphasis in the Negro movement is in part a pragmatic adjustment to the reality of a serious defect in American democracy.

Another issue is related to the nature of the business forms and their relationship to power. The simplest form of black businesses, which could be and is now being successfully established, is the small retail or service proprietorships. However, the economic power derived from this type of activity cannot be effective unless it represents an overall increase in individual economic welfare with an aggregate increase in economic power. The presence of small black retail firms in ghetto areas would mollify the contention that white retail firms in these areas cause all surplus and investable funds to flow out of the ghetto for non-ghetto economic development. This is an unexamined premise. The share of funds retained in the ghetto may or may not be greater if firms were black-owned and -operated, and only comparative analysis of actual cases would substantiate this. It is probable that any increase in the share of funds retained within the ghetto would be only the owner's profit. The black owners must spend and invest within the black community. The remainder and most of the cash flow of these firms would be paid out for inventory purchases, advertising expenditures, taxes, labor costs, etc. At this time, only the wage payments would remain in the ghetto. This occurs usually whether the firm is white- or black-owned (assuming that white businessmen would hire Negro employees).

An alternative is the concentration on black ownership of industrial firms. The size of these undertakings and the associated economic power could be significant. The capitalization for industrial activities of large size would be obtained by the dispersal of ownership through sale of shares of stock. But there is a fairly complete separation tendency, particularly in the ownership in corporations, from effective stockholder control. The actual economic power represented by widely dispersed ownership is probably not very significant.

The assumption of correspondence between acquisition of economic power and political and social leverage is critical. If this relationship can be verified, then the successful development of economic power is essential to the aspirations of both militants and nonmilitants. It is imperative that the modes of economic development undertaken have the greatest possibility for success. It is important that the assumptions under which economic development is undertaken be verified and the means chosen be effective.

Kain and Persky of Harvard have made several careful studies of the various economic development programs designed to attack the sources of economic deprivation of the Negro. Their comments are illuminating and potentially helpful:

Despite the urgency of the current situation, alternative policies must be evaluated in terms of their long-run impact. The selection of specific program tools should be governed by a careful definition of the underlying problems. Few existing programs have such a legitimate birth.

. . . . .

The Negro in this country clearly faces a broad range of pressing problems, problems that challenge the basic structure of our social and physical environment. While there are many proposals and counterproposals aimed at the ultimate solution, it is clear now that no easy way out exists.[10]

Limited Progress

Any assessment of the outlook for the success of black economic development programs must be cautiously pessimistic. In the past two years symbolic progress in the attack on the problems that make the Negro disadvantaged has occurred. National Negro organizations reflect a vital concern with the economic plight of the Negro by identifying a series of causal factors in programs oriented toward the eventual removal of economic ills. In a symbolic way, the existence of these programs is a sign of progress in the manner in which the Negro has elected to deal with economic ills. In white corporate programs, the incidence of the number of firms, and the variety of programs now in existence, are symbolic reflections of a recognition of the nature of deprivations that face black Americans. The expansion of federal government manpower programs to include a larger number of individuals and a relatively larger number of the hard-core unemployed is also the basis for a positive evaluation of the "symbolism of efforts" to improve the economic lot of the Negro.

The black may in fact be looking toward this symbolic evidence of progress as the essential sign of the willingness of the American people to alter predispositions on discrimination and implicit racism. But unfortunately, symbolism is not implementation. Symbolic efforts will not change the steady course of the movement of the American system toward separate black and white communities.

On the practical matter of the progress made in implementing black development programs, it is necessary to separate the programs into the two elemental types referred to in earlier chapters of this book: (1) those programs that emphasize jobs employment access or skills training, and (2) those programs that are oriented toward the economic development of the black community, within or without the system, through the control of economic resources, either by individuals as entrepreneurs or by the black community as a whole. Most positive progress has occurred in the jobs-oriented programs, which are the most traditional way of improving the blacks' economic position. The Urban League's job-placement and apprenticeship program is progressing at about the same rate and has been receiving funds from the federal government and private agencies for implementation.

Increasingly more federal efforts have been devoted to the jobs-oriented approach through programs administered under the Manpower Development and Training Act. The progress in the JOBS program, as a reflection of increased private sector–public sector cooperation, increased the number of job options available to the unemployed. It should be noted, however, that federal-government support of manpower programs were reassessed in late 1969. President Nixon proposed a reorganization of the Job Corps, which eliminated most of the training centers. A small number of new training centers were established but tied to existing manpower training programs. The JOBS program under the Nixon administration would continue to provide additional jobs with the government paying any special training costs incurred by public agencies that hire the hard-core unemployed. Despite the steady expansion in the number of individuals participating in federal manpower programs, enrollment opportunities in all federal training programs will not surpass a cumulative eight-year total of 3.2 million until the fiscal year 1970. Federal assistance manpower programs, however, will have approximately 1.2 or 1.7 million first-time enrollees in fiscal year 1970. Despite the increase in the number of people involved in these programs, there will still be approximately 250,000 nonwhites unemployed in poverty areas and 170,000 nonwhites unemployed outside of poverty areas. The nonwhite unemployment rate in central cities will continue in the short run at about 7 per cent, with the teen-age unemployment rate about four times higher. The unemployment rate for nonwhites in American suburbs will remain, in the short run, at about 7 per cent. At issue in the federal employment programs is the rate at which the federal government continues to expand programs designed uniquely for the hard-core urban unemployed. On the basis of several years' experience of JOBS and other similar private-public cooperation efforts, the federal government relies more and more heavily on private sector-created job opportunities for placing the hard-core unemployed. There is ample evidence in the case of Ford and other automobile manufacturers, who have participated in the JOBS program that the hard-core workers are the first to be "laid off" during cutbacks in production. These job openings are not provided in response to "normal" economic demand for productive resources, but are artificially created jobs that have no long-term tenure either because of exigencies of economic conditions or because of the rapid outdating of skills required. In terms of jobs created exclusively by the private sector, there is no indication that the private sector is willing to undertake employment programs of the magnitude necessary to significantly reduce the number of hard-core unemployed or to provide jobs of the type that would significantly improve the earnings of people who have been traditionally unable to maintain a steady stream of income. White corporations that have established industries in ghetto areas to provide local employment options has created an insignificant number of new employment opportunities. The magnitude of the white effort is not large enough.

In all the job-oriented approaches there have been no well-designed efforts to serve the peculiar and particular needs of the young Negro, age 19 to 24. This problem is crucial because this youth group is more prone to aggressive activity in militant separatist organizations. No effective employment solutions can be implemented without emphasis on the needs of this group of young unemployables, a disenchanted group that has not been affected by the jobs-oriented approach.

There are fewer reasons for optimism about the rate of progress in the elimination of poverty in the case of the economic development programs advocated by the black and white community. No black development program has been funded. Thus, none of the broad-gauged economic development programs which could provide resource control for a large number of the indigent population has been implemented. The CORE program, which is highly structured and well designed, is in limbo in the congressional-committee labyrinth. No other program has been able to produce even symbolic evidence of implementation.

The black capitalism thrust of the National Business League continues at about the same pace. It is through NBL programs that the most extensive evidence of the establishment of small black businesses has occurred.

One important reason why black capitalism of the NBL type has not increased the number of establishments has been the change in policy environment in the Commerce Department and the Small Business Administration. Under former SBA head, Howard Samuels, the Small Business Administration's Project OWN made a brief, but satisfactory record in the financing of minority enterprises. Prior to late 1968, the SBA exhibited a dismal record of support of small black businesses. In fiscal year 1968, only 1,700 out of 13,000 loans by SBA were for minority-owned businesses. In that same fiscal year only $30 million, or 3.7 per cent, of the $800 million in direct, shared, guaranteed loans went to minority-owned businesses. In August, 1968, Project OWN was initiated. Although Project OWN was not a magic formula to correct past years of neglect, it did make an impressive record in the few months in which it was effectively managed. For example, the number of minority loans increased dramatically in the first three months of OWN's operation. The rate of minority loans tripled. Private-sector cooperation and participation in making minority loans increased sixfold. A managerial assistance program was initiated as a logical first step in providing private-sector managerial assistance to the minority businesses. A black and Spanish-American advisory-council system had been established. This advisory group seemed to be functioning and participating in making suggestions for changes in government-loan policy.

But the actions of the federal government during the first half of 1969 failed to match this record or the campaign promises on black capitalism. President Nixon had called for programs on black capitalism. He indicated that an imaginative enlistment of private funds, private agencies, and private talents were needed to develop opportunities of Negro businesses. But the federal government moved away from willingness to make high-risk loans to minority businesses. The concept of compensatory capitalism, which had provided guidelines for financing minority businesses during Samuel's period, assumed that high risks are acceptable for higher priority social and economic objectives. It now appears that the Nixon officials have pulled back because of concern with the loss rate of loans to minority businesses. The loss rates on loan to minority businesses is about four times higher than for white-owned businesses. But it should be noted that on a cost-effectiveness basis, regardless of the loss rate of the loan, a program using compensatory capitalism principles is an extremely low-cost method of achieving selected economic and social objectives within the inner city.

The loans made under Project OWN are declining in number and are far below targets. Furthermore, the dollar volume of loans to minority-owned businesses has stabilized well below the target. Insufficient progress has been made in involving the private sector in programs to provide needed managerial assistance to potential black and minority businessmen. It is necessary to close the "management gap" as well as the poverty gap.

There is no apparent real effort on the part of the federal government to reduce the fragmented federal effort to aid minority businesses. The Nixon administration inherited this fragmented approach from the earlier Democratic administration. President Nixon did ask his Secretary of Commerce to help coordinate government efforts, but the Office of Minority Business is still a separate office in both the Commerce Department and the Small Business Administration. There is still no effective coordination of minority programs in Washington. There is inadequate financing and no policy commitment to the black-capitalism concept. Unless more money is forthcoming and administration coordination is improved, and until there is a full commitment in policy actions, there is no basis to assume that small business enterprises will receive increasing support from the federal government.

The federal government's role in the development of the infra-structures is tied principally to education and housing programs. For fiscal year 1970, the Republican administration reduced requests for appropriations by $1.25-billion for the Model Cities Program, in addition to a $1.25-billion reduction for urban renewal. An amount of $7 million was dropped from the Johnson budget request for rent supplements, and this was reduced to a total of only $23 million. A $75-million reduction was requested in special grants for Model Cities. The administration expanded the scope of the Model Cities Program from the central city core and pro-vided for an increase in block grants to the locality that makes the initial use of the money. In total, the request for housing programs will be slightly higher than in the fiscal year 1969, but will be less than the amount requested by the former Demo-cratic administration in their fiscal year 1970 budget. But well-established, institutionalized resentments plus insufficient funding of public housing militate against any short-term improvement in the number of low-cost homes or rental residences available for the central-city black. The short-run outlook, then, for improvements in the housing environment for Negroes is not bright. Particular problems associated with reallocating responsibility and redesign-ing administrative structures further reduce the probability that the intent of the Housing Act of 1968 or Model Cities Act can be realized at the pace suggested when these programs were enacted. In terms of design and quality of the housing under these pro-grams, the total housing and living environment within the ghetto will not be changed. Establishing residences and employment and development opportunities within the ghetto itself is not a feasible way of eliminating the root causes or the factors that account for black economic deprivation.

In the period since blacks have become oriented toward their own economic problems, there has been symbolic progress, and little else. The rate of progress in implementation of programs has been intolerably slow, and the incipient poverty and other institu-tionalized causes of deprivation have not been dissipated. Economic conditions have, however, improved for the working, middle-class Negro. But the pace of change in socioeconomic status for the hard-core unemployable is imperceptive. Furthermore, the only feasible manner now available for the black youth, the unemployables, and for the aggressively competitive able and skilled black worker to gain economic improvement or advancement is through the evolutionary upward path within white institutions. There are no unique opportunities yet available for black resource control through individual or cooperative entrepreneurship. There are no functioning development schemes for blacks other than those that also function for the more institutionally favored white.

The Kerner Report thesis that the nation is moving toward two distinct systems is not challenged by events of the past two years, despite an expanding number of private- and public-sector economic programs. Action by the public and the private sector is still inadequate. Some of the economic programs are ill-conceived and inoperative or implemented only at great cost. The cost is too high in terms of the malallocation of resources or in terms of economic efficiency for the benefits that result. Economic development programs, or programs that improve the economic position of the Negro, cannot produce the power base necessary to bring about the pattern of policies necessary to solve the Negroes' economic ills. On the larger question of origin and type of appropriate policies, the next chapter provides some pathways to the development of an aggregate approach oriented toward the restructuring of the environment within which these economic ills are exhibited.

CHAPTER 10

Future Tasks —A New Urban Policy

It is the current tragedy of the United States that the simultaneous problems of racism, poverty, and the declining inner city confront the society and challenge its cohesiveness. Any one of these problems taxes the ability of our society to find creative and effective remedial solutions or to free the resources that will be necessary to alleviate them. Moreover, any one problem probably taxes our willingness to deal directly and effectively with it. "Willingness" is perhaps the more critical issue, because the system possesses the economic and innovative capacity to undertake solution-oriented programs.

There is no option or luxury of confronting these issues one at a time. The problems that confront our society are now of critical

For Notes to Chapter 10 see pages 349–351.

dimensions. The action imperative cannot be denied if the society is to be preserved in its present institutional form. These three great domestic crises are integrally related and cannot be separated. The failures of past and present solution-oriented policies indicate that any meaningful and effective action must be comprehensive. To continue to approach each of these problems exclusive of their interrelationship with the others is futile. The existence of the three issues simultaneously and cumulatively compounds the adverse effects. The magnitude of the crisis is greater than the sum of its integral parts.

In addition, the foreign crisis in Vietnam aggravates the triad of domestic problems. The economic demands of the war have drained resources and impaired the ability and willingness to undertake a massive, comprehensive solution of the domestic problems. The government demand for goods and services for the Vietnam War, plus the high level of consumer and investment demand, has created an undesirable rate of inflation. Priorities have been established to attempt to control inflation. These policies have in turn eliminated the possibility of a large public-sector financial commitment for the solution of this triad of domestic problems.

Inflation constitutes a "cruel tax" on most individuals in the society. But the attempt to control this inflation also has severe adverse effects on people with incomes below the poverty level. A slowdown in economic expansion cannot be accomplished without the cost of increased unemployment. Those who will become unemployed first will be those who have only recently been absorbed into the productive sector of the economy, whether through the increasing economic prosperity or through jobs and skills-training programs. The policy of firing those who were most recently hired negates the positive effects of the manpower programs, which are the most effective of all antipoverty techniques presently employed.[1] Thus the Vietnam War and the resulting inflation create conditions that militate against implementing meaningful programs to alleviate domestic problems.

For years prior to the war, the problems of poverty and the

Negro were long ignored or unseen. There has been a lack of effective organization of individuals concerned with these problems. Their inability to demand vociferously the recognition of the social and economic disparities existing in this country and their threat to the systems of special privileges existing within the society has now been ended. Black groups now demand that social and economic impoverishment be recognized. They are no longer willing to wait for the benefits of increased economic prosperity to trickle down to them as future productive components in the economic system. Society is no longer able to ignore poverty and economic disparities. The imperatives for effective action on social and economic impoverishment of a large segment of the population are clear. The need for a humane society with social justice is obvious to most Americans. In addition, blacks of a more radical or militant posture are willing to disrupt or to destroy the structures of society if they do not gain a meaningful place in economic and social institutions. For the society as a whole, additional time and an evolutionary process are luxuries no longer permitted. The urgency in both the mood and circumstances of the impoverished must be dealt with through a sense of crisis.

The existence of a racial and economic ghetto is not a new phenomenon in America's urban environment. The existence of the inner city, the circumstances of life within it, and the unrest of the urban poor and the Negro have now become an integral part of the overall crisis developing in large metropolitan areas. Immediate attention was focused upon the plight of the ghetto after the riots of the summer of 1967. The Report of the National Advisory Commission of Civil Disorders highlighted the conditions of the inner city for the millions of citizens who had been oblivious to the tragedy of life in these areas. In the ghetto of a large urban area, the high rates of physical deterioration, the diseconomies in transportation and other public services, the staggering fiscal problems, the increasing mood of psychological frustration, and the deterioration of the environmental quality of the urban areas are elements of the impending crisis in the functioning of metropolitan areas. The cities have become the newest frontier in America. The myriad of problems of these urban areas, stemming from rapid, unplanned growth and equally rapid deterioration, have created a challenge to be met with effective and concentrated action. It is not an overstatement to say that the battle for the survival of America's metropolitan areas is now enjoined. The luxury of time to cope in an evolutionary fashion with these problems cannot be permitted.

The existence and interaction of racism, poverty, and the declining inner city, which are incredibly complex issues, make three factors quite clear. First, the problems are crucial and demand immediate solutions, which does not permit a leisurely approach or postponement until the country can be disengaged from the Vietnam War. Second, any meaningful approach must be on a massive scale. The problems cannot be fragmented or dealt with as separate and independent problems. Any effective solution will demand a massive reallocation of resources and a national commitment. Third, the effective remedial policy must be comprehensive, unified, and coordinated. Identification of particular aspects of any one problem and unidimensional programs to meet these specific elements are no longer sufficient. A successful approach must include the diverse facets of each problem while retaining recognition of the interrelatedness in the coordination of remedial activity. Only a unified national policy will be effective.

The Need for Research

At this juncture, the lack of insight or understanding of the complexity and the interrelatedness of these problems and the absence of essential research are critical. Our understanding of the dimensions of the problems and their relationships is deficient. It is problematic and probabilistic to design solutions for a poorly understood problem. It is critical that additional research be undertaken to increase understanding of the complexities of the issues. The imperatives and urgency of these problems will not allow the time necessary to undertake careful and systematic studies. It is necessary that some procedure be designated which will "buy" the time to complete these studies. One technique for "buying time" is some form of guaranteed annual income.

The Guaranteed Annual Income The Report of the National Advisory Commission on Civil Disorders pointed out that the present system of public welfare has contributed to the tensions and social disorganization that led to the civil disorders of the summer of 1967. There are few familiar with the present system of social welfare who dispute this conclusion. The system does not provide for the basic needs of people living in poverty. The limitations of the system have created strong social tensions both among recipients of welfare and in the larger society who provides this aid but does not understand the nature of poverty.[2] The Commission on Civil Disorders concluded that the "present policies choice," under which the nation would continue the present welfare system, allocating the same relative or percentage share of the federal budget to welfare assistance with the absolute magnitude of this aid changing with federal revenues, is insufficient even to hold the line in the inner cities and is certainly inadequate to improve the condition of the residents of these areas.

The shortcomings of the present welfare system have been discussed at length elsewhere and need not be examined here beyond enumerating its major deficiencies.[3] First, the present system is categorical. This necessitates extensive investigations of a recipient's circumstances to determine if he is qualified for aid in a given category (such as the Aid for Dependent Children program). Investigation activity has occupied the social worker and eroded his capacity to perform his casework function. Investigations have created animosity between the case worker and his client. In addition, such activity results in an infringement on the privacy of the person receiving welfare and has created an incentive to circumvent the requirements of qualifying for aid. The categorical system has generated a large bureaucracy with a maze of red tape that impedes the successful fulfillment of the welfare function. Second, there are significant social stigmas attached to receiving welfare aid under the present system. It is difficult for an individual on welfare to live in dignity or with a sense of personal pride in his life style. The present social attitudes towards welfare and the perpetual circumspection of their private lives are functions of the categorical system. Any welfare system that fosters these stigma cannot fulfill the major aim of permitting individuals a life characterized by personal dignity and relief from the degradation of economic privation. Third, the federal welfare system provides welfare aid only to the nonworking poor. A large proportion of the impoverished in the United States are the employed poor. Those persons have jobs but earn extremely low incomes or incomes that are low relative to large family sizes. These individuals do not qualify for welfare in any category under the present federal system.[4] Thus, it is possible that a man might have productive employment but receive lower income than if he did not work or if he subsisted on the welfare payments. Fourth, the present welfare system does not create positive incentives to seek gainful employment and creates a disincentive for any individual presently receiving welfare. The welfare income of an individual is reduced by the amount of any nonwelfare income he receives; every dollar of nonwelfare income reduces his welfare payments by a dollar. This is a 100 per cent tax on any nonwelfare income. There is little monetary incentive to seek a nonwelfare source of income. There is a positive disincentive involved, especially if the person disqualifies himself from receiving aid by accepting employment.

Fifth, welfare payments are distributed at the state and municipal levels. The size of these payments is determined by local governments. This administration system has resulted in a wide disparity between the size of the welfare payments in different categories between different cities and states, and particularly between the welfare payments in some southern states and in large northern cities. Welfare has created an incentive for persons to leave southern rural areas and migrate into the urban areas. New York City is a prime example of the problems created when a region attempts to provide satisfactory welfare payments when other areas of the country do not. New York has incurred a large influx of persons seeking welfare aid, and its welfare rolls have swelled beyond manageable dimensions. These regional welfare disparities create a situation where the poor migrate from the rural areas aggravating problems in the urban areas.

The recommendation of the National Advisory Commission on Civil Disorders call for an overhaul of the present system. The changes recommended are major: the establishment of minimal-income standards for welfare recipients; extension of Aid for Dependent Children; payment for needy families with two unemployed parents; the removal of many of the restrictions on eligibility and welfare for employed poor. The final recommendation of the Commission was that the United States move toward a national system of income supplementation to provide a minimum standard of living for all Americans. The Commission argued for some form of guaranteed annual income, which would be available to all in the poverty category with no categorical restrictions and qualifications.

The potential for some form of guaranteed annual income to eliminate the differential between the actual income of those living in poverty and the incomes necessary to raise them to an acceptable standard of living depends upon the size of the "poverty income gap" and its rate of elimination in the absence of programs for income redistribution. The Council of Economic Advisors estimated that given the rate of decrease in the number of poor between 1961 and 1968, poverty could be eliminated in ten years. If the record of 1968 were maintained, this timespan could be reduced to approximately five and a half years.[5] However, the Council pointed out that this rate of reduction will be extremely difficult to maintain. Those remaining in poverty have no direct participation in the economic system and thus will be affected only slightly by any increase in general prosperity. The average rate of increase in income of the nonpoor is 3 per cent per year. If the incomes of those persons in poverty categories were to increase at this same rate, twelve to seventeen years will be required to eliminate poverty. Thus, action must be taken to increase the incomes of the poor more rapidly than those of the nonpoor, and this can occur only through some form of redistribution of income. The Council of Economic Advisors conclude that this redistribution process could be accomplished with small sacrifices from nonpoverty income categories.

Only a relatively small redistribution of the benefits of growth is needed to speed greatly the reduction in poverty. If approximately 85% of households that are not poor and receive about 95% of total income are willing to make only a small sacrifice of the estimated at 3% of yearly growth in their real income per capita, the prospects for poverty reduction could be greatly transformed. If increase in real income for the nonpoor is lowered, merely from 3% to 2½% a year, and that differential of about 2.8 billion dollars annually is effectively transferred to those in poverty, then family incomes for those now poor can grow about 12% annually. This redistribution would eliminate the 1967 "poverty gap" of 9.7 billion dollars in less than 4 years. Since any program of redistribution would be likely to reach some of the near poor and might raise some poor families substantially above the poverty line before others are affected, perhaps a better projection of the time required would be 6 to 8 years.[6]

The most direct and efficient technique for redistribution of income is through a program of guaranteed annual income in the form of the negative income tax. Proposals for the negative income tax take many forms. The basic design of all these programs is to identify the size of the poverty-income gap for a family or individual and fill all or part of this gap by a direct income transfer. The logic of this approach is to make the progressive income tax structure progressive throughout. Those receiving incomes below taxable levels should receive payments or "negative taxes."

The cost of such programs depend upon several factors. First, is the program designed to be a supplement for the present welfare system or a substitute for it? If its purpose was to supplement the existing welfare system and to fill the entire income gap, the cost would range from $9.7 to $11.5 billion. If the program were designed as a substitute for the existing welfare system and to fill the entire income gap, the cost would be considerably higher. A second factor would be the rate of negative income taxation that was employed. The unique feature of the negative income tax is that a negative taxation rate of less than 100 per cent could be used to provide a strong incentive for recipients to seek employment. Milton Friedman's plan incorporates a 50 per cent rate of negative taxation.[7] In this case negative tax payments would be reduced only by 50 per cent of each dollar earned in addition to welfare. In positive terms, an individual would be allowed to retain 50 per cent of every dollar earned, as opposed to the 100 per cent rate of taxation under the present welfare system. Other plans call for diminishing rates of negative taxation as incomes rise, for the dual affect of increasing the incentive factor as incomes increase and reducing the cost of the programs. The cost of a program of this nature is unknown. This would depend upon the rate of negative taxation utilized and its effects upon work incentives. The incentive effects are not known and only actual experimentation could provide estimates.

The negative income tax as a system of income supplementation has many excellent features. Milton Friedman, a conservative economist, supports a welfare system of this nature because it substitutes the rules of the income-tax structure for the discretion of welfare workers and eliminates red tape in the present welfare system. Second, the system is noncategorical and requires a single qualification of income below whatever poverty line is established. Third, the welfare system based on the negative income tax would reach all those living in poverty, including the employed who are not eligible for welfare payments under the present system. Fourth, it builds an incentive to work and seek productive employment by the use of a negative tax rate of less than 100 per cent. Fifth, it removes the regional inequities in the magnitude of welfare payments that presently exist.

John F. Kain of the MIT-Harvard Joint Center for Urban Studies, an accomplished researcher on problems of the urban area and the urban poor, has become an outspoken advocate of some form of negative income-tax system.

Recently I attended five days of hearings held by the U.S. Commission on Civil Rights in Montgomery, Alabama as a consultant to the Commission. During the course of these hearings I got religion. I was converted to the absolute necessity of the immediate enaction of some form of guaranteed annual income. Now this does not mean that I was ever against the concept. Quite the contrary. I had long regarded some form of guaranteed annual income as a desirable piece of legislation and one that was well past due. Moreover, I was certain that the nation in the not-so-distant future would adopt such a scheme. My conversion involved moving the guaranteed annual income from a long list of desirable legislative enactments to the position of number one priority. In my opinion there is no single piece of domestic legislation that would do so much to solve the problems of our cities and our nation.[8]

In late summer 1969, President Nixon proposed a sweeping reform of the welfare system, which he characterized as "a bureaucratic monstrosity" and "a legacy of entrenched programs that have outlived their time." One proposed reform, The Family Assistance System, implemented the concept of the negative income tax. According to government statistics, $3,300 is a subsistence standard for a family of four. The reform proposal provides $500 for each of the first two members of a family, and $300 for each additional member. Thus a family of four would receive $1,600, or $50 less than 50 per cent of the minimum subsistence income.

The 50 per cent negative tax rate in the new measure introduces work incentives. Nixon argues work incentives provide for "workfare" rather than "welfare." A family of four would be allowed to retain all of the first $60 per month or $720 per year of earned income. The $720 represents the estimated cost of being employed in terms of clothing, transportation costs, etc. Every dollar earned beyond the initial $720 reduces welfare payments by 50 per cent. Thus a family of four with earned income of $2,000 would be eligible for a family assistance payment of $960 for a total income of $2,960. A family of five with the same earned income could receive an FAS payment of $1,260 and a total annual income of $3,260.[9] This work incentive feature is to be reinforced by a "work requirement." Eligibility for FAS payments is contingent on the willingness of an employable or qualifiable head of a household to work or to undergo training for work. To facilitate this measure, the size of the manpower training program must be increased by 10 per cent and more money ($600 million) must be made available to establish day care centers.

The merits of the welfare reform measure are significant. For the first time welfare payments may be made to the employed poor. State eligibility requirements would be eliminated and minimum benefits for all states established. Welfare payments will probably be increased in twenty states with the effect of reducing interstate welfare differentials. The incentive for fathers to desert a family to become eligible for AFDC payments would be eliminated. Much of the burdensome "red tape" should be eliminated. Disincentives to work are reduced. Thus the Family Assistance System may represent a major improvement in welfare aid.

However, the shortcomings of the measures are significant. (1) The most critical issue is the size of the FAS payments. $1,600 for a family of four provides only $33.33 per person per month or $1.11 per person per day. This amount is inadequate. States which have attempted to maintain adequate welfare assistance may be forced to provide supplemental payments. In thirty states, the federal payments would be less than the present levels of combined federal and state payments. Under the new measure, these states would be required to maintain the current level of benefits although no state would be required to spend more than 90 per cent of its present welfare costs. The twenty states in which the FAS payments exceed the present average levels would be required to spend at least half of current spending on welfare to supplement the federal base.

(2) The measure can be criticized because it provides the opportunity for some states, principally in the south, to manipulate the system of work requirements to guarantee a cheap, largely Negro, labor supply.

(3) The measure may eliminate or downgrade the food stamp program. Thus the actual purchasing power of the poor would decrease in forty-four states. The administration has indicated that this unforeseen element of the reform measure will be altered to assure that FAS payments are supplemental to the food stamp program.

(4) The work requirement and incentive features of the measure are questionable because they rest upon the assumption that a significant number of welfare recipients are employable. Available data does not support that position. Breaking down the 9,603,700 persons participating in federal assistance programs in March of 1969, the various categories are shown in Table 1.

Table 1*

Blind	80,000
Disabled	728,000
Aged	2,000,000
Children (AFDC)	4,815,000
Mothers of preschool children	1,500,000
Total	9,123,000

* *Source:* Christian Science Monitor, August 14, 1969.

The difference in the total in these categories and the total enrollment in welfare programs is approximately a half million. Of this group, roughly 400,000 are mothers with school age children. There are 80,700 employable males acting as single heads of households receiving AFDC payments. Thus the size of this "welfare manpower" source is very small.

These statistics reflect the extremely tight labor market existing in late 1969. Any induced unemployment as an anti-inflation device would be borne largely by those whom the work incentive and requirement measures are designed to move into the labor force. Any positive effects of work incentives are speculative and the real impact unknown. If jobs are not available, any effects will be negligible. The Nixon proposal ignores entirely the demand side of the market. There is no provision for generating jobs in the business sector or with the government serving as an employer of the last resort. Such deficiency may cripple the reform measure.

In balance, the reform proposal represents a long needed overhaul of welfare assistance and a sharp improvement in the existing system. However, there are critical deficiencies, namely the inadequate levels of FAS payments and the restrictive work requirement provisions. Mitchell I. Ginsburg, New York City's Human Resources Administrator has provided a similar critical evaluation.[10]

Despite major limitations, the welfare proposal, in concept and potential, can represent the beginning of a turnabout in national welfare policy.

The establishment of national minimum standards, even though woefully inadequate; the provision of assistance to the working poor; the setting of national criteria for eligibility and the involvement of the Social Security Administration in administering the income program are of major importance. I believe these steps will inevitably and appropriately lead to the assumption by the national government of the entire income maintenance program, thus allowing the local community to concentrate on services.

Urban Alternatives

The National Advisory Commission on Civil Disorders had identified two fundamental questions affecting the future of American cities: Should future population be concentrated in the central cities, as in the past twenty years, where the Negro and white populations become even more residentially segregated? Should our society provide greatly increased special assistance to Negroes and other relatively disadvantaged population groups? The Commission concluded that three basic choices confront the United States in attempts to provide socially effective answers to the above questions.

The first of these alternatives, "the present-policies choice," has been rejected on the grounds of existing inadequacy. The second alternative, "the enrichment choice," involves attempts to offset the adverse affects of the continued separation and deprivation of the ghetto, and to generate significant improvements in the environmental quality of these areas. This effort would not appreciably affect the pattern of segregation in the inner city, but would make the ghetto areas more habitable. Under the final alternative, "the integration choice," efforts would be made to improve the quality of life in racial enclaves, but would include a concomitant emphasis of creating incentives for emigration from inner-city ghettoes, or integration into the social, economic, and political fabric of American life.

The choice of the policy alternative to be implemented is a decision that represents a crucial crossroads in the future of American social philosophy and practice. As a question of social philosophy, the decision should be made without economic considerations as the primary determining factors. However, when social and political institutions fail to transmit effectively social valuations in policy choices, decisions are made by default through the market mechanism. These market-dictated policies may not reflect conscious social planning. At the present juncture in its history the United States is confronted with a social crisis that threatens the cohesiveness and continuance of the system's culture and institutions. In this crisis American society and its political institutions cannot afford to default in making social valuations explicit in the choice of alternatives for the future of the city.

Although an urgent imperative exists to alleviate the economic disparities in the metropolitan areas and the plight of the Negro within the urban environment, careful consideration must be taken in selecting development alternatives. The chosen alternative must correspond to the pervasive social values and policies of the society. It is probable that the "integration alternative," which permits every citizen an exercise of free choice without racial barriers, corresponds most closely to the historical idealism expressed in American social philosophy. But it is now evident that economic programs have been formulated by government industries and in the black community without consideration of the long-run consequences, inadvertently fostering the enrichment of "gilding-the-ghetto" choice. For example, the present emphasis on ghetto economic development and black capitalism implies that the ghetto can serve as an effective unit for economic development. Other attempts have been made to bring industry into the inner city, to provide sources of income for ghetto residents, and to make capital funds available to assist Negro entrepreneurs catering to a market composed of Negro consumers.

These "gilding-the-ghetto" alternatives present a high risk both for the Negro and for society at large. It is unlikely that the effort to establish successful black businesses, other than small retail or service firms, can prove successful. Purchasing power concentrated within the ghetto area will prove insufficient to provide a market for any commodity produced in quantities reflecting existing economics of scale, thus output cannot be competitive with products produced outside the ghetto. Lack of adequate purchasing power within the ghetto area will force ghetto industry into competition with the larger market external to the ghetto. Black enterprise will then incur competitive disadvantages. It is difficult to argue that there are any strong, locational advantages to influence the location of any capital intensive industry within the ghetto. The two positive locational factors in the ghetto environment are a source of cheap, unskilled labor and relative proximity to urban markets. Technological developments and transportation have greatly reduced the importance of the market-proximity factor. Any successful black capitalistic industry must be designed to take advantage of the unique comparative advantage of the ghetto: the cheap labor supply. Any new industry must be designed to be labor intensive to utilize low levels of skills; for example, the tent- and bat-making endeavors of the Watts Manufacturing Company. However, enterprises of this type must remain on a small scale, thus there will be an extremely small impact on employment within the ghetto. The firm will ultimately be faced with the prospect of becoming less competitive with other capital intensive industries. It is difficult to perceive of black capitalism based in the ghetto as a successful development option.

The absence of any positive location incentives and the significant disincentive of the low environmental quality of the ghetto militate against the feasibility of any industrial enterprise locating within the ghetto. It would be necessary to provide for artificial incentives such as tax rebates or subsidies to insure the profitability of the undertaking. It is unlikely the businessman will be willing to initiate business ventures that are destined to be commercially unprofitable. Most industries entering a ghetto enterprise would be forced to use less than the most efficient technology available elsewhere in order to take advantage of an unskilled labor supply. Firms would be utilizing a lower level of technology than employed in competitive nonghetto industries. The combination of factors of inefficient technology utilization, high training costs, adverse environmental quality, and high-risk factors force a ghetto industry to be noncompetitive with similar nonghetto industry. Thus, unless an industry is willing to absorb higher costs through lower profit margin, or can be insured that profit margins would not be impaired through subsidies, they are unlikely to establish ghetto industries. If tax incentives are used to entice industries into the ghetto it is problematical as to how long firms will be willing to remain once the incentive is withdrawn. Any use of tax incentives in a long-run policy requires that these incentives be continued until the total environment of the ghetto is improved for industrial activity.

Efforts to create black economic development or black capitalism within the ghetto area are unrealistic and cannot be successful.[11] This approach may prove disastrous if programs by blacks, or whites, are concentrated on this goal. In addition, the inherent risk of creating more rigid patterns of racial separation, segregation, or further polarization from this approach will strain existing social cohesiveness in this country. There is basic logic in the arguments of the early black utopians and many contemporary black activists and white liberals, that the Negro must separate himself psychologically and culturally, if not physically, from the predominant culture of the white society in order to achieve a sense of nationhood, cultural identity, and awareness and a sense of pride in their Negritude. At some later date the races could then attempt to get together in a unified society. However, recognition of the validity of this aim, does not justify undertaking separatist development schemes that exhibit an extremely high probability of eventual failure. In addition to the difficulty of establishing black-controlled economic enterprises within the ghetto, the rate of physical deterioration of the inner city is so rapid that, perhaps, no action short of razing these areas could improve environmental quality. Thus, the enrichment choice must be viewed as an historical alternative that was not implemented at the time when it could have been a realistic possibility. Therefore, the economic infeasibility of large-scale, black-owned, black enterprises within the ghetto area, the lack of significant locational factors creating incentives for white-owned industries to establish within the ghetto area, and the extremely high rate of urban deterioration within the inner city make infeasible the enrichment or "gilding-the-ghetto" alternative. This approach offers no realistic hope of alleviating the economic plight of the urban Negro. In an evaluation of the "gilding-the-ghetto" alternative, Kain and Persky of the MIT-Harvard Joint Center for Urban Studies conclude that . . . "it is nothing less than a complete change in the metropolis that will solve the problems of the ghetto."[12]

The present policies alternative has been rejected as inadequate. The enrichment alternative must be rejected as an uneconomic technique for economic development, regardless of beneficial political, social, psychological effects on the ghetto inhabitants. The economic inadequacies of this alternative negate any advantages from other noneconomic values. The remaining alternative on which social policy must be concentrated is the ghetto-dispersal choice. Under this alternative, efforts should be made to improve the quality of life in the inner city by improving the environmental quality of the area, that is, improve the level of public services, education, housing, transportation, recreational access, etc. This approach offers only a stop-gap measure because of the current high rate of physical deterioration of these areas. Programs need to slow the rate of deterioration and improve environmental quality in the short run, while recognizing that these efforts would probably not be sufficient to reverse the trend of the physical environment. Thus, the permanent policy solution must be to remove people from this environment.

Black militants vehemently reject this dispersal alternative. Some argue that for the first time in their history they are beginning to develop political power based on the concentration of Negroes in urban areas. Any policy that would destroy this political power base is opposed, In addition, the time factor is critical in attempting to implement the dispersal choice. The rate of desegregation and integration has been extremely slow. Effective implementation of the dispersal policy through integration would require a considerable period of time. Blacks simply are unwilling to have another generation or series of generations of Negro people sacrificed to existing poor conditions. Militants are actively seeking an alternative to avoid integration into an alien society.

However the dispersal alternative does not necessarily imply integration. It could be implemented through "segregated dispersal." This policy would require incentives to encourage people to move from the inner-city ghetto into smaller enclaves that would have higher environmental quality and would be closer to job opportunities. The Department of Housing and Urban Development has recently changed its urban renewal policy to permit construction of new urban-renewal housing facilities other than at demolished sites. This new policy may indirectly lead to "segregated dispersal" if new housing projects are high-rise apartments located in selected areas throughout the urban areas. Population concentrations would permit the Negro to retain a fragmented power base and to seek the necessary social and cultural cohesiveness.

The segregated dispersal alternative, however, still preserves segregation. Although it may be understandable that a great many Negroes have opposed attempts to achieve integration, it is difficult to understand arguments for the continued existence of invidious segregation. Voluntary separation by blacks from the larger white society may differ in kind from imposed external segregation and would permit the Negro to build the social and cultural pride necessary to achieve political, economic, and social power. However, it is possible that this policy may result in polarization of the society and erect insurmountable barriers to integration. The segregated dispersal alternative would exhibit the characteristics of the South African apartheid policy, which locates blacks in reservations surrounding the industrial areas. Apartheid permits exploitation of the black as a source of physical labor while prohibiting any movement into society external to his reservation. This policy as implemented in South Africa is anathema to Negroes and the majority of whites in the United States. Thus, it is difficult to understand any willingness to accept a domestic policy so close in form to the apartheid policy.

The only policy that conforms to the idealism expressed in American social philosophy is that of "integrated dispersal." It is the only policy that retains any hope of allowing the United States to achieve the social cohesiveness essential to sustain society in its present institutional form. The challenges of implementing the integrated-dispersal alternative should be the primary focus for remedial development programs. The goal of achieving the reconstruction of the ghetto and integration of the Negro into the larger white society should be the primary criterion for evaluating all developmental alternatives. Programs inconsistent with this goal should be eliminated from consideration on incompatibility grounds.

It is easy to argue that the enrichment alternative is not economically feasible or is unlikely to succeed regardless of its compatibility or incompatibility with social goals and evaluations. Thus, this alternative is undesirable as a social goal. It is similarly simple to argue that the integrated dispersal alternative is compatible with social goals and should be advocated on social and philosophical grounds. But although the enrichment alternative is economically unfeasible, it is difficult to demonstrate the economic validity of the integration approach. It is necessary to argue for integrated dispersal on other than social grounds, including economic feasibility. Thus, it seems appropriate to examine and evaluate economic policy alternatives or components of comprehensive programs for black economic development that are consistent with the integrated-dispersal alternative.

Stemming Migration
from Rural Poverty
Areas

The Report of the President's National Advisory Commission on Rural Poverty has stated that

The urban riots during 1967 had their roots, in considerable part, in rural poverty. A high proportion of people crowded into city slums today came from rural slums. This fact alone makes clear how large a stake the people of this nation have in an attack on rural poverty.

. . . . .

Because rural Americans have been denied a fair share of America's opportunities and benefits, they have migrated by the millions to the cities in search of jobs and places to live. This migration is continuing. It is, therefore, impossible to obliterate urban poverty without removing its rural causes. Accordingly, both reason and justice compel the allotment of a more equitable share of our national resources to improving the condition of rural life.[13]

Only 30 per cent of this country's population lives in rural areas, but these regions possess 40 per cent of those persons falling into the poverty category. Thus, the magnitude of the poverty problem is greater in rural areas than in the urban environment. But the manifestations of poverty are more obvious in urban areas because of its high concentration.

A significant component of the social and economic problems of the ghetto area is directly attributable to the concentration of people into a relatively restricted, declining, physical environment. Of course, many people presently living in inner city areas previously immigrated from rural areas to escape the poverty conditions existing there. But rural emigration is not the major cause of the density or high rate of population increase within the inner city.

The rate of reproduction of the indigenous people of these areas is the causal factor. The immigration into the ghetto environment from rural poverty pockets does, however, compound the magnitude of this problem. Any solution-oriented remedial policies for economic development for the ghetto must incorporate some policy to alleviate the conditions existing in rural poverty environment and to stem the inflow of people from rural areas.

Kain and Persky of the MIT-Harvard Center on Regional Economics conclude:

While job creation, like other "gilding" programs, might initially reduce Negro unemployment, it must eventually affect the system that binds the northern ghetto to the rural urban areas of the south. The system will react to any sudden changes in employment-income opportunities in northern ghettos. If there are no offsetting improvements in the south, the result will be increased rates of migration into still restricted ghetto areas. While we need to know much more about the elasticity of migration to various economic improvements, the direction of the effect is clear. Indeed it is possible that more than one migrant might appear in the ghetto for every job created. Even at lower levels of sensitivity a strong wave of in-migration could prove extremely harmful to many other programs . . . . a serious program of southern economic development is worthwhile in its own right as a cure to a century of imbalance and distribution of economic activity in the country. From the narrow viewpoint of the north, however, the economic development of the south can play a crucial role in providing leverage in the handling of metropolitan problems.[14]

The development potential for rural poverty areas, particularly in the South, is much greater than the potential for the development of urban ghetto areas. Ghetto areas are undeveloped in the sense that the level of economic prosperity is extremely low. The potential for further development is based on the supply of available or unexploited resources. Many rural areas are underdeveloped but do exhibit a high potential for economic development because of unexploited resource bases and positive locational factors. Therefore, the problems associated with economic development and poverty reduction in rural areas are of a lesser magnitude.

. . . . The deep south is not a declining area unsuitable for further investment. It is rich in resources, poor in capital—both human and physical, a program of southern economic development conceived on a regional scale could serve to rectify a major imbalance of distribution of economic activity while providing new alternatives for the native population, white and black.[15]

The most effective and comprehensive current national effort designed to combat rural poverty is the Appalachian Regional Development Act of 1965. This Act was an outgrowth of the Area Redevelopment Act implemented in 1961 but phased out in the Public Works Acceleration Act of 1962. The Area Redevelopment Act was designed to "alleviate conditions of substantial persistent unemployment . . . in certain economically distressed areas."[16] The earlier act was designed to provide loans to industry, to attempt to create an infrastructure in underdeveloped regions, to provide technical assistance to aid in local development planning in these areas, and to provide for training and retraining in an effort to upgrade labor force skills.[17] The Public Works Acceleration Act was to supplement the development and infrastructure of public works to increase the employment impact of these activities. The Economic Development Agency indicated that the economic impact of this program was positive; 7,700 projects were supported and an estimated 2 million man months of employment resulted.[18]

The Appalachian Regional Development Act is designed to "assist the region in meeting its special problems . . . and to establish a framework for joint federal-state efforts towards providing the basic facilities essential to the common problems in meeting its common needs on a coordination and concerted basis."[19] This program is a broad-guaged effort to meet many of the manifestations of rural poverty. But it is too early to evaluate the contributions of this program to development efforts in the Appalachian area. Limited current evidence indicates constructive progress in the EDA programs.

The emphasis on rural development through the Economic Development Administration has been sharply curtailed under the Nixon administration. The level of activity of EDA seems to be diminished and many of its present programs are in disarray. A central function of this agency was to create a favorable climate for investment in redevelopment areas. The most promising EDA effort is the Economic Development District Program designed to identify areas with common economic problems and potentials, and to create an administrative agency charged with research, planning, and implementation. Through the establishment of larger development districts, resources could be pooled to take advantage of various economies in any cooperative effort. The larger development districts contain at least two regional areas, including economic development centers, composing a population of less than 250,000 people.

The President's Commission on Rural Poverty has moved far beyond the present authority of the Economic Development Agency in recommendations for action to combat rural poverty. The Commission proposed a broad-gauged program to strike at every cause and manifestation of poverty in rural areas. The program is designed to meet three basic requirements: (1) a job for every rural person willing and able to work; (2) jobs paying high enough wages to allow every individual to achieve a decent standard of living; and (3) ending discrimination against rural peoples whether by statute or administration.[20]

The policies directed to achieve full employment have several current and future dimensions. The Commission urged establishment of a comprehensive and active manpower delivery system. Several of the recommendations have been implemented. For example, the Cooperative Area Manpower Planning System (CAMPS) coordinates efforts of the Manpower Development and Training Agency and the Office of Economic Opportunity. CAMPS makes manpower services available to all workers and employers in locations throughout the country and provides a system with flexibility to meet diversified problems occurring in these regions. The Commission recommended that the system of labor-market information be improved to create the widest possible dissemination of data on job opportunities and on those seeking employment. The Commission urged that the U.S. government serve as an employer of the last resort and provide jobs at the national minimum wage for every unemployed person seeking work. The Commission recommended that the wages-and-hours provisions of the Fair Labor Standards Act be extended uniformly to all occupations and all regions, and advocated that the Department of Labor undertake a program to relocate disadvantaged workers unable to find employment in the region in which they live. Programs seek to increase mobility rather than emphasize worker relocation in urban areas.

The other Commission recommendations are oriented toward breaking down rural discrimination by extending Title IV of the Civil Rights Act of 1964 to all labor unions and employers, both private and state and local governments; programs that drastically improve the quality of rural education through increases in federal funds and technical services available to state education agencies; a massive program to alleviate health and deficient medical care programs in rural areas; the establishment of family-planning programs; a broad revision in welfare standards applying to rural poor; and an extended program of conservation and development of natural resources.

Finally, the Commission recommended a comprehensive area-and-redevelopment program. This program would be to establish area-redevelopment districts such as those under consideration by the Economic Development Administration and would extend federal funds and public works in the Economic Development Act of 1965 and the Housing Act of 1954. In efforts to attract industry into poverty regions, liberalized investment tax credits, accelerated depreciation schedule, and broader carry-forward carry-backward provisions would be provided. The Commission urged that local industrial subsidies be discouraged if they adversely affect the fiscal position of communities or reduce ability to finance and construct public facilities and services.

Another positive focus, although not included by the President's Commission on Rural Poverty, would be an attempt to offset the competitive advantage of already developed areas in attracting industry. Congress should enact legislation to prohibit the use of tax exempt municipal securities for industrial development except in programs identified with national policy for regional development.

Development of the rural south, particularly the black belt, should be the number one priority of such a national policy of regional development. Such legislation would restore the previously competitive edge in the south in attracting industry. These legislative changes should be accompanied by a much larger program of business loans, community facilities loans, and other initiatives designed to further accelerate southern economic development.[21]

Policies to achieve rural economic development should rank relatively high on a list of development priorities. The lack of rural opportunities relates directly to the problems of the cities. This is perhaps the easiest link to approach in the spectrum of urban problems. In addition to stemming the immigration into urban areas, emigration from urban areas might even result. Balanced growth is a desirable national policy. There appears to be sufficient information to proceed to identify effective remedial economic development policies. Rural development contrasts with the problems of the cities. The cities' problems are less easily defined. Thus, any urban policy alternative possesses a high-risk coefficient.

Strategies Against Poverty

Remedial action to alleviate poverty can take two basic forms. Distributive policies can be designed to fill the poverty income gap through programs such as the negative income tax. Structural policies may be designed to increase the capacity of the poor to become productive participants in the economy.[22] Until automation is more extensively introduced in the economy, necessitating a system of distribution not based on productivity, distributive policies should be directed toward improving conditions of the poor in the short run, or until the time when the poor can be incorporated productively into the economy.[23] Long-run policy efforts should focus on changes within the economy to help the individual enjoy the full potential of his earning capacity. Structural-type policies should be aimed at inadequate urban transportation, racial discrimination, inadequate job information, and lack of job access. In addition, remedial policy must be directed towards the individual or structural improvement in the abilities, skills, and capacities of the nonwhite poor. This policy must be designed to increase public investment in human capital. Investment in human capital refers to expenditures to increase the economic productivity of the individual, such as education, jobs and skills training, and sources of capacity of market participation and behavior.[24]

Any effective long-run policy must concentrate on structural changes. Such structural changes encompass two areas of potential action: market changes and changes in qualifications of individuals. Policies designed to implement the "integrated-dispersal choice" in urban areas can be consistent with both these categories. It is important to note that structural changes can take place only over a long period of time because institutions and personal characteristics do not change quickly. It is necessary to be assured that distributive and structural policies complement one another.

Implementing the Integrated-Dispersal Alternative For ghetto dispersal via structural market changes to be a realistic alternative to ghetto enrichment, a massive effort must be made to break down restrictions that limit the out-mobility of residents. Out-mobility is now restricted by inadequate transportation facilities, inadequate job market information, limited opportunity for employment outside of ghetto, segregated housing outside the ghetto, discrimination in hiring practices, and labor union codes. Policies oriented toward structural market improvement must be more strategically directed toward these market deficiencies in urban institutions.

Increasing Mobility Through Transportation The policy of attempting to use the ghetto for economic development requires one type of job mobility, that of moving jobs to the unemployed.

A logical alternative would be to attempt to expand labor mobility by making nonghetto job opportunities more accessible to the ghetto unemployed. Employment opportunities, particularly in manufacturing, are increasingly outside the central urban areas in suburban fringes. This trend in industrial location has created a time and distance constraint on job access for the ghetto residents. For some inner-city residents, public transportation may not be accessible. For others, the time involved in traveling on existing facilities and making many transfers for long trips to the suburbs make jobs inaccessible. For others the cost of the fares is just too high. For some with extremely low reading skills, the complexity of signs and instructions precludes their use of transportation systems in the city.

Researchers studying the problem of urban transportation indicate that major difficulties occur in making jobs accessible to the unemployed. Improvement in the urban transportation systems is one of the most promising techniques for attaining economic progress through outmobility for the ghetto unemployed.[25] Urban areas with underdeveloped center cities should evaluate programs for improving and expanding public urban transportation. Improvement should be directed towards providing direct lines between job opportunities and the ghetto, reducing the number of transfers necessary to reach all employment centers, making transportation faster, and subsidizing transportation facilities to reduce the fares for the inner-city workers. The cost of providing subsidized or even free transit between ghetto areas and suburban job opportunities may be high. But relative to the cost of ghetto enrichment, or tax subsidies and incentives for industry locating in ghetto areas, this cost is quite low. Other factors, such as increasing urban size, pollution, congestion, and too many automobiles, will make improved urban transit systems necessary at some time in the near future. Improved transit linkages between ghettoes and adjacent areas should be the first priority in an improved metropolitan transit system.

Improved System of Providing Employment Information   It is known that census records greatly understate the number of

Negro males in inner-city areas and that the actual rate of Negro unemployment and subemployment is higher than recorded. In addition, an unknown number of ghetto residents have simply dropped out of the labor force. They do not actively seek jobs because of disillusionment about ever finding employment opportunities, or because other factors have eliminated incentive. The Kerner Report indicated that underemployment, or employment in jobs using less skill than actually possessed, represents a greater problem than unemployment. Underestimates of unemployment statistics, unemployment not recorded, exclusion from the labor force, and underemployment indicate that productive employment opportunities are a critical need of the ghetto dweller.

Increased employment is in part a function of the inadequate information on existing employment opportunities. Additional methods must be introduced to bring existing employment opportunities outside to the attention of the ghetto residents. Individual firms need to set up more ghetto storefront labor-recruiting offices. Public employment bureaus need to expand recruitment efforts. Public employment bureaus must set up additional agencies within the inner city and staff these offices with employees who are acquainted with the environment, the stresses, and complex burdens of the inner-city residents. Employment agency staff must be capable of providing a chain of communication with potential indigenous workers. Presently, employment bureaus are to establish data banks on jobs and potential employees. Information on the individual worker, such as his record in previous jobs, will be accessible on short notice. Now public employment agencies are often unable to provide complete information on employment opportunities outside state or local areas. Structural modifications must be made in the method in which job information is disseminated to ghetto residents. More complete job information should be compiled and distributed within the ghetto. Coordination between potential employers and potential employees can be improved by more extensive use of computerized job banks.

Improved Housing   A policy of establishing cheap, expanded, urban transit will induce out-mobility of labor from the ghetto. A concomitant policy to improve job opportunities is improved housing to permit ghetto residents to live outside the inner-city area closer to suburban job opportunities. More rigorous enforcement of open-housing codes and more low-cost public housing in the suburban areas is needed. The Model Cities Act may foster public housing construction outside urban areas at some future time. If housing becomes available that is convenient to suburban job opportunities, ghetto laborers may emigrate to these more desirable environments. If dispersal of the black-ghetto residents into suburbs causes white residents to move away from existing job opportunities, whites may then begin to pay the cost of their discrimination. In economic terms, whites creating the external cost would be forced, in part, to internalize this cost, thereby creating more efficient allocation. As the preceding chapter noted, the available supply of low-cost housing has fallen behind the need for these facilities. There is reason for extreme pessimism about the capacity of public policy to prevent further market imbalance. A massive public effort is required to increase the supply of public housing. This effort should be coordinated with the "integrated-dispersal alternative" approach. New housing should be dispersed throughout urban and suburban areas and located close to employment opportunities. Complete and strict compliance with open-housing codes is mandatory. In Columbus, Ohio, the private sector has effectively entered the arena concerning open housing. A group of twenty-five leading businessmen of that city have been working with realtors and using their leverage to insure that the open-housing regulations are observed.

Private Enterprise, Hiring Practices, and Labor Unions

Because of the extremely slow rate of implementation of economic development programs, there is little basis for optimism that these current programs can make any extensive contribution to the elimination of poverty. Through a process of default on other programs, manpower-training programs offer the best chances of facilitating economic improvement. A willingness of private industry to undertake adequate programs is perhaps the most critical of the issues in the economic development of black America. Unless blacks can be absorbed into the economy in a productive manner, the present direction of public effort cannot be justified. The most successful public effort has been the man-power-training and development programs. These public programs have provided skills training for private-sector jobs but have not greatly expanded public employment opportunities.

It must be re-emphasized that there is only limited evidence that the private sector is willing to undertake employment pro-grams of the magnitude necessary to significantly reduce the number of hard-core unemployed or to provide the type of jobs that would significantly improve the earnings of people who have been traditionally unable to maintain a steady stream of income. Michael Harrington, who was largely responsible for bringing the problem of poverty to public attention, is extremely pessimistic about the possibility of private industry ever making a significant contribution to the alleviation of poverty.[26]

Businessmen, even at their most idealistic, are not prepared to act in a systematically un-business-like way that such amenities require.[27]

. . . . .

So America, whether it likes it or not, cannot sell its social conscience to the highest corporate bidder. It must build new institutions of democratic planning which can make the uneco-nomic, commercially wasteful, and humane decision about educating and urban living, this society so desperately needs.

Another distinguished analyst of the America dilemma, Gunnar Myrdal, has expressed a more optimistic view of the possibilities for mobilization of private enterprise:

. . . . I believe we shall see big business taking a leading part in the war against poverty. The change in business opinion is, in my opinion, one of the most significant trends in the U.S. of particular consequence because of the extraordinary influence businessmen have in politics in this country. Potentially, it may be among the most important causes for allowing the rapid and steady growth in that it is conditioned for success in the war against poverty.[28]

Charles Silberman, a noted author, has placed the question in more problematical and conditional terms. Rather than expressing extreme optimism or pessimism about the capabilities of business to contribute to the alleviation of poverty, he argues that the manner in which the business sector reacts to these needs will be critical in determining the racial situation in the United States.

The way in which business responds to Negro pressures, perhaps more than any other single factor, will determine the character and tone of race relations over the rest of this decade. Businessmen like to think of themselves as conservatives. They have a rare opportunity to conserve American society by repairing what has to be repaired and changing what has to be changed. As we have seen, Negroes have become increasingly cynical about the efficacy of law and the integrity and good faith of white leadership. If they act on their own initiative to create jobs for Negroes, businessmen may be able to convert that distrust and cynicism into some degree of confidence and so, in the phrase of Edmund Burke, "make the revolution a parent of settlement and not a nursery of future revolutions." If they are to do this, however—if they are to play a truly constructive role—businessmen will have to look beyond the rules and canons of business management. They will have to learn the art of politics in the highest sense of that term, for they will be engaged in what has been called the "politics of repair."[29]

Silberman's position seems most relevant. It is futile to engage in debates on whether the problem can best be tackled by the private or public sector, or whether business can make, or is willing to make, a significant contribution to the alleviation of poverty. The national imperative is that every facet of the American system must make a maximum feasible contribution to the alleviation of the problems of race, poverty, and the urban areas. Much precious energy has been dissipated in the false dichotomy of private- and public-sector action. The competition and debate should be ended. Both private and public sectors must mobilize to their capacity to attack these problems. The critical question is the willingness of the private sector to establish a partnership with the public sector. The efforts of the National Association of Businessmen are encouraging, as are the efforts of a number of individual corporations and firms in the business sector. However, the great majority of the private-industry sector remains adamant in refusing to accept their historical responsibility for present circumstances. Business does have a responsibility to initiate and take action to bring the Negro into our economic structure. If the business sector chooses to remain intransigent on this issue, no other hope remains than a massive juxtapositioning of the public sector to resolve the manifestations of the problem exclusive of the established business community.

Such action would be disastrous, simply because of the untapped resources that private industry can bring to bear on these problems.

Structural Changes in the Individual and His Market Qualifications

The elimination of structural barriers to mobility, job opportunity, and accessibility have little significance to the individual who does not possess the skills or other qualifications to take advantage of increased opportunities. Any programs designed to bring about structural changes for the individual must be coordinated with and complementary to efforts that create structural changes in the market. The programs that improve the individual's market qualifications through investment in human capital should be focused on at least three elements: (1) the quality of education and the level of educational opportunity available to the Negro; (2) manpower-training and development activities designed to train individuals in particular market skills; and (3) market-oriented behavior and motivations.

Comprehensive programs designed to move the black into the economic and social mainstream must cope directly with the educational deficiencies in existence. The 1954 school desegregation decision affirmed that segregated schools were not equal and that the quality of segregated education was inadequate. The pace of school desegregation has been slow; it is inconceivable that complete implementation of the 1954 concept will be accomplished in the near future. Complete desegregation of the schools is an extraordinarily effective way to improve the quality of education accessible to the Negro, and desegregation efforts should be greatly intensified. But where school desegregation pulses along at a slow pace, some form of compensatory education for the black is mandatory. The Headstart Program is one significant illustration of needed compensatory education. Although the effects of the Headstart education may often be abrogated when the child returns to his ghetto environment, the objectives of the program are valid. Similar programs should be pursued as vigorously as understanding of the total educational needs of the ghetto child will permit. At the other end of the educational spectrum the Upward-Bound programs financed by the federal government and operated through colleges and universities are designed to bring the product of a substandard primary and secondary education up to college-level qualifications so that he may embark on a college education. Upward-Bound has proven to be relatively successful, but needs to be expanded to make this compensatory education available to greater numbers of the educationally disadvantaged. Upward-Bound and other public-sector remedial programs have been felled by the parsimonious effort to cut the level of government expenditures. No new Upward-Bound programs are being funded.

The concept of compensatory education needs to be extended to children between the Headstart and Upward-Bound age groups. Public-sector resources on a large scale must be devoted to creating educational opportunities so that the Negro will be able to offset the debilitating effects of ghetto life. An effective program of compensatory education would eliminate the need for later programs such as Upward-Bound. School desegregation is mandatory. But until the time when desegregation is a reality, compensatory education is a legitimate process to help the Negro become a functioning participant in the economic development of black America.

A second dimension in increasing the level of human capital in the black community must be directed to individuals no longer participating in the formal education process in primary, secondary, or college levels. Those individuals in the black community who have very low skill levels but who have the potential for benefiting from training should be given increased opportunities for remedial training. Institutional arrangements now exist to facilitate skills training—primarily on-the-job training through Operation Mainstream, New Careers, and the JOBS programs. At issue is the level at which these programs will operate given current efforts to hold back the level of federal funding. Current policy seems to be a reduction in the rate of expansion of programs available to train the hard-core unemployed. With the current institutional emphasis on remedial programs, employment and skills training efforts should be expanded to reach even larger numbers of the hard-core unemployed. Jobs and skills training have been a traditional technique utilized by the black in seeking integration into the white economic structure. This employment expansion effort is consistent with the integrated-dispersal alternative. Although black activists may become disillusioned about the possibilities of achieving economic improvement through this slowly evolving training process, this effort is consistent with the existing social values of society. It would be extremely unfortunate if the government reduced its most effective programs through short-term financial cutbacks to control inflation. Inflationary trends must be brought under control, but the major cost of cutbacks in spending should not fall upon the impoverished.

The third area of emphasis to provide the Negro with improved market qualifications is concerned with motivational attitudes, market-oriented behavior, or economic versus uneconomic behavior patterns. Studies of the economic development of under-developed countries indicate clearly that some cultures are "uneconomic." An intellectual and empirical controversy permeates the literature of economic development on the direction of causality and the relationship between economic development and cultural change. On the one hand, economic development can precede social and cultural change. The nature of economic change and economic imperatives of the society will be instrumental in bringing about social and cultural change and in determining the nature of the society and institutions. An alternative position suggests that social and cultural conditions create the environment in which economic life of the society is transacted. Therefore, the cultural environment circumscribes the characteristics and scope within which the economic changes can take place. Thus, social and cultural change are the antecedents to significant economic development. Can economic development precede and thus induce cultural change, or must traditional cultural patterns be interrupted as a precondition for economic development? Economists and psychologists now emphasize the latter position. Economic development cannot precede until given cultural changes are induced that will create market-oriented behavior and economic rationalization.

David McClelland, in *The Achieving Society*, has carried out an extensive study of the factors conducive to economic development which create economic attitudes in the population.[30] He has concluded that there is a significant relationship between achievement motivations in a society and the presence or absence of entrepreneural activity. Achievement motivation is inculcated in the individual at an early age and by the culture in which he resides. An uneconomic culture is one which assigns priority to other nonmaterial values. If the thesis is correct that cultural and motivational attitudes must change before economic development can precede, then development efforts must be directed toward "rationalizing" the culture by inculcating market-achievement motivations in the populace. If cultural change must precede economic development, then development cannot be a rapid process. Cultural changes and changes in motivational attitudes occur very slowly.

Thus, policy must emphasize the creation of a high-achievement motivation within the Negro populace if economic development is to be pursued. The utilization of mass media, educational systems, and, to a lesser extent, the values emphasized within the family must be incorporated. An ideological campaign with such slogans as "black power" and "black pride" appears to be logical and coherently constructive. An ideological appeal designed to mobilize the black population which can generate a high-achievement motivation within this group is vital. The "black power" and the "black pride" concepts within the black movement should not be discouraged.

The Negro, the City, and Economic Development

Society must provide answers to the question of which national priorities are to be emphasized in social policy. The societal choices must insure continuity in existing institutions but generate changes conducive to creating a system not inconsistent with broad social and philosophical goals. The historical ambivalence between American idealism and social reality has created social tension which cannot be ignored if present institutional forms are to be preserved. Social transformations involving high-priority national commitments and social mobilization must include effective solutions to the problems of race and poverty and the decline of the cities. Nothing less than a national mobilization of resources in realistic remedial actions will suffice to dissipate the tendency toward atrophy in metropolitan areas.

The extensive fragmentation of policy and token efforts, both within the public sector and between the public and private sectors, present a prescription for national tragedy. Finding the appropriate manner in which to bring to whites a realization of the dimensions of the domestic crises presently confronting this society is the greatest task facing policy-makers, teachers, and researchers. Many scholars exhibit profound pessimism regarding the possibility of accomplishing this task. They recognize that the United States possesses both the resources and the imaginative and creative ability to cope with these problems. There is, however, pessimism about the possibilities and probabilities of bridging the chasm between social attitudes and social realities concerning societal problems. Changes in attitudes and values in this society occur very slowly and in an evolutionary manner. The need for change traditionally has outpaced institutional and value system changes in this society. Technology has generated changes in property relationships, which make the mores pertaining to individualism and the institution of private property unrealistic. A dynamic for change within the black community has created a social force that makes present attitudes toward the Negro and the measured worth of a man untenable. The rate of urban deterioration has fostered a situation in which social attitudes on individualism and responsibilities of local and state governments or intergovernmental relations are incompatible with the need and dynamics for change. The rate at which social values and social institutions can be transformed to generate humanistic and realistic solutions to the dehabilitating conditions under which the Negro lives in poverty in the inner city are crucial in determining whether these anachronistic social attitudes will produce a destructive cataclysm.

A large number of alternative policies have been examined in this book. Only those policies compatible with and inclusive of techniques for implementing the "integrated-dispersal" alternative should be initiated or supported as public policies. It is a valid conclusion that the Negro, because of discrimination, has never been given the opportunity to make a place for himself in the economic system. The Negro has provided exploited or cheap labor and has contributed to the present prosperity and thus deserves a just share of the benefits of the economic system. Public policy must be directed towards integrating the Negro into the system by providing him a more equitable share of the fruits of the system or the means to obtain them. The concept of black capitalism is an integral component of the overall drive for black self-respect and pride and is meaningful. Black entrepreneurship and black ownership of capital should be promoted and encouraged. This effort, however, must be removed from the context of the ghetto. Black production and black retailers catering to a completely black market will not be successful on any profitability scale. Until full economic integration can be achieved, an alternative possessing a much greater probability of success is the creation of an effectively functioning biracial economy where black entrepreneurs compete for white- and black-consumer demand. Although the black businessman will face formidable competition across the color line, this difficulty would be slight compared to the problems associated with the conduct of black business that caters only to black consumers. There is reason for cautious optimism that consumer preference between businesses will be related to price and quality differentials rather than the race of the entrepreneur.

A more effective means for the Negro to obtain economic power is the training of black management and executive personnel to infiltrate the sources of economic power in the industrial establishment and the government. The economic cost to the Negro community of achieving economic power through the management route is significantly lower than establishing new industrial sites. The risks involved are fewer. Negroes have not traditionally chosen education in management, partly because of the inaccessibility of both management training and job opportunities. The constraints upon Negro participation in this occupational field are eroding.

Another thrust within the black movement compatible with the integrated dispersal alternative that possesses a high potential for success is creation of black cooperatives. This economic organization is an effective way to pool economic resources and capital sources as an effective means of distribution of the income to these enterprises. In cooperatives, ownership and control are closely aligned in the communal nature of the decision-making processes. Thus, cooperatives provide an effective means for the Negro to obtain a larger share of the return to capital and to control the economic power associated with the ownership of means of production.

Among the militants, the concepts of economic development of James Boggs and the programs of the Congress of Racial Equality illustrate an insight into economic processes and understanding of the economic needs and techniques for obtaining economic development. James Boggs argues that some form of guaranteed annual income must become a reality in the United States in the near future because of increasing automation. Boggs does not believe this change in the property-income relationship can occur under the existing institutional arrangements. His view is understandable in the context of the experiences and the environment of the Negro in the United States. But it now appears possible that a guaranteed annual income may be initiated under existing institutional forms caused by the breakdown and inadequacy of other forms of social welfare.

The emphasis of the Congress of Racial Equality upon making every man a capitalist by providing him a share of the return to capital and its program for implementing this goal are realistic. The program possesses a high probability of success if it can be extracted from the ghetto environment. A community development corporation has proved a successful model in underdeveloped countries as well as in some cases within the United States. The chances for this model are much greater outside the ghetto environment in other regions of the metropolitan area. There is nothing in the nature of this development model that would preclude its extraction from the ghetto. Implementation in the broader context of the urban environment would make it compatible with the integrated-dispersal alternative. It is an effective technique for mobilizing black resources, industrial and public support, and for applying these elements to the problem of the economic development of the Negro. However, if CORE insists upon retaining the emphasis on separation in the ghetto environment, it is unlikely to receive the financial support necessary to undertake economic activity on any significant scale. The separation emphasis may threaten this organization's economic activities already underway.

The public sector has emphasized skills and training in efforts to provide the black with the qualifications to obtain productive employment in the private sector. Other public-sector "poverty programs," such as those of the Small Business Administration, the Minority Entrepreneurship Program, plus the current orientation of welfare programs, can best be interpreted as programs of tokenism or "pacification" of the Negro. Thus, if the current policy focus is to be maintained, the manpower development and training programs should be intensified in quality and expanded in scope. The future critical question is the ability and willingness of the private sector to absorb blacks who receive job training through the public- and private-sector skills-training programs. From this frame of reference, programs such as the jobs in business sector (JOBS), Sullivan's OIC, and other industrial training programs should be supported. The role of the government as an employer of last resort must receive more attention and greater emphasis. Jobs in the public sector should be greatly expanded.

The alternative policies within the cities have been analyzed in this chapter. In addition to structural changes within the metropolitan area, other specific programs designed to eliminate the ghetto, achieve desegregation, and create incentives for emigration from centralized urban areas must be implemented. One plan designed to accomplish the dual goals of desegregation and decentralization is a ten-year program of de-ghettoization of urban areas. This technique of achieving desegregation has three elements: First, it proposes a ten-year program of building "new towns" in outlying areas that will accommodate the projected Negro and white population growth. The concept of new towns is not new, and has its origins in England in the postwar period, but the coordination of the new towns concept with a program of desegregation is unique. A new-town program designed as a fully integrated environment is rapidly becoming a reality in Columbia, a suburb of Washington, D.C.[31] Second, 350,000 more subsidized housing units would be constructed in each year of the ten years of the program. Third, public expenditures would be allocated for social capital construction, such as sewers, water, roads, electricity, etc.

A totally effective new-towns program would require not only housing but also extensive improvement in transportation and new industries. Experimentation in Europe and in the United States has demonstrated that "new towns linked to the central city and to each other by mass transportation are important in improving the quality of the urban environment and in solving the problems of suburban sprawl."[32] White industry may be willing to take advantage of these areas.

New towns offer an opportunity to bring together ghetto residents with available jobs and industries which have demonstrated a preference for one-story plans in outlying areas. At the same time, these industries provide economic base for the new towns.[33]

The trend in plant location is outside the metropolitan center city. Development of new towns would tend to reduce worker-to-job distances.

It may be argued that *desegregated* decentralization in new towns will provide the most efficient means of confronting the problems of urban society.

The new towns program costs the least of any program for dealing with the problem. By building on outlying land we are using the cheapest land. By concentrating development, the cost of utilities and roads are decreased. Moreover, since we are working with the market factors and in the direction of normal population growth, the economic forces of the market place add to, rather than compete with, the subsidized effort. For example, additional older housing will become available to lower income persons and this will help to eliminate the irrationalities of constructing expensive public housing on valuable inner city land.[34]

The new town plan is extremely attractive because it eliminates the ghetto, achieves desegregation, brings ghetto workers and industrial jobs together, accomplishes a more efficient transportation system, and creates a better urban environment. These goals correspond with the overall social strategy of integrated dispersal.[35]

A National Urban Policy

This study has explored the multivarious nature of the problems of race, poverty, the inner city, and has emphasized the staggering complexities and vast dimension of these problems. It is clear that present policies of alleviation are fragmented and do not suffice either in terms of sophistication or magnitude. The imperative is clear that the federal government must design and implement a "national urban policy" capable of generating a coordinated and massive attack on the syndrome of problems of race, poverty, and the inner city. Only a policy of this scope is capable of structuring national urban priorities or allocating expenditures massive enough to implement these policies, or overriding local governmental units which prove incapable of providing a meaningful strategy. The Advisory Commission on Intergovernmental Relations has documented this conclusion:

On balance, therefore, the Commission concludes—taking particular account of its findings as to diseconomies of urban congestion, the locational mismatch of jobs and people, the linkage of urban and rural problems, and urban sprawl—that there is a specific need for immediate establishment of a national policy for guiding the location and character of future urbanization, involving federal, state, and local governments in collaboration of the private sector of the national economy.[36]

Summary

The elimination of poverty in the United States has and will prove to be a difficult task. Economic prosperity has greatly reduced the number of individuals falling into poverty categories in the post-World War II period. Those remaining are people who possess tenuous relationships with the functioning economic system, despite the resources, innovative ability, and knowledge and insight available to reduce poverty. This society proves unwilling to undertake the necessary tasks. Race and racism compound the difficulties of establishing and implementing appropriate policies. Racial discrimination must end. The enforcement of existing legislation against discriminatory patterns must be carried out as a crash program. Overt or covert discriminatory behavior is a principle barrier to the economic development of the Negro. Stokely Carmichael has argued that elements of racial constraint are built into all American institutions. If this position is correct, black economic integration into the capitalistic system as presently constituted is not possible. Institutionalized racism cannot be challenged or destroyed by legal means. The Reverend Albert Cleage, Minister of the Church of the Black Madonna in Detroit, argues that racism is institutionalized. Thus, existing economic institutions offer little hope for the economic development of the Negro.

. . . . I think as far as the black community is concerned, the capitalistic economy doesn't work for us because we don't have any stake in it. It just happened that when we got to a place where we were able to do something, we were outside. The concentration of wealth in the white capitalistic set-up is so complete now that you can't break into that. With all the other racist elements in American society, we are not only outside of it, but we are frozen outside of it.[37]

Appendix

Exhibit 1—Poverty trends

(From *Economic Report of the President,* January, 1969, pp. 153–54).

With the general rise in family incomes in the postwar period, the incidence of poverty has declined sharply from 30 to less than 12 per cent. The number of persons in poverty declined about 20 million over the past twenty years, including a drop of 12 million since 1963 —an estimated 4 million in 1968 alone.

The "poverty gap"—that is, the difference between the actual incomes of the poor and the incomes necessary to place them above the poverty line—has been reduced. The poverty gap fell from $13.7 billion in 1959 to $9.7 billion in 1967, measured in current dollars.

The incidence of poverty is highest in those rural areas not in metropolitan counties, with the heaviest concentrations in the South and Appalachia. The incidence is also quite high in the smaller cities and towns outside of major metropolitan areas. In the central cities, the incidence is 16 per cent and in their suburbs about 9 per cent.

Most of the poor are white. In 1967, 71 per cent of all poor families and 83 per cent of all poor unrelated individuals were white. The

323

incidence of poverty is far higher among nonwhites: about one household in three compared with about one in seven among whites.

Of the 2.4 million nonwhite households in poverty, 2.3 million are Negroes; the remainder are mostly the original Americans—Indians and Eskimos. A 1964 survey revealed that 74 per cent of the 55,000 families living on Indian and Eskimo reservations had incomes under $3,000.

Only recently has the reduction of poverty among nonwhites matched the reduction among whites. Between 1959 and 1962, the number of whites in poverty declined 2.8 million, but during the same period the number of poor nonwhites rose by 0.9 million. Between 1962 and 1967, white poverty was reduced another 7 million, or about 28 per cent, while poverty among nonwhites fell by 3.2 million, also about 28 per cent.

Table 1 **Concentration of U.S. Nonwhite Population by Region—1960 and Projected 1985**

Region	METROPOLITAN AREAS[a]		CENTRAL CITIES OF METROPOLITAN AREAS	
	1960	1985	1960	1985
United States	64.4%	78.3%	50.5%	58.4%
Northeast	93.9	94.5	76.0	77.4
North Central	89.7	91.5	78.8	81.9
South	45.7	63.9	34.1	42.2
West	77.9	89.6	53.5	59.1

[a] 1960 boundaries of SMSA's used for 1960; 1967 boundaries used for 1985.

Source: Hodge-Hauser Table III–6, page 28, based on U.S. Bureau of the Census, *U.S. Census of Population, 1960 Selected Area Reports, Type of Place,* Final Report PC(3)–1E, Table 1.

Table 2 **Distribution in United States of Total Population, Contrasted with Distribution of Total Poor Population, by Type of Place—1966**

	ALL PERSONS		WHITE PERSONS		NONWHITE PERSONS	
	Total Population	Poor Population	Total Population	Poor Population	Total Population	Poor Population
Metropolitan	64.7%	51.0%	64.3%	50.0%	67.9%	53.2%
Central City	30.2	31.5	27.0	26.5	53.4	43.6
Ring	34.6	19.5	37.3	23.5	14.5	9.6
Nonmetropolitan	35.3	49.0	35.7	50.0	32.1	46.8
	100.0	100.0	100.0	100.0	100.0	100.0

Table 3 **Negroes as a Percentage of Total Population by Location, Inside and Outside Metropolitan Areas, and by Size of Metropolitan Areas—1950, 1960, 1966, and 1968**

	PERCENTAGE OF NEGROES			
	1950	*1960*	*1966*	*1968*
United States	10	11	11	11
Metropolitan areas	9	11	12	12
Central cities	12	17	20	20
Central cities in metropolitan areas of :[a]				
1,000,000 or more	13	19	26[b]	25
250,000 to 1,000,000	12	15	20[b]	18
Under 250,000	12	12	12[b]	12
Suburbs	5	5	4	5
Smaller cities, towns, and rural areas	11	10	10	10

[a] In metropolitan areas of population shown as of 1960.
[b] Percentage nonwhite, data for Negroes are not available.

Source: U.S. Department of Commerce, Bureau of the Census.

Table 4 **Percentage of U.S. Population That is Nonwhite, in Central City and Suburb, by Region—1960 and Projected 1985**

Region and Residence	Percentage Nonwhite, 1960	Percentage Nonwhite, 1985
United States		
Central city	17.8%	30.7%
Ring	5.2	6.1
Northeast		
Central city	13.8	26.4
Ring	3.1	3.7
North Central		
Central city	17.1	32.0
Ring	2.8	2.2
South		
Central city	26.0	38.8
Ring	11.7	13.2
West		
Central city	13.0	23.3
Ring	4.9	5.3

Source: Hodge-Hauser Table III–7, p. 31, based on U.S. Bureau of the Census, *U.S. Census of Population, 1960, Selected Area Reports, Type of Place,* Final Report PC(3)–1E, Table 1.

Table 5 **Population Change by Location, Inside and Outside Metropolitan Areas—1950-1968 (Numbers in Millions)**

| | Total Population | | | | | |
| | NEGRO | | | WHITE | | |
	1960	1966	1968	1960	1966	1968
United States	18.8	21.5	21.9	158.1	170.9	173.7
Metropolitan areas	12.2	14.8	15.0	99.2	109.3	110.7
Central cities	9.7	12.1	11.8	47.5	46.6	45.8
Suburbs a	2.5	2.7	3.2	51.7	62.7	64.9
Smaller cities, towns, and rural areas	6.7	6.7	7.0	58.9	61.6	63.0

| | Population change, 1950–1968 | | | | | |
| | NEGRO | | | WHITE | | |
	1950–60	1960–66	1966–68	1950–60	1960–66	1966–68
United States	+3.8	+2.6	+.4	+23.7	+12.8	+2.8
Metropolitan areas	+3.8	+2.6	+.2	+19.3	+10.2	+1.3
Central cities	+3.2	+2.2	−.2	+2.2	−.8	−.8
Suburbs a	+.6	+.2	+.4	+17.2	+11.0	+2.2
Smaller cities, towns, and rural areas	(b)	(b)	+.2	+4.3	+2.7	+1.5

a Comprises the part of metropolitan area outside central cities.
b Less than 50,000.

Source: U.S. Department of Commerce, Bureau of the Census.

Table 6   **Persons Below the Poverty Level[a]—1959-1967**

	PERCENTAGE		NUMBER (IN MILLIONS)	
	Nonwhite	White	Nonwhite	White
1959	55%	18%	10.7	28.2
1960	55	18	11.4	28.7
1961	55	17	11.6	26.5
1962	54	16	11.6	25.4
1963	51	15	11.2	24.1
1964	49	14	10.9	23.4
1965	46	13	10.5	21.4
1966	41	12	9.6	20.1
Based on revised methodology:[b]				
1966	40	12	9.3	19.5
1967	35	10	8.3	17.6

[a] The poverty definition (as developed by the Social Security Administration) is based on the minimum food and other needs of families, taking account of family size, number of children and farm-nonfarm residence. As applied to 1967 incomes, the poverty threshold for a nonfarm family of four was $3,335.

[b] Reflects improvements in statistical procedures used in processing the income data.

Source: U.S. Department of Commerce, Bureau of the Census, and U.S. Department of Health, Education, and Welfare, Social Security Administration.

Table 7   **Percentage of Nonwhite Families in Poverty Areas[a] of Large Cities—1960, 1966, and 1968 (Numbers in Thousands)**

	NONWHITE FAMILIES			FAMILIES IN POVERTY AREAS[a] AS A PERCENTAGE OF NONWHITE FAMILIES		
	1960	1966	1968	1960	1966	1968
All large cities[b]	2,024	2,558	2,543	77	62	56
Central cities in metropolitan areas of:						
1,000,000 or more	1,392	1,770	1,816	76	59	53
250,000 to 1,000,000	633	788	728	79	69	63
New York City	260	388	406	77	62	59
Chicago	187	239	247	80	54	48
Los Angeles	100	128	150	61	47	40

[a] Poverty Areas were determined by ranking census tracts in metropolitan areas of 250,000 or more in 1960, according to the relative presence of each of the following equally weighted poverty-linked characteristics: (1) family income below $3,000, (2) children in broken homes, (3) persons with low educational attainments, (4) males in unskilled jobs, (5) substandard housing. It includes an adjustment for changes brought about since 1960 by urban renewal. In general, the lowest 25 per cent of census tracts are included.

[b] In metropolitan areas of 250,000 or more in 1960.

Source: U.S. Department of Commerce, Bureau of the Census.

Table 8 **Labor Force and Unemployment In and Outside the Poverty Areas in Large Metropolitan Areas**[a]**—1967 and 1968 (First 6 Months) (Numbers in Thousands)**

	NONWHITE		WHITE	
	1967	*1968*	*1967*	*1968*
In poverty areas:				
Civilian labor force	2,747	2,713	3,856	3,831
Unemployed	241	217	212	199
Unemployment rate	8.8	8.0	5.5	5.2
Outside poverty areas:				
Civilian labor force	2,691	2,951	33,688	34,324
Unemployed	167	172	1,110	1,053
Unemployment rate	6.2	5.8	3.3	3.1

[a] In the 100 largest metropolitan areas in 1960.

Source: U.S. Department of Labor, Bureau of Labor Statistics.

Table 9 **Unemployment in Central Cities and Suburbs of the 20 Largest Metropolitan Areas**[a]**—1967**

	UNEMPLOYMENT RATE		Ratio of Nonwhite to White	NUMBER UNEMPLOYED (IN THOUSANDS)	
	Nonwhite	*White*		*Nonwhite*	*White*
Central cities	7.6	3.7	2.1	222	332
Adult men	4.9	2.8	1.8	75	148
Adult women	6.6	3.5	1.8	76	109
Teenagers	31.6	11.5	2.4	71	73
Suburbs	7.0	3.1	2.3	53	407

In the 20 largest metropolitan areas in 1960.

Source: U.S. Department of Labor, Bureau of Labor Statistics.

Table 10   Subemployment Indicators[a] for Men—1966 and
1967
(Numbers in Thousands)

	Nonwhite	White
Subemployment rate :[a]		
1966	21.6	7.6
1967	(c)	(c)
Indicators of subemployment[b]		
Number of low earners :		
1966	635	1,417
1967	505	1,176
Percentage of change	—31%	—17%
Monthly average number unemployed 15 weeks or more :[b]		
1966	69	255
1967	53	202
Percentage of change	—23%	—21%

[a] *The Manpower Report of the President,* issued April 1968, published a new national subemployment measure for 1966 (pp. 34–36). This measure includes (1) workers unemployed 15 weeks or more and (2) workers who made less than $3,000 in 1966 for year-round full-time work (taken as a proportion of the entire labor force with a week or more of work experience during the year). This indicator is, therefore, on an annual basis and considerably different from the subemployment rate in a specific week arrived at last year for workers in urban slums. (See page 97 in *Social and Economic Conditions of Negroes in the United States,* October 1967, Report No. 332, and Current Population Reports, Series P–23, No. 24.)

[b] Annual data for those unemployed 15 weeks or more in 1967 are not yet available; therefore a rate is not computed but two subemployment indicators are presented. These are not precisely the same as those required for the national subemployment rate published for 1966.

[c] Data not available.

Source: U.S. Department of Labor, Bureau of Labor Statistics.

Table 11   **Nonwhite Commuting from Central City to Suburban Jobs—1960**

	PERCENTAGE OF WORK FORCE			
	Nonwhite Male Commuters	Central-City Nonwhite Males	Total Suburban Employment, 1959	Total Suburban Employment,[a] 1959
Baltimore	9,546	16.0%	6.9%	138,069
New York	7,007	3.1	1.3	524,799
Philadelphia	8,570	8.6	1.8	480,821
St. Louis	3,156	9.0	1.4	233,505
San Francisco	7,272	15.3	2.0	370,790

[a] Employment data by county not available for 1960.

Source: U.S. Census of Population 1960, *Journey to Work: County Business Patterns,* 1959, as quoted in "The Impact of Housing Patterns on Job Opportunities," National Committee Against Discrimination in Housing, New York, 1968.

Table 12 Unemployment Rates[a]—1948-1967 and 1968 (First 6 Months)

	Nonwhite	White	Ratio of Nonwhite to White
1948	5.2	3.2	1.6
1949	8.9	5.6	1.6
1950	9.0	4.9	1.8
1951	5.3	3.1	1.7
1952	5.4	2.8	1.9
1953	4.5	2.7	1.7
1954	9.9	5.0	2.0
1955	8.7	3.9	2.2
1956	8.3	3.6	2.3
1957	7.9	3.8	2.1
1958	12.6	6.1	2.1
1959	10.7	4.8	2.2
1960	10.2	4.9	2.1
1961	12.4	6.0	2.1
1962	10.9	4.9	2.2
1963	10.8	5.0	2.2
1964	9.6	4.6	2.1
1965	8.1	4.1	2.0
1966	7.3	3.3	2.2
1967	7.4	3.4	2.2
1968[b]	6.8	3.2	2.1

[a] The unemployment rate is the percentage unemployed in the civilian labor force.
[b] First 6 months seasonally adjusted.

Source: U.S. Department of Labor, Bureau of Labor Statistics.

Table 13 Employment by Occupation,[a] 1967, and Change, 1960-1967
(Numbers in Thousands)

| | Employed, 1967 | | Change, 1960–1967[a] | | | |
| | | | NUMBER | | PERCENTAGE | |
	Non-white	White	Non-white	White	Non-white	White
Total	8,011	66,361	970	6,721	14	11
Professional and technical	592	9,287	263	2,141	80	30
Managers, officials, etc.	209	7,286	31	396	17	6
Clerical	899	11,434	391	2,158	77	23
Sales	138	4,387	25	99	22	2
Craftsmen and foremen	617	9,228	203	1,083	49	13
Operatives	1,882	12,002	465	1,434	33	14
Service workers, except private household	1,519	6,037	287	1,136	23	23
Private household workers	835	934	—169	—278	—17	—23
Nonfarm laborers	899	2,634	—70	—61	—7	—2
Farmers and farmworkers	423	3,131	—453	—1,389	—52	—31

[a] The 1967 data pertain to persons 16 years of age and over, while in 1960 the age cutoff was 14 years. Since 14–15-year-olds make up less than 2 per cent of total nonwhite employment, it can be assumed that they have almost no effect on the 1960–1967 occupational change.

Source: U.S. Department of Labor, Bureau of Labor Statistics.

Table 14 Percentage of Occupied Housing Not Meeting Specified Criteria[a] by Location—1960 and 1966

| | NONWHITE | | WHITE | |
	1960	1966	1960	1966
United States	44	29	13	8
Large cities[b]	25	16	8	5
Suburbs	43	29	7	4
Smaller cities, towns, and rural	77	64	23	14

[a] Housing is classified as "not meeting specified criteria" if it either is dilapidated or lacks one or more of the following basic plumbing facilities: hot running water in the structure, flush toilet for private use of members of the household, and bathtub or shower for private use of members of the household.

Housing is reported as "dilapidated" if defects are so critical or so widespread that the structure would require extensive repairs, rebuilding, razing, or was of inadequate original construction. Information is collected also on housing condition rated as "deteriorating," that is, having one or more defects of an intermediate nature that require correction if the unit is to continue to provide safe and adequate shelter.

Based on these classifications, deteriorating and dilapidated housing for nonwhite households in the nation as a whole was 45 per cent in 1960 and 39 per cent in 1966.

[b] Of 50,000 population or more in metropolitan areas.

Source: U.S. Department of Commerce, Bureau of the Census. Data for 1966 are preliminary.

Notes

Notes to Chapter 1: The Problem and Strategy

1. Report of the National Commission on Urban Problems, Introduction. Washington, D.C.: U.S. Govt. Printing Office, 1969, pp. i and ii.

2. *Ibid.*, Ch. 1, p. 23.

3. *Ibid.*, p. 30.

4. Elliott Liebow, *Tally's Corner*. Boston: Little, Brown, 1967, p. 53.

5. Frank H. Cassell, "Realities and Opportunities in the Development of Jobs." *Business and Society*, Vol. 8, No. 2 (Spring 1968), p. 25.

6. *Ibid.*, p. 61.

7. *Ibid.*, p. 62.

8. Report of the National Commission on Urban Problems, *op. cit.*, Part II, "Housing Programs," Ch. 1, pp. 31–41.

9. See Dick Netzer, *The Urban Fiscal Problem* (Institute of Local Government) (University of Pittsburgh, 1967), Ch. 8.

10. Report of the National Commission on Urban Problems, *op. cit.*, Part IV, "Government Structure, Finance and Taxation," pp. 15 and 16.

11. *Ibid.*

12. *Ibid.*, p. 44.

13. Herbert Hill, "Planning the End of the American Ghetto: A Problem of Economic Development for Equal Rights," in *Focus,*

NAACP document. Paper presented at White House Conference, "To Fulfill These Rights," June 2–3, 1966, Washington, D.C.

14. Nora Sayre, "Blacker Theatre." *The Progressive,* April 1969, pp. 37 and 38.

15. Bayard Rustin, "Funding Full Citizenship." *Council Journal,* Vol. 6, No. 3, 1967, p. 4.

16. *Ibid.,* p. 5.

17. *Ibid.*

18. Personal interview with James Boggs, Granville, Ohio, March 1969.

19. Advisory Commission on Intergovernmental Relations, "Urban and Rural America: Policies for Future Growth." A Commission Report, Washington, D.C., April 1968, p. 124.

Notes to Chapter 2: Black Economic Philosophies: Historical Antecedents

1. *Report of the National Advisory Commission on Civil Disorders.* New York: Bantam, 1968, p. 235.

2. The most authoritative source on these communities is *Black Utopia: Negro Communal Experiments in America,* by William and Jane Pease (Madison: The State Historical Society of Wisconsin, 1963). Abortive attempts to establish black communities occurred in Brown, Mercer, and Miami counties in Ohio. The following were more successful attempts: (1) Frances Wright's Nashoba in Tennessee, the only true utopian experiment among them; (2) Wilberforce in Ontario, Canada; (3) Dawn in western Canada; (4) Elgin in Ontario, Canada; (5) The Refugee Home Society in Canada near Detroit; and (6) the Port Royal experiments on the Sea Islands of South Carolina.

3. See Arthur E. Bestor, Jr., *Backwoods Utopias* (Philadelphia: University of Pennsylvania Press, 1950).

4. The following information is derived from Pease, *op. cit.,* pp. 18–20.

5. *Ibid.,* p. 20.

6. *Ibid.,* p. 163.

7. Samuel R. Spencer, Jr., "The Achievement of Booker T. Washington," in *Booker T. Washington and His Critics,* ed. by Hugh Hawkins. Boston: D. C. Heath, 1962, p. 108.

8. *Ibid.*

9. Kelley Miller, "Washington's Policy," in *Booker T. Washington and His Critics, op. cit.,* pp. 50–51.

10. Booker T. Washington, *The Future of the American Negro.* Boston: Small, Maynard, 1899, pp. 222–223.

11. *Ibid.,* p. 132.

12. *Ibid.,* p. 86.

13. *Ibid.,* p. 93.

14. This address is reprinted in Booker T. Washington, *Up from Slavery* (New York: Doubleday, Page, 1902), pp. 218–225.

15. Washington, *op. cit.*, p. 99.

16. *Ibid.*, p. 153.

17. Horace Mann Bond, "The Influence of Personalities on the Public Education of Negroes in Alabama," in *Booker T. Washington and His Critics, op. cit.*, p. 75.

18. Washington, *op. cit.*, p. 69.

19. W. E. B. DuBois, "Of Mr. Booker T. Washington and Others," in *Booker T. Washington and His Critics, op. cit.*, pp. 35–36.

20. C. Vann Woodward, "The Atlanta Compromise," in *Booker T. Washington and His Critics, op. cit.*, p. 105.

21. *Ibid.*

22. W. E. B. DuBois, *The Souls of Black Folk.* Chicago: A. C. McClurg, 1903, pp. 58–59.

23. W. E. B. DuBois, "The Talented Tenth," in "Booker T. Washington and Others," in *The Negro Problem: A Series of Articles by Representative Negroes of Today.* New York: James Pott, 1903, pp. 33–75.

24. Francis L. Broderick, *W. E. B. DuBois: Negro Leader in a Time of Crisis.* Stanford, Calif.: Stanford University Press, 1959, p. 102.

25. DuBois, *op. cit.*, p. 3. *Souls of Black Folk.*

26. See Broderick, *op. cit.*, p. 150. In his book *Dusk of Dawn,* DuBois asserted that his program for the Negro "can easily be mistaken for a program of complete racial segregation and even nationalism among Negroes . . . [but that] this is a misapprehension."

27. Harold Cruse, *The Crisis of the Negro Intellectual.* New York: William Morrow, 1967, p. 309.

28. W. E. B. DuBois, "Segregation." *The Crisis,* Vol. 41 (January 1934), p. 20.

29. Broderick, *op. cit.*, p. 167.

30. Quoted by Broderick, *op. cit.*, p. 51.

31. Quoted by Broderick, *op. cit.*, p. 103.

32. W. E. B. DuBois, "The Immediate Program of the American Negro." *The Crisis,* Vol. II (April 1915), p. 311.

33. See Broderick, *op. cit.*, p. 167.

34. Broderick, *op. cit.*, p. 166.

35. W. E. B. DuBois, "Socialist of the Path," and "Negro and Socialism." *Horizon,* Vols. 1 and 2 (February 1907), pp. 7–8.

36. T. Nelson, "W. E. B. DuBois: Prophet in Limbo." *Nation,* Vol. 186 (January 25, 1958), p. 78.

37. W. E. B. DuBois, *Dusk of Dawn,* Harcourt Brace & Co., New York, 1940, pp. 319–322.

38. UNIA Manifesto, quoted by Edmund D. Cronon in *Black Moses: The Story of Marcus Garvey and the Universal Negro Improve-*

ment Association (Madison: University of Wisconsin Press, 1955), p. 17.

39. Cronon, *Black Moses, op. cit.,* p. 172.

40. Quoted by Cronon in *Black Moses, op. cit.,* p. 153.

41. *Philosophy and Opinions of Marcus Garvey,* 2nd ed., compiled by Amy Jacques Garvey. London: Frank Cass, 1967, p. 21.

42. *Ibid.,* p. 24.

43. *Ibid.,* p. 23.

44. *Ibid.,* same page.

45. Cronon, *op. cit.,* p. 65.

46. *Philosophy and Opinions of Marcus Garvey, op. cit.,* p. 121.

47. Cronon, *op. cit.,* p. 132.

48. *Philosophy and Opinions of Marcus Garvey, op. cit.,* p. 8.

49. Cronon, *op. cit.,* p. 51.

50. *Philosophy and Opinions of Marcus Garvey, op. cit.,* p. 38.

51. *Ibid.,* p. 39.

52. *Ibid.,* p. 9.

53. Marcus Garvey, quoted by Cronon in *Black Moses, op. cit.,* p. 60.

54. Cronon, *op. cit.,* p. 60.

55. W. E. B. DuBois, *Dusk of Dawn, op. cit.,* p. 277.

Notes to Chapter 3: Moderate and Militant Diversity in Ideology

1. See Kenneth B. Clark, "The Crisis: Attitudes and Behavior," in *Business Leadership and the Negro Crisis,* ed. by Eli Ginsberg (New York: Columbia University Press, 1968), p. 27.

2. See E. E. Thorpe, *The Mind of the Negro: An Intellectual History of Afro-Americans* (Baton Rouge, Ortlieb Press, 1961), p. 425.

3. *Ibid.,* p. 426.

4. Personal interview, July 18, 1968, New York City. Mr. Fitzhugh is a former academician and a vice-president of the Pepsi-Cola Company.

5. *Ibid.*

6. *Ibid.*

7. *Ibid.*

8. Personal interview, at NAACP headquarters, New York City, July 17, 1968.

9. *Ibid.*

10. *Ibid.*

11. R. H. Kinzer and Edward Sagarin, *The Negro in American Business, The Conflict between Separatism and Integration.* New York: Greenberg Publisher, 1960, p. 1.

12. See remarks by B. G. Burrell, before the Annual Banquet of the Booker T. Washington Business Association, Detroit, July 13, 1968.

13. B. G. Burrell, address before the Mt. Vernon Avenue Improvement Association, Columbus, Ohio, February 8, 1968, p. 3.

14. B. G. Burrell, address at Bethpage, N.Y., May 24, 1968. Mimeographed.

15. *Ibid.*

16. *Ibid.,* p. 3.

17. See remarks by the Reverend Leon Sullivan, "Employment and Manpower Problems in the Cities: Implications of the Report of the National Advisory Commission on Civil Disorders." Hearings before the Joint Economic Committee, Ninetieth Congress, Second Session, May 28, 29 and June 4, 5, 6, 1968. Washington, D.C.: U.S. Govt. Printing Office, 1968, p. 204.

18. *Ibid.*

19. *Ibid.,* p. 220.

20. *Ibid.,* p. 225.

21. Personal interview with Mr. Watts, July 18, 1968, New York City.

22. The other is Harold Cruse, author of *The Crisis of the Negro Intellectual.* (New York: William Morrow, 1967).

23. James Boggs, *The American Revolution: Pages from a Negro Worker's Notebook.* New York: Monthly Review Press, 1964.

24. James Boggs, "Black Power: A Scientific Concept." *The Liberator,* April and May 1967.

25. James Boggs, *Manifesto for a Black Revolutionary Party.* Philadelphia: Pacesetters, 1968, p. 15.

26. *Ibid.,* p. 11.

27. Grace L. and James Boggs, "The City is the Black Man's Land," unpublished paper, 1966, p. 5.

28. James Boggs, *Manifesto for the Black Revolutionary Party, op. cit.,* p. 8.

29. *Ibid.,* p. 33. The terms *militant* and *revolutionary* should be interpreted cautiously. As utilized by many blacks, these terms refer to radical confrontation with the system from within the system, but not necessarily to a violent overthrow of the system itself. The differing interpretations of these terms again illustrate the problems of categorization of individuals and groups within the Negro movement, and they should be approached with extreme circumspection.

30. *Ibid.,* p. 17.

31. *Ibid.,* p. 36.

32. Remarks by James Boggs on Ray Franklin's "The Political Economy of Black Power," a paper presented at the Socialist Scholar's Conference, New York, September 10, 1967.

33. James Boggs, "Jobs and Politics—The Revolution of the Self-Governing Man," a paper presented at a meeting of the Alliance for Jobs or Income Now, New York, December 5, 1964.

34. Designation on title page of Elijah Muhammad, *Message to the Blackman in America.* Chicago: Muhammad Mosque of Islam, No. 2, 1965.

35. Elijah Muhammad, "The Break-up of the Old World!" in *Message to the Blackman in America*. Chicago: Muhammad Mosque of Islam, No. 2, 1965, p. 266.

36. *Ibid.*, "Make America Know Her Sins," p. 281.

37. See *Ibid.*, "The Battle in the Sky," p. 293. In the same volume, see also the articles entitled "On Universal Corruption," "The Day of America's Downfall," "America is Falling, Her Doom is Sealed," and "The Resurrection of Our People."

38. See *Ibid.*, "Explanation of What Muslims Want and Believe," p. 167.

39. *Ibid.*, "Program and Position," p. 164.

40. *Ibid.*, "Program and Position," p. 163.

41. See *Ibid.*, "A House of Our Own," p. 224.

42. See *The Islamic News*, July 6, 1959.

43. E. Muhammad, speech in Washington, D.C., quoted by E. U. Essien-Udom, in *Black Nationalism*, New York: Dell, 1964, p. 386.

44. E. Muhammad, "Of Land and a Nation," in *Message to the Blackman in America, op. cit.*, p. 223.

45. C. Eric Lincoln, *The Black Muslims in America*. Boston: Beacon Press, 1961, p. 97.

46. See E. Muhammad, "A Nation Within a Nation," in *Message to the Blackman in America, op. cit.*, p. 230.

47. See Lincoln, *op. cit.*, p. 85.

48. Malcolm X, "God's Judgment of White America." Manuscript of unpublished speeches, New York, December 1, 1963, quoted by George Breitman in *The Last Year of Malcolm X: The Evolution of a Revolutionary* (New York: Merrick, 1967), pp. 57–58. This book perhaps provides the best interpretive source of the evolution of Malcolm X's philosophy during the last year of his life. Other sources are *Malcolm X Speaks: Selected Speeches and Statements*, edited by George Breitman (New York: Grove Press, 1965). For more information concerning the life of Malcolm X and his tenure as a Black Muslim, see *The Autobiography of Malcolm X* (New York: Grove Press, 1964).

49. *Malcolm X Speaks, op. cit.*, p. 10.

50. *Ibid.*, p. 51.

51. *Ibid.*, pp. 226–227.

52. Breitman, *op. cit.*, p. 68.

53. *Ibid.*, p. 138.

54. *Malcolm X Speaks, op. cit.*, p. 121.

55. Bayard Rustin attacked Malcolm X on his economic philosophy. He argued against the policy of establishing small businesses at a time when these were declining under the pressure of big businesses. And further he believed that Malcolm X did not understand the radical changes in the structure of the economy which were being created by the technological revolution. See Breitman, *op. cit.*, p. 88.

56. Phonograph recording, "Malcolm X Speaks Again," 20 Grand Records, New York, 1965. Quoted by Breitman, *op. cit.*, pp. 88–89.

57. These programs are published in appendices A and B of Breitman, *The Last Year of Malcolm X, op. cit.*

58. Breitman, *op. cit.*, p. 151.

59. *Black Panther,* November 23, 1967, p. 7.

60. *Ibid.*

61. Eldridge Cleaver, "The Land Question." *Ramparts,* Vol. 6, (May 1968), pp. 51–53.

62. *Ibid.*, p. 52.

63. *Black Panther,* November 23, 1967.

64. E. Cleaver, *op. cit.*, p. 53.

65. "Black Business: Its Role in the Liberation Struggle," *Black Power,* February 1967, p. 10.

66. *Ibid.*

67. David Llorens, "Black Separatism in Perspective," *Ebony,* Vol. 33 (October 1968), p. 88.

68. Richard B. Henry, Minister of Information of the Republic of New Africa, quoted in D. Llorens, *op. cit.*, p. 95.

69. *Ibid.*

70. "All about CORE," (pamphlet of the Congress of Racial Equality, 1963). Reprinted in *Negro Protest Thought in the Twentieth Century,* ed. by Francis L. Broderick and August Meier (New York: Bobbs-Merrill, 1965), p. 301.

71. Quoted in "Is Black Capitalism the Answer?", *Business Week,* August 3, 1968, p. 60.

72. Statement by Roy Innis, National Director of Congress of Racial Equality, to subcommittee on Equal Opportunity in an Urban Society, Resolutions Committee for the Republican National Convention, July 30, 1968, Miami Beach. Mimeographed.

73. *Ibid.*, p. 6.

74. Personal interview with Kermit Scott, Director of Chapter Development and Director of Community Relations, Congress of Racial Equality, Columbus, Ohio, July 8, 1968.

75. *Ibid.*

Notes to Chapter 4: Economic Programs of Militant Separatists

1. James Boggs, *Manifesto for A Black Revolutionary Party,* Philadelphia: Pacesetters, 1968, p. 13.

2. James Boggs, "The Rights of Man in an Age of Abundance." Paper presented to the Northern Negro Grass Roots Leadership Conference, Detroit, November 9–10, 19

3. James Boggs, "Jobs and Politics—The Revolution of the Self-Governing Man," p. 3. Mimeographed paper.

4. James Boggs, "Practical Applications of Automation." Paper prepared for the automation seminar, March 23, 1965, in Detroit.

5. Remarks by James Boggs on Ray Franklin's "The Political Economy of Black Power." Paper presented at the Socialist Scholars Conference, New York, September 10, 1967.

6. James Boggs, "Black Power: A Scientific Concept Whose Time Has Come," p. 9, *Liberator,* April 1967.

7. Report of National Commission on Technology, Automation, and Economic Progress (mimeographed), January 29, 1966, Ch. I, p. 1.

8. E. U. Essien-Udom, *Black Nationalism,* New York: Dell, 1964, p. 189.

9. Elijah Muhammad, "A Sound Economic Plan I," in *Message to the Blackman in America.* Chicago: Muhammad Mosque of Islam, No. 2, 1965, p. 194.

10. Quoted by C. Eric Lincoln, *The Black Muslims in America.* Boston: Beacon Press, 1961, p. 123.

11. E. Muhammad, *op. cit.,* pp. 177–186.

12. Eleventh Report to the 1961 Regular California Legislature in Sacramento, California.

13. E. Muhammad, *op. cit.,* pp. 169–171.

14. E. Muhammad, *op. cit.,* "An Economic Blueprint," pp. 173–175.

15. E. Muhammad, *op. cit.,* "Economic Program to Help Fight against Poverty and Want," pp. 192–193.

16. E. Muhammad, *op. cit.,* "A Sound Economic Plan I," p. 195.

17. E. Muhammad, *op. cit.,* "An Economic Blueprint," p. 172.

18. See *Ibid.,* pp. 174–175.

19. E. U. Essien-Udom, *op. cit.,* p. 183.

20. *Ibid.,* p. 185.

21. *Ibid.,* p. 183.

22. W. W. Rostow, *The Stages of Economic Growth.* Cambridge, England: Cambridge University Press, 1961.

23. See E. Muhammad, *op. cit.,* "Up! You Can Accomplish What You Will!" pp. 200–201.

24. See E. Muhammad, *op. cit.,* "To Help Fight Against Poverty and Want," p. 193.

25. E. U. Essien-Udom, *op. cit.,* p. 189.

26. *Ibid.*

27. E. Muhammad, *op. cit.,* "What do the Muslims Want?" p. 161.

28. *Ibid.,* p. 162.

29. Kurt Samuelsson, *Religion and Economic Action.* London: Heinemann, 1961.

30. Open Application for Funding Grants to CORE Development Corporation and Invitation to Cooperate with CORE Development Corporation in Projects to Raise the Economic Productiveness of Ghetto Residents and Other Poor. Congress of Racial Equality, Inc., 1968.

31. See Lewis Kelso and Mortimer Adler, *The Capitalist Manifesto,* and *The New Capitalists,* 1961, New York: Random House.
32. Open Application for Funding Grants, *op. cit.,* p. 15.
33. *Ibid.,* p. 7.
34. CORE uses the terms "second economy" to refer to a "black economic substructure" or synonymously with "black capitalism."
35. *Ibid.,* p. 14.
36. *Ibid.,* p. 21.
37. *Ibid.,* p. 20.
38. *Ibid.,* p. 25.
39. *Ibid.*
40. *Ibid.,* p. 26.
41. Community Self-Determination Act of 1968, H.R. 18709, Ninetieth Congress, Second Session, July 18, 1968; Rural Development Incentive Act of 1968, H.R. 14600, Ninetieth Congress, Second Session, January 15, 1968.
42. Community Self-Determination Act, *op. cit.,* preface.
43. *Ibid.,* p. 5.
44. *Ibid.,* p. 67. This bill recognizes that one of the contributing factors to the problems of the city is the migration into the inner city from rural areas. To slow this rate of immigration, the bill provides that any community development corporation in an area that lies completely outside any standard metropolitan area would have a factor of five subtracted from its development index. This procedure would have the effect of making it appear that the regions level of development relative to others was lower, and in fact it actually was. It would introduce a bias towards development of rural areas.
45. *Ibid.,* p. 39.
46. *Ibid.,* p. 21.
47. *Ibid.,* p. 121.
48. Rural Development Incentive Act, *op. cit.,* p. 1.
49. These two bills have received wide support among particularly Republican congressmen and leaders of black communities. However, Chairman of the House Ways and Means Committee, Wilbur Mills, is reported not to be in favor of it because of the so-called tax gimmicks built into it. Both bills were reintroduced in the Ninety-first Congress, First Session (S. 33). The bills have not been scheduled for hearings, and there presently appears little or no possibility that they will be passed by Congress. Many of the original proponents have now withdrawn their support.
50. The "professions" and franchised retail outlets are exceptions within this category.
51. Personal interview with the Reverend Albert B. Cleage of the Central United Church of Christ, in Detroit, July 24, 1968.
52. *Ibid.*

53. Harold Cruse, *The Crisis of the Negro Intellectual.* New York: William Morrow, 1967, p. 93.

54. Ibid., pp. 88–90, 258–259.

55. Theora Makeda, "A Challenge for Black Leadership." *The Liberator,* Vol. 7 (June 1967), p. 10.

56. *Ibid.,* pp. 10–11.

57. James Boggs, *Manifesto for a Black Revolutionary Party.* Philadelphia: Pacesetters, 1968, p. 1.

58. *Ibid.,* p. 3.

59. *Ibid.,* pp. 6–7.

Notes to Chapter 5: Development Programs Within the Institutional Framework

1. See Proceedings of the National Business League, 1900, and E. E. Thorpe, *The Mind of the Negro: An Intellectual History of the Afro-American,* Baton Rouge, Ortlieb Press, 1961, p. 422.

2. Operations Manual for Project Outreach of the National Business League, prepared by Samuel E. Harris, economic consultant, New York, pp. 4–5. Undated.

3. National Business League, "Project Mainstream," published by N.B.L., Washington, D.C., undated brochure. *Ibid.,* p. 14.

4. See Project Mainstream brochure, National Business League, (3418 Georgia Avenue, N.W., Washington, D.C.), p. 4.

5. *Ibid.,* p. 3.

6. B. G. Burrell, statement presented at hearings before the Joint Economic Committee, Ninetieth Congress. Washington, D.C.: U.S. Govt. Printing Office, 1968.

7. Statement on Inner-City Economic Development, Project Outreach (4325 Georgia Avenue, N.W., Washington, D.C.), p. 1.

8. Editorial, *Mainstream,* publication of the National Business League, Vol. 1, No. 1 (January 1968), p. 31.

9. See Benjamin Mays, *The Negro's God* (Boston: Chapman and Grimes, 1939).

10. See Committee on Government Operations, "Federal Role in Urban Affairs," U.S. Senate, Eighty-Ninth Congress, December 14 and 15, 1966, Part 14, p. 2921.

11. See *ibid.,* pp. 2932–2940.

12. See "A Call to Action," recommendations on the Urban and Racial Crisis, submitted to President Richard M. Nixon by the National Urban League, January 20, 1969, p. 50.

13. *Ibid.,* pp. 1 and 2.

14. See Herbert Hill, "Planning the End of the American Ghetto: A Problem of Economic Development and Equal Rights," in *Focus,* NAACP document. Paper presented at White House Conference, "To Fulfill These Rights," June 2–3, 1966, Washington, D.C., pp. 24–28.

15. Personal interview with William Morris, at NAACP headquarters, New York City, July 17, 1968.

16. See A. Philip Randolph Institute, "A 'Freedom Budget' for All Americans," New York, October 1966, pp. 5ff.

17. A. Philip Randolph, "Toward a Freedom Budget." *Dissent,* Vol. 13 (March-April 1966), p. 125.

18. Statement by Dr. Ralph D. Abernathy, President, Southern Christian Leadership Conference, Resolutions to Subcommittee on Equal Opportunities in an Urban Society, Republican National Convention, Miami Beach, July 31, 1968, p. 6.

19. United Press International release, January 9, 1969.

20. See "Business and the Urban Crisis," *Business Week,* February 3, 1968, p. C-6.

21. Statements by the Rev. Leon Sullivan, "Employment and Manpower Problems in the Cities: Implications of the Report of the National Advisory Commission on Civil Disorders." Hearings before the Joint Economic Committee, Ninetieth Congress, Washington, D.C., May 28, 29 and June 4, 5, 6, 1968, p. 208.

22. A. S. Venable, "Mobilizing Dormant Resources: Negro Entrepreneurs." Remarks made available by the Business and Defense Services Administration, May 1967.

23. Personal interview with F. Naylor Fitzhugh, former academician and a vice-president of the Pepsi-Cola Company. New York City, July 18, 1968.

24. GHEDIplan, An economic development plan prepared for the Human Resources Administration of the City of New York. April 1968, p. 4.

25. See Charles G. Bennett, "City Development Plan Seeks to Aid Slum Area Businesses," New York *Times,* April 11, 1968.

26. See "Asks Building Business for Ghetto," *New York Amsterdam News,* April 13, 1968.

27. GHEDIplan, *op. cit.,* p. 6.

28. See New York *Times,* "More Boston Negroes Enter Business," March 9, 1969.

29. See "Will an Ethnic Pitch Sell the Black Market?" *Business Week,* April 12, 1969, pp. 88 and 92.

30. See memorandum of Milton Kotler (Institute for Policy Studies, Washington, D.C.), "The Neighborhood Corporation as a Unit of Economic Development," in "The Federal Role in Urban Affairs," Committee on Government Operations. U.S. Senate, Eighty-ninth Congress, 1966, pp. 2058–2061.

31. *Ibid.,* p. 2057.

32. Harold Cruse, *The Crisis of the Negro Intellectual,* New York: William Morrow, 1967, pp. 88–90; 258–259.

33. *Ibid.*

Notes to Chapter 6: Programs of White Majority Businesses

1. David M. Kennedy, "Business Takes a New Look at the Disadvantaged," *The Role of Banks and the Urban Challenge.*" Continental National Bank and Trust Company of Chicago, December 9, 1968, p. 4. Monograph.

2. *Ibid.*

3. George Champion, "Creative Competition." *Harvard Business Review,* May-June 1967, p. 67.

4. See Kodak's *Highlights,* Vol. 22, No. 1, (February 1969), p. 4.

5. Thomas Calcerano, former Director of Procurement and Placement of the National Business League, now an employee of American Telephone and Telegraph System, in *The Bell Telephone Magazine,* January-February 1969, p. 16

6. "Hard Core Jobless Get a Friend at the Top." *Business Week,* March 1969, pp. 69 and 71.

7. Samuel M. Burt and Herbert E. Striner, "Toward Greater Industry and Government Involvement in Manpower Development." Upjohn Institute for Employment Research, Kalamazoo, Mich., September 1968, p. 3.

8. Manpower Report of the President, U.S. Dept. of Labor, April 1968, p. 201.

9. S. M. Burt and H. E. Striner, *op. cit.,* p. 6.

10. "New Plants Dot the Black Slums," *Business Week,* March 22, 1969, p. 100.

11. "An Industry's Cure for Slums," *U.S. News and World Report,* September 2, 1968, p. 59.

12. *Ibid.*

13. "Business and the Urban Crisis, a Special Report from McGraw-Hill." *Business Week,* February 3, 1968, p. C-12.

14. *Ibid.*

15. G. Champion, *op. cit.,* p. 62.

16. Statement by Peter F. McNeish, Executive Secretary, Committee on Urban Affairs, American Bankers' Assn., Washington, D.C., in letter of October 2, 1968.

17. Donald M. Graham, "Financial Institutions and the Urban Challenge," in *The Role of Banks and the Urban Challenge,* Continental National Bank and Trust Company of Chicago, October 4, 1968.

18. *Ibid.*

19. Statement by former Small Business Administrator Howard J. Samuels, in "Small Business Administration," news release of August 13, 1968.

20. *Ibid.*

21. See Projects 200–1, 300–1, 400–1, 500–1, published by the Business and Defense Services Administration, U.S. Dept. of Commerce, Washington, D.C.

22. John Garrity, "Red Ink for Ghetto Industries," *Harvard Business Review*, May-June 1968, p. 5.

23. "What Business Can Do for the Poor," *Nation's Business*, Vol. 55 (October 1967), pp. 67 and 68.

24. *Ibid.*, p. 68.

25. Statement by Lester C. Thurow, "Employment and Manpower Problems in the Cities: Implications of the Report of the National Advisory Commission on Civil Disorders." Hearings before the Joint Economic Committee, Ninetieth Congress, Second Session, Washington, D.C.: U.S. Govt. Printing Office, 1968, p. 146.

26. *Ibid.*, p. 10.

27. *Ibid.*, p. 146.

28. Statement by Allen L. Otten, "Employment and Manpower Problems in the Cities," *op. cit.*, quoted in *The Wall Street Journal*, April 26, 1968.

29. Hazel Henderson, "Should Business Tackle Society's Problems?" *Harvard Business Review*, July-August 1968, p. 82.

30. *Ibid.*, p. 83.

31. James L. Sunquist, "Jobs Training and Welfare for the Underclass," *Agenda for the Nation*, ed. by Kermit Gordon. Brookings Institution, Washington, D.C., 1968, p. 62.

32. Statement by John F. Kain, "Employment and Manpower Problems in the Cities," *op. cit.*, p. 78.

33. *Ibid.*, p. 80.

34. See S. O. Woodard and V. M. Pinachi, "Investment Influences of the Tax Credit Program," *National Tax Journal*, Vol. 18, No. 3 (September 1965), pp. 275–276; and Robert E. Hall and Dale W. Jorgenson, "Tax Policy and Investment Behavior," *American Economic Review*, Vol. 17, No. 3 (June 1967), p. 413. Also see E. C. Brown, "Tax Incentives for Investment," *American Economic Review*, May 1962, pp. 335–345.

35. Ralph Gray, "Industrial Development Subsidy and Efficiency in Resource Allocation." *National Tax Journal*, Vol. 17, No. 2 (June 1964), p. 165.

36. Advisory Commission on Intergovernmental Relations, "Urban and Rural America: Policies for Future Growth." A commission report, Washington, D.C., April 1968, pp. 141–142.

37. Benjamin Bridges, "State and Local Inducements for Industry," *National Tax Journal*, Vol. 18, No. 2, Part 2 (June 1965), p. 192. See Seymour Sacks, "State and Local Government Finances and Economic Development," in *State and Local Taxes on Business*, Tax Institute of America, Princeton, N.J., 1965, pp. 209–224.

38. Richard M. Bird, "Tax Subsidy Policy for Regional Development," *National Tax Journal*, Vol. 19, No. 2, 1966, p. 123.

Notes to Chapter 7: Private- and
Public-Sector Cooperation

1. James L. Sunquist, "Jobs Training and Welfare for the Under-class," in *Agenda for the Nation,* ed. by Kermit Gordon. Garden City, N.Y.: Doubleday, 1968, p. 67.

2. U.S. Chamber of Commerce, *Task Force on Economic Growth and Opportunity, the Disadvantaged Poor,* Third report, 1966, pp. 89–90. The U.S. Chamber of Commerce has a voluntary program on racial-urban problems. It is a three-pronged attack on problems of hard-core unemployment, crime, substandard housing, and race relations. "Forward Thrust" is an effort to encourage voluntary working relationships among business; government; and economic, religious, cultural, labor, civil rights, neighborhood, and other groups to mobilize community resources. The emphasis is on local initiative, with an accompanying recognition of the need to cooperate with government. The Chamber's position is that, because of the distinctive character of the programs, this approach avoids the pitfalls that plague many programs designed to impose national remedies on local problems.

"Urban Action" is an exchange and information-sharing project in which sixty national organizations cooperate to help combat urban problems. It provides information on consumer relations, crime prevention, health, and manpower training.

The Urban Action Clearing House is designed to make available documented results as to what communities have accomplished in the urban crisis. Case studies discuss major urban needs, such as improved education, job training, better law enforcement, low-cost housing, and modernized government. Each study points up the pitfalls and the principles that can be applied elsewhere.

The Chamber acknowledges that there are no easy answers to city problems, but its programs basically tell how citizens can take a more vigorous part in attacking them.

3. Samuel M. Burt and Herbert E. Striner, "Toward Greater Industry and Government Involvement in Manpower Development." Upjohn Institute for Employment Research, Kalamazoo, Mich., September 1968, p. 3.

4. *Ibid.,* p. 13.

5. White House Executive Order proscribing arrangements for developing and coordinating a national program for minority business enterprises. Office of White House Press Secretary, March 5, 1969.

6. U.S. Dept. of Commerce, news release, Washington, D.C., March 5, 1969.

7. See U.S. Dept. of Commerce, Economic Development Administration, "Regional Economic Development in the United States," Part 1, October 1967.

8. Manpower Report of the President, including a Report on Manpower Requirements, Resources, Utilization and Training by the U.S. Department of Labor, transmitted to Congress, April 19, 1968, p. xiii.

9. *Ibid.*, pp. 197–206.

10. James Tobin, "Raising the Incomes of the Poor," in *Agenda for the Nation,* ed. by Kermit Gordon. Garden City, N.Y.: Doubleday, 1968, p. 86.

11. *Ibid.*, p. 98.

12. See Peter B. Doeringer, "Ghetto Labor Markets Problems and Programs." Discussion paper 35, presented at the Program on Regional and Urban Economics, MIT-Harvard Joint Center for Urban Studies, Harvard University, Cambridge, Mass., May 1968, p. 23; also Garth L. Mangrum, "Government as Employer of the Last Resort," in *Towards Freedom of Want,* Industrial Labor Research Association, Madison, Wisc., 1969, p. 153.

13. See Luther Gulick, "The Financial Plight of the Cities." *Current History,* December 1968, pp. 334, 337.

14. See Report of the National Commission on Urban Problems, "Building the American City" (House Document 91–34). U.S. Govt. Printing Office, Washington, D.C., 1969, p. 172.

15. *Ibid.*, pp. 174–178.

16. John F. Kain and Joseph J. Persky, "The Ghetto, the Metropolis, and the Nation." Discussion paper 30, presented at the Program on Regional and Urban Economics, MIT-Harvard Joint Center for Urban Studies, Harvard University, Cambridge, Mass., March 1968, pp. 6–10.

17. *Ibid.*, p. 11.

Notes to Chapter 8: The Financial Dimension of Development Programs

1. Theodore L. Cross, *Black Capitalism: Strategy for Business in the Ghetto.* New York: Atheneum Press, 1969, Ch. V and VI.

2. Eugene P. Foley, *The Achieving Ghetto.* Washington, D.C.: The National Press, 1968, pp. 103–148.

3. A. Philip Randolph Institute, "A 'Freedom Budget' for All Americans," New York, October 1966, p. 5.

4. Committee on Government Operations, "Federal Role in Urban Affairs," U.S. Senate, Eighty-ninth Congress, December 14 and 15, 1966, Part 9, p. 1993.

5. A. Philip Randolph Institute, *op. cit.,* p. 11.

6. A. Philip Randolph, "Toward a Freedom Budget." *Dissent,* Vol. 13 (March-April 1966), p. 125.

7. See Charles G. Bennett, "City Development Plan Seeks to Aid Slum-Area Businesses," The New York *Times,* April 11, 1968.

8. "McLaurin Offers Plan to Aid Slum Sections," Mount Vernon, N.Y., *Daily Argus,* April 12, 1968.

9. Lawrence S. Ritter, *A Capital Market Plan for the Urban Areas.* New York: Goodbody, undated, p. 12.

10. *Report of the National Advisory Commission on Civil Disorders,* New York: Bantam, 1968, p. 411.

11. "Employment and Manpower Problems in the Cities: Implications of the Report of the National Advisory Commission on Civil Disorders." Hearings before the Joint Economic Committee, Ninetieth Congress, Second Session, May 28, 29, and June 4, 5, 6, 1968. Washington, D.C.: U.S. Govt. Printing Office, 1968, pp. 116–117.

12. An earlier House bill, H.R. 244 (January 10, 1967) provided tax deductions for businesses that provided new jobs for skilled and unskilled workers and domestics. The deduction was to be equal to 25 per cent of the annual salary rate for each new job.

Businesses, large and small, would be encouraged to hire these hard-core unemployed for the first six months, or less the employer would be allowed a 75% credit; 50% for more than six months but not more than one year, and 25% for the employee who works for one year but not more than two years. The individual must be retained at least six months. The worker would receive the higher of the minimum wage or the prevailing wage. The employer would be restricted on the number of green-card employees he could hire and could not substitute green-card employees for existing employees.

See "Employment and Manpower Problems in the Cities: Implications of the Report of the National Advisory Committee on Civil Disorders," *op. cit.,* p. 280.

13. Advisory Commission on Intergovernmental Relations, "Urban and Rural America: Policies for Future Growth." Washington, D.C., April 1968, p. 141.

14. T. L. Cross, *Black Capitalism, op. cit.,* pp. 169, 188, 189, 191, 198 and 201–202. Eugene P. Foley in his *The Achieving Ghetto,* also advocates a variety of tax concession incentives to foster indigenous ghetto economic development.

15. Report of the National Commission on Urban Problems, Part IV, "Government Structure, Finance and Taxation," Ch. 5, pp. 2 and 3.

16. Harvey S. Perloff and Richard B. Nathan, eds., *Revenue Sharing and the City.* Baltimore, Resources for the Future, Inc., John Hopkins Press, 1968.

17. Advisory Commission on Intergovernmental Relations, "Fiscal Balance in the American Federal System," Vol. I, Washington, D.C., October 1967, p. 67.

18. Report of the National Commission on Urban Problems, *op. cit.,* Part 4, Ch. 5, p. 9.

19. *Ibid.,* p. 13.

20. Economic Report of the President, January 1969. Washington, D.C.: U.S. Govt. Printing Office, 1969, p. 187.

Notes to Chapter 9: Progress and Poverty

1. Report of the Joint Economic Committee on the January 1969 Economic Report of the President, April 1, 1969, Washington, D.C.: U.S. Govt. Printing Office, p. 47.

2. Report, the National Commission on Urban Problems, Part II, Housing Programs, pp. 3–68.

3. "Are Model Cities the Business of Business?" *Nation's Business,* February 1969, p. 44.

4. *Ibid.*

5. Report of the National Commission on Urban Problems, Part II, "Housing Programs," Washington, D.C.: U.S. Govt. Printing Office, Ch. 3, pp. 68–69.

6. See James Bailey, "Housing Yes, Cities No," *Architectural Forum,* September 1968, p. 37.

7. John F. Kain and Joseph J. Persky, "Alternatives to the Gilded Ghetto." Discussion paper 21, presented at the Program on Regional and Urban Economics, MIT-Harvard Joint Center for Urban Studies, Harvard University, Cambridge, Mass., February 1968, pp. 18–19.

8. Samuel M. Burt and Herbert E. Striner, "Toward Greater Industry and Government Involvement in Manpower Development," Upjohn Institute for Employment Research, Kalamazoo, Mich., September 1968, p. 2.

9. See Grace L. Boggs, "The Black Revolution in America" (No. 6 in a series) in *A Black Look at White America.* University Center for Adult Education, Detroit, November 12, 1968.

10. J. F. Kain and J. J. Persky, *op. cit.,* pp. 1 and 31–32.

Notes to Chapter 10: Future Tasks—A New Urban Policy

1. It has been reported that the current administration is willing to accept a substantial increase in unemployment (750,000 workers) as the cost of reducing inflation. See "The Cities: Waging a Battle," *Newsweek,* March 10, 1969, p. 50.

2. Report of the National Advisory Commission on Civil Disorder, New York: Bantam, 1968, p. 57.

3. See Clair Wilcox, *Toward Social Welfare,* Homewood: Richard D. Irwin, 1969.

4. Some state welfare systems do provide for supplemental assistance for the working poor.

5. Economic Report of the President, January 1969. Washington, D.C.: U.S. Govt. Printing Office, 1969, p. 159.

6. *Ibid.,* p. 160.

7. Milton Friedman, *Capitalism and Freedom,* Ch. 12, "The Alleviation of Poverty," Chicago: University of Chicago Press, 1962. Friedman's program would substitute the negative income tax for all other forms of welfare programs.

8. Statement of John F. Kain (Department of Economics, Harvard University, MIT Joint Center for Urban Studies). Hearings before the Joint Economic Committee, Ninetieth Congress, Second Session, May 29, 1968. Washington, D.C.: U.S. Govt. Printing Office, 1968.

9. Under this program, states could choose to reduce the work incentive by up to 17 cents, so that the worker would only receive 33 cents in welfare aid for every dollar earned above $720. The motive is a possible cost saving which might or might not be realized depending on the reaction of the recipient worker to the reduced incentive.

10. New York *Times,* August 17, 1969.

11. Black-owned businesses which have succeeded in ghetto environments have been service facilities which depended upon racial discrimination to ensure a market for their product. However, even these enterprises are experiencing competitive disadvantages as social barriers are eliminated.

12. John F. Kain and Joseph J. Persky, "Alternatives to the Gilded Ghetto." Discussion paper 21, presented at the Program on Regional and Urban Economics, MIT-Harvard Joint Center for Urban Studies, Harvard University, Cambridge, Mass., February 1968, pp. 18–19.

13. President's National Advisory Commission on Rural Poverty, "The People Left Behind." Washington, D.C.: U.S. Govt. Printing Office, September 1967, pp. XI and XIII.

14. J. F. Kain and J. J. Persky, *op. cit.,* pp. 13 and 16.

15. *Ibid.,* p. 27.

16. U.S. Department of Commerce, Economic Development Administration, "Regional Economic Development in the United States," Part 2, October 1967, p. V–3.

17. *Ibid.*

18. *Ibid.,* p. V–5.

19. *Ibid.*

20. President's National Advisory Commission on Rural Poverty, *op. cit.,* p. 17.

21. John F. Kain, "Notes from the Black Belt." Testimony before the U.S. Commission on Civil Rights, Montgomery, Ala., May 2, 1968.

22. See James Tobin, "Raising the Incomes of the Poor," in *Agenda for the Nation,* ed. by Kermit Gordon (Garden City, N.Y.: Doubleday, 1968), p. 90.

23. Distributive policies might also have a long-run structural impact if high levels of income maintenance reduced the inheritance of poverty traits by disrupting the "culture or vicious cycle of poverty."

24. *Ibid.*

25. See Eli Ginsberg *et al., Manpower Strategy for the Metropolis.* New York: Columbia University Press, 1968.

26. *The Other America: Poverty in the United States.* New York: Macmillan, 1962.

27. Michael Harrington, *Towards a Democratic Left.* New York: Macmillan, 1968, pp. 102–103 and 109.

28. Gunnar Myrdal, "A Summing Up" in *Poverty in America,* ed. by Margaret S. Gordon. San Francisco: Chandler, 1965, p. 444.

29. Charles E. Silberman, *Crisis in Black and White.* New York: Random House, 1964, pp. 247–248.

30. David C. McClelland, *The Achieving Society.* Princeton, N.J.: Van Nostrand, 1961.

31. Bernard Weissbourd and Herbert Chaney, "An Urban Strategy." *The Center Magazine,* Vol. 1, No. 6 (September 1968), pp. 56–65.

32. *Ibid.,* p. 60.

33. *Ibid.,* p. 61.

34. *Ibid.,* p. 63.

35. For further information on "New Towns," see Advisory Commission on Intergovernmental Relations, "Urban and Rural America: Policies for Future Growth," Ch. 4, "New Communities in America and Their Objectives," (Washington, D.C.: U.S. Govt. Printing Office, 1968), pp. 60–105.

36. *Ibid.,* p. 129.

37. Personal interview with the Reverend Albert B. Cleage of the Central United Church of Christ, in Detroit, July 24, 1968.

Index

Index

DATE